MASTERING THE FINANCIAL DIMENSION OF YOUR PSYCHOTHERAPY PRACTICE

Written by two therapists with extensive business experience, *Mastering the Financial Dimension of Your Psychotherapy Practice* addresses the clinical and financial challenges of establishing and maintaining a successful private practice. This book contains updated content on investing strategies, changes in the insurance marketplace, and trends in the marketing of a psychotherapy practice. The first of five sections explores the life cycle of the modern therapy practice, offering best business and investing practices for each phase. In the second and third sections, the authors consider the emotional dimension in the development of a private practice. The fourth section offers a basic course in financial planning, including an investigation into five common financial mistakes therapists make and various solutions to each situation. The fifth section is designed to offer a road map of actions to take in establishing a financial plan. Concluding the book is an inspirational discussion of how the therapist in private practice can create a career with meaning, fulfillment, personal satisfaction, and solid financial rewards.

Peter H. Cole, LCSW, and **Daisy Reese, LCSW,** have been teaching and practicing psychotherapy for more than 25 years. Peter is an assistant clinical professor of psychiatry at the University of California, Davis School of Medicine and a chartered financial consultant (ChFC®), specializing in work with mental health professionals. Daisy owns a private practice. They are also founders and co-directors of the Sierra Institute for Contemporary Gestalt Therapy, where they continue to train and mentor therapists in Northern California.

MASTERING THE FINANCIAL DIMENSION OF YOUR PSYCHOTHERAPY PRACTICE

The Definitive Resource for Private Practice

Peter H. Cole and
Daisy Reese

Routledge
Taylor & Francis Group

NEW YORK AND LONDON

First edition published 2018
by Routledge
711 Third Avenue, New York, NY 10017

and by Routledge
2 Park Square, Milton Park, Abingdon, Oxon, OX14 4RN

Routledge is an imprint of the Taylor & Francis Group, an informa business

© 2018 Peter H. Cole and Daisy Reese

The right of Peter H. Cole and Daisy Reese to be identified as the authors
of this work has been asserted by them in accordance with sections 77 and
78 of the Copyright, Designs and Patents Act 1988.

All rights reserved. The purchase of this copyright material confers the
right on the purchasing institution to photocopy or download pages which
bear the photocopy icon and a copyright line at the bottom of the page.
No other parts of this book may be reprinted or reproduced or utilized in
any form or by any electronic, mechanical, or other means, now known
or hereafter invented, including photocopying and recording, or in any
information storage or retrieval system, without permission in writing from
the publishers.

Trademark notice: Product or corporate names may be trademarks or
registered trademarks, and are used only for identification and explanation
without intent to infringe.

Library of Congress Cataloging-in-Publication Data
Names: Cole, Peter H., 1955– author. | Reese, Daisy, 1947– author.
Title: Mastering the financial dimension of your psychotherapy practice :
    the definitive resource for private practice/Peter H. Cole and Daisy Reese.
Description: First edition. | New York : Routledge, 2017. |
    Includes bibliographical references and index.
Identifiers: LCCN 2016059850 | ISBN 9781138906051 (hbk : alk. paper) |
    ISBN 9781138906068 (pbk. : alk. paper) | ISBN 9781315692340 (ebk)
Subjects: | MESH: Psychotherapy—economics | Practice Management—economics |
    Financial Management | Private Practice—economics
Classification: LCC RC480 | NLM WM 21 | DDC 616.89/1400681—dc23
LC record available at https://lccn.loc.gov/2016059850

ISBN: 978-1-138-90605-1 (hbk)
ISBN: 978-1-138-90606-8 (pbk)
ISBN: 978-1-315-69234-0 (ebk)

Typeset in Sabon
by Apex CoVantage, LLC

We dedicate this book to our children: Ananda, Reese, Alex, Elizabeth, and Hannah. Since the first edition of this book, you have grown into adults that we respect and love with all our hearts.

CONTENTS

List of Figures	x
List of Tables	xi
Foreword by Melinda Douglass	xiii
Acknowledgments	xvi

INTRODUCTION **Why a Financial Planning Book for Therapists?** **1**

SECTION I: THE LIFE CYCLE OF A PSYCHOTHERAPY PRACTICE **7**

CHAPTER 1 **Moving Through the Seasons** **9**

CHAPTER 2 **The Internship Phase: Having a Good Experience While Preparing for Licensure** **13**

CHAPTER 3 **The Launching Phase** **17**

CHAPTER 4 **The Establishing Phase** **28**

CHAPTER 5 **The Prime Phase** **37**

CHAPTER 6 **The Elder Phase** **48**

SECTION II: PSYCHOLOGICAL AND THERAPEUTIC CONSIDERATIONS **65**

CHAPTER 7 **Raising Your Money Consciousness: An Important Journey of Individuation** **67**

CHAPTER 8 **The Psychological Dimension** **72**

vii

CHAPTER 9	**Characterological Defenses Around Money Wounds**	**76**
CHAPTER 10	**What Is Financial Well-Being?**	**83**
CHAPTER 11	**The Couple's Money Dance**	**87**
CHAPTER 12	**Complementary Work: Referring to and Working With a Financial Planner**	**94**
CHAPTER 13	**Money as a Transference Object in Therapy**	**99**

SECTION III: CURRENT PRACTICE CONSIDERATIONS   **101**

CHAPTER 14	**Sustaining Your Prosperous Practice Through Changing Economic Times**	**103**
CHAPTER 15	**The Affordable Care Act and Beyond: Making Managed Care Work for You**	**108**
CHAPTER 16	**Your Online Presence**	**113**
CHAPTER 17	**Utilizing Practice Management Software Systems for Your Office**	**119**

SECTION IV: A THERAPIST'S MONEY GUIDE   **123**

CHAPTER 18	**Filling in the Financial Knowledge Gap**	**125**
CHAPTER 19	**Five Common Financial Mistakes of Private Practitioners**	**130**
CHAPTER 20	**Tax-Advantaged Investing Plans for Self-Employed Psychotherapists**	**146**
CHAPTER 21	**A Therapist's Guide to Fundamental Investing Concepts**	**154**
CHAPTER 22	**Securities That Therapists Commonly Invest In**	**162**
CHAPTER 23	**Socially Responsible Investing**	**174**
CHAPTER 24	**Debt and Credit Issues**	**176**
CHAPTER 25	**An Insurance Primer**	**192**
CHAPTER 26	**Estate Planning: Financial Planning for After a Death**	**202**

SECTION V: YOUR MONEY PAGES **215**

CHAPTER 27 **Introduction to a Lifetime Plan for Your Financial Well-Being** **217**

CHAPTER 28 **Financial Worksheets and Process Pages** **220**

CHAPTER 29 **Looking Forward** **261**

Addenda **265**
Addendum I: Further Resources 267
Addendum II: Using QuickBooks® for
  Your Bookkeeping 270
Addendum III: Glossary of Financial Terms 272
Index 287

FIGURES

1	Example of Maximum Growth Asset Allocation	15
2	Example of Growth Asset Allocation	36
3	Example of Growth and Income Asset Allocation With 40% in Bonds and Cash	44
4	Example of Growth and Income Asset Allocation With 50% in Bonds and Cash	45
5	Example of Balanced Asset Allocation With 60% in Bonds and Cash	46
6	Conservative Model Portfolio	59

TABLES

4.1	Monthly Savings Toward Goal of $1 Million	35
6.1	Social Security Chart of Retirement Ages With Reductions for Early Retirement	52
6.2	Medicare Part B Model	63
19.1	Example of Current Revenues	132
19.2	Example of Target Revenues	133
19.3	Target Revenues Worksheet	143
19.4	Actual Revenues Worksheet	144
21.1	S&P 500 Selected Dates	156
21.2	Asset Classes	156
21.3	Taxable vs. Tax-Deferred on $7,500 in Income—Year One	161
22.1	Major Asset Classes Defined	167
24.1	Amortization	183
24.2	Loan Repayment Plans	186
26.1	Fee Simple Ownership	207
26.2	Joint Tenancy With Right of Survivorship	208
26.3	Tenancy in Common	209
26.4	Community Property	210
26.5	Living Will and Durable Power of Attorney	212
28.1	Personal Information Worksheet	220
28.2	Lifetime Financial Planning Objectives Worksheet	222
28.3	Private Practice Basic Worksheet	225
28.4	Income Worksheet	228

28.5	Balance Sheet	230
28.6	Personal Expenses Worksheet	235
28.7	Debt Maintenance Worksheet	237
28.8	Cash Flow Worksheet	239
28.9	Social Security Worksheet	244
28.10	Retirement Age Worksheet	244
28.11	Yearly Living Expenses Now and in Retirement Worksheet	244
28.12	Risk Profile Worksheet	246
28.13	Life Insurance Worksheet	246
28.14	Pension Worksheet	246
28.15	Special Income Worksheet	248
28.16	Special Expenses Worksheet	250
28.17	Higher Education Expenses Worksheet	252
28.18	Basic Benefits Package in the Life Cycle of Your Practice	259

FOREWORD

Mentors give us tools to work with and a hand on our shoulder. I benefited from the mentorship of Peter and Daisy during my postgraduate training in group therapy. They provided strategic, effective input on my work and life decisions. As a management consultant at Bain & Company who moved into psychology and private practice, I believe that it is useful to integrate the business aspects with psychological understanding to create a fulfilling and prosperous practice. Starting out, I knew to diversify my practice and think long-term, yet I did not know about priorities at each stage, psychological defenses I would face, or the financial tools and systems to realize these priorities. When I later read their academic text on practice development and financial planning, it came as no surprise that their financial acumen ably covered the big picture and was deeply rooted in experience.

Peter Cole draws upon over 20 years as a chartered financial consultant at Securities America and the Insight Financial Group. His financial work with practitioners and counseling people in various life stages inform his extensive view of how to plan for the future. This includes both typical issues (such as building your network, securing necessary insurance, retirement and estate planning, etc.) and complex variations that an individual may face. Daisy Reese, who is co-director of the Sierra Institute for Contemporary Gestalt Therapy with Peter, has a gift for articulating psychological defenses and styles. Her descriptions and

xiii

reflective prompts will help you see your emotional patterns with money with a fresh eye and may also act as a clinician's diagnostic tool.

As you read anecdotes and examples in each chapter, you will come to appreciate the crossroads I think each of us faces in private practice: down one path the familiar status quo and down the other approaching life as a proactive, disciplined business owner and investor. The authors provide well-researched information and instruments to become more systematic, engendering a proactive and deliberate frame of mind. Most therapists are smart, creative people who are not trained in business or financial planning. Therefore, the knowledge and recommendations you will gain reading this book can empower you to bring your talents to bear and address money matters head-on, as you will see in the case examples provided.

New and returning readers will want to focus on the section covering current practice concerns. This will get you up to speed on contemporary concerns such as recession-proofing your practice, the Affordable Care Act, software tools, and your business presence online. Read the whole book to gain a holistic picture of financial health and utilize the authors' framework: an original phase model of private practice development. Orient yourself to the major tasks at each stage and note where your strengths and growth areas are. Then keep going back, as you would a cookbook, to fine-tune specific facets of your practice plan as you advance through the stages of development. The worksheet and process pages help you connect sophisticated (often new) financial concepts with insight into historical conditioning and lingering feelings about money. Your practice and personal financial analysis is sorted into manageable chunks, while the writing prompts provide emotional support. These activities will help you to calculate numbers that will guide wiser choices as a practitioner and investor.

One unanticipated outcome from reading this guide was that I found myself becoming a more positive, empowered, and creative listener with colleagues, friends, and family who also struggle with financial anxieties and important decisions. Peter and

Daisy's guide is comprehensive in scope and resourceful in the frameworks, psychological insight, and tools provided. I believe it will help countless early career and established health practitioners clean up, reorganize, expand, and carefully design their dream practice.

Melinda Douglass
San Francisco Psychologist

ACKNOWLEDGMENTS

First thanks go to George Zimmar, PhD, of Routledge/Taylor & Francis. You have been supportive from the first day we talked. This book could never have come into being without you. Your unflagging support, encouragement, and valuable feedback have meant a great deal to us. Also at Routledge we would like to thank Anna Moore for encouraging us to bring this second edition to fruition. You have been incredibly helpful every step along the way—thank you!

We would like to thank the mental health professionals who generously gave of their time, knowledge, and insight in agreeing to be interviewed for this book: Claude Arnett, MD; Alison Buckley, MFT; James Hansell, PhD; Phillip Littman, LCSW; Karin Nilsson, PhD; John Robinson, PhD; Leslye Russell, MFT; and Shani Simon, LCSW. We are particularly appreciative of the wisdom of the elder therapists we interviewed: Hilde Burton PhD; Joan Cole, PhD; and Betty Russell LCSW. Your insights and examples were truly inspiring.

We would also like to thank the folks at Securities America for your ongoing excellence and support, especially David Bastoni. Special thanks go to our loyal staff at Insight Financial Group, especially Shila Vardell—we truly could not have done this without you. You are like family to us.

Finally, a heartfelt "thank you" to our daughter Elizabeth Collentine-Cole who served as editor of this manuscript. The dedication and skill you brought to this project, even while you were juggling the demands of graduate school and internship, was truly amazing.

To the many therapists who have chosen Insight Financial Group for your financial planning and investing needs, we thank you for placing your trust in us. We hope to earn it every day.

INTRODUCTION

Why a Financial Planning Book for Therapists?[1]

Most psychotherapists enter private practice with a sense of excitement—a feeling of fulfilling a long-held dream. It's true. Private practice can indeed be a source of tremendous satisfaction, intellectual stimulation, and personal enrichment. Private practitioners are able to set their own hours, create their own environment, and connect with stimulating people—both colleagues and clients. Private practitioners are able to follow their own path in a way possible for people in few other professions.

For private practice to be viable, however, it must pay the bills. It must cover overhead expenses, support a comfortable lifestyle, and assure a secure financial future for the therapist and perhaps for his or her family as well.

For many psychotherapists, the business end of the practice is the one with which they feel least comfortable and with which they have the tools to deal least effectively. It is the recognition of this that led to the writing of this book. We have dealt with hundreds of therapists during our years in practice. We have acted as therapists, trainers, and mentors. Peter has worked with many therapists as their financial planner. Having gone through the

---

1   Peter H. Cole, ChFC, Director and Financial Services Specialist, Insight Financial Group, 2011 "P" Street, Sacramento, CA 95811, Phone 916-444-1122, Fax 916-553-4373. Securities through Securities America Inc., a registered broker/dealer, member FINRA/SIPC, Peter Cole, Registered Representative. Advisory services through Securities America Advisors, an SEC-registered investment advisory firm, Peter Cole, investment advisor representative. CA Insurance Lic. 0D04931. Insight Financial Group is not an affiliated entity of the Securities America companies.

struggle of establishing a successful private practice and having helped many others to do so, he has a unique understanding of the necessary steps for making a practice thrive—personally, professionally, and financially.

This book is designed to specifically address the challenges faced by private practitioners:

1) A therapist's career is often lifelong, with different professional and financial goals emerging into the foreground as he/she passes through the stages of practice development.

    Section I of this book, "The Life Cycle of a Psychotherapy Practice" (Chapters 1–6), takes an in-depth look at the life stages of the therapist along with the developmental tasks and financial planning strategies appropriate to each stage.

2) Therapists are attuned to the emotional dimension of human experience, including the emotional dimension of finances.

    We recognize that emotional issues can sabotage the best intentions. In working with this book, you will come to a clearer understanding of your own emotional issues around money and be better able to avoid the unconscious pitfalls that may have hindered you in the past. Section II, "Psychological and Therapeutic Considerations" (Chapters 7–13), covers a range of issues concerning the powerful influence our emotional lives has on our financial behavior.

3) Therapists must deal with current challenges and opportunities in marketing their practices, making them thrive and having them function efficiently.

    To address some of the most challenging and salient current issues in private practice, Section III, "Current Practice Considerations" (Chapters 14–17), is specifically written to help you with:
    - Sustaining your practice through tough economic periods
    - Working effectively with the Affordable Care Act
    - Enhancing your online presence
    - Utilizing practice management software.

4) Therapists must deal with money as an issue in their psychotherapy practices.

We understand that the private practice of psychotherapy necessarily involves a complex interweaving of a service business with deeply intimate work. In Section II we also explore the fascinating terrain of money as an issue in psychotherapy.

5) Many therapists are highly skilled clinicians but have underdeveloped financial skills.

We offer comprehensive financial information designed to help you develop the essential skills necessary to be financially successful in private practice. Section IV, "A Therapist's Money Guide" (Chapters 18–26), is designed to be both a crash course and ongoing resource for you to turn to in understanding the fundamentals of your personal financial planning.

6) Therapists in private practice do not have the safety net of benefits provided by an employer.

We encourage you to recognize the fact that you are your own employer, with all the responsibilities that being a good employer entails (even if you are your only employee, this does not let you off the hook from being a responsible employer). We provide you with extensive information on arranging an appropriate benefits package for yourself. Chapter 20 takes you through the pros and cons of every major tax-advantaged retirement vehicle open to sole proprietors in private practice. Chapter 25 provides you with essential insurance information.

7) Because most therapists' retirement plans are self-directed, therapists need input about appropriate investment choices.

Throughout the text, we address appropriate investment strategies given the life stage and financial situation of the therapist and his or her family. In the discussion of the life cycle of a therapy practice in Section I, appropriate asset allocation and investment choices are discussed for each phase. Chapter 22 is a guide to investment choices commonly used in today's retirement plans.

8) Many therapists have been reluctant, for whatever reasons, to seek out professional financial advice and have put together

informal financial plans for themselves without an in-depth understanding of what this requires.

We provide a road map to sound financial and estate planning that can be individualized to fit your unique situation. Section V, "Your Money Pages" (Chapters 27–29), provides you with worksheets designed to get you started with your individualized financial plan. In Chapter 12 we address how to find a qualified and suitable financial planner.

9) Due to financial constraints, many therapists are responsible for their own bookkeeping.

This book will help you put your practice bookkeeping in good order. In Addendum II, we provide you with a step-by-step guide to getting started with QuickBooks®, an accounting package for small business that many therapists are using successfully.

10) Therapists, who earn most of their money by providing psychotherapy in the 50-minute hour, have difficulty leveraging their time-to-money ratio.

Throughout the text, we look at ways of adding to your income through making your money work for you.

This book is organized into five sections.

1) The Life Cycle of a Psychotherapy Practice
2) Psychological and Therapeutic Considerations
3) Current Practice Considerations
4) A Therapist's Money Guide
5) Your Money Pages.

You may find that you flip around the book as you enter into the material. For example, if you are reading about your phase of therapy practice in Section I and are at the discussion of asset allocation for your retirement plan at your phase, you may want to flip to a discussion of asset allocation in Section IV for more in-depth information. This book is intended to be used interactively. Write in it, use it, and flip through it! We have packed this book with a wealth of financial information. The more engaged you are with the material, the more you will get out of it.

To be an effective therapist requires compassion, knowledge, insight, patience, humor, and generosity of spirit. It is our hope that this book will help you to provide well for yourself so that you can continue offering these qualities to your clients.[2]

---

2 Names of clients in this book have been changed to protect their identities.

SECTION I

THE LIFE CYCLE OF A PSYCHOTHERAPY PRACTICE

SECTION I

THE NEW LOGIC OF
PSYCHOTHERAPY PRACTICE

CHAPTER 1

Moving Through the Seasons

More than any profession we can think of, psychotherapy involves the whole person. Who we are—our dreams, our fears, our strivings, and our Achilles' heels—directly impact how, and how well, we do our work. As therapists ourselves, we have had an "insider's view" of therapist professional development. In observing our own development over the course of our careers and observing friends, colleagues, interns, and trainees, we've become interested in trying to define the "life cycle" of a therapist—from graduate school through retirement. What are the clinical, personal and practice development tasks at each phase? What are the pitfalls? We have paid particular attention to the financial planning issues at each phase and looked at the way they are integrated into the larger picture.[1] Certainly, we can't claim to have come up with the definitive answers to these questions. However, we hope you will share some of our fascination with the questions themselves. Our hope is that this section will be a springboard for your reflection on where you are in your own professional development, so that you are in a strong position to plan for your future.

In writing this chapter we interviewed therapists across the spectrum—from a 32-year-old intern to a semi-retired therapist in her eighties. We came away from these interviews with a

---

1   Although we have considered practice development issues without regard to chronological age, by necessity the financial planning questions will be addressed with age as an important factor.

heightened respect and affection for our chosen profession and the people who practice it. Our sincere thanks to our thoughtful and generous interviewees, all of whom are credited in the notes at the end of the chapter.

LAUNCHING PHASE—LAYING A SOLID FOUNDATION

"Tell me, what is it you plan to do with your one wild and precious life?"

—*Mary Oliver (1993a, p. 94)*

Characteristic Tasks and Goals
- Creating a space of your own—leasing and furnishing your own office;
- Finding/creating your niche;
- Learning how to market—developing a plan for referrals;
- Finding and developing relationships with mentors;
- Finding a professional community that fits for you;
- Setting up your bookkeeping;
- Initiating your financial/retirement plan—asset allocation could be rather aggressive at this stage;
- Arranging the health and disability insurance coverage you need.

ESTABLISHING PHASE—BEGINNING TO BUILD

"The slow and difficult trick of living, and finding it where you are."

—*Mary Oliver (1993b, p. 239)*

Characteristic Tasks and Goals
- Balancing work and family commitments without losing yourself;
- Developing a reputation with centers of influence and referral sources;
- Learning to value your expertise and reflecting that in the fees you charge;
- Beginning to assume leadership roles in your professional community;

- Keeping on track with your retirement funding—your asset allocation should probably become somewhat less aggressive with the inclusion of more investment-grade bonds;
- Purchasing or upgrading your life insurance policy;
- Considering the possibility of buying real estate—a home, rental property, maybe an office building to house your practice.

PRIME PHASE—REAPING REWARDS

"To everything there is a season . . . a time to sow and a time to reap."

—Ecclesiastes 3:1

Characteristic Tasks and Goals
- Sharing your wisdom—becoming a mentor;
- Developing your skills at writing and speaking;
- Shaping your practice—working at what interests you and learning to say "no" to what does not;
- Giving back to the community—through pro bono work and leadership in professional organizations;
- Maintaining the discipline of amply funding your retirement plan—moderately conservative asset allocation is appropriate at this stage;
- Seriously evaluating long-term care insurance by the time you're in your mid-fifties;
- Paying off the mortgage on earlier real estate purchases.

ELDER PHASE—REWARDS FOR WORK WELL DONE

"To live so that which came to me as seed goes to the next as a blossom and that which came to me as a blossom, goes on as fruit."

—Dawna Markova (2000)

Characteristic Tasks and Goals
- Determining how much work feels right at this phase of your life—because most therapists love what they do, they often don't want to relinquish work completely;

- Aligning your spending with your retirement income so that work is by choice and not financial necessity;
- Developing a new lifestyle that feels satisfying—redefining what a balanced life means for you;
- Attending to estate planning issues;
- Making sure that appropriate advanced medical directives are in place;
- Assuring that your asset allocation is increasingly conservative, with the majority of holdings in income-producing securities and growth securities de-emphasized.

REFERENCES

Markova, Dawna. *I Will Not Die an Unlived Life* (Kindle Locations 129–142, Red Wheel Weiser, Kindle Edition, 2000)

Oliver, Mary. "The Summer Day." *New and Selected Poems* (Boston: Beacon Press, 1993a)

Oliver, Mary. "Going to Walden." *New and Selected Poems* (Boston: Beacon Press, 1993b)

CHAPTER 2

The Internship Phase

Having a Good Experience While Preparing for Licensure

The Internship Phase, the period during which you have completed your graduate degree, but have not yet gained licensure, can be a challenging time in your professional life. Spending time as an intern (i.e.. working under a licensed professional's supervision) is a requirement for licensure in all states. It can (and should) be an opportunity for learning, professional and personal development, and building connections that will last throughout your professional career.

However, it can also be a period that feels like wasted time—an experience of feeling exploited and frustrated.

As an intern, you have the right to expect support, training, and mentoring. Unfortunately, many internship positions don't offer this or offer only a pale facsimile. To get the experience you want and need as an intern, you must think carefully about what your options are and what they offer. You must also do your best to objectively assess your own capabilities and be willing to offer a fair exchange for the experience you hope for.

What does this mean? First, ask yourself, "What are my strengths and weaknesses?" If you are freshly out of school (perhaps you entered a graduate program right after college), you are probably a bit light in the experience department. You may have a fair amount of (normal) anxiety and feel awkward and unsure in dealing with clients. In this case, you will probably be better supported and more successful interning at an agency or clinic. Having supervisors close at hand and being in an environment with more experienced colleagues can help you gain confidence and perhaps give you the opportunity to work with a population that is more challenging. You are also more likely to be in an environment that allows you to develop and experiment with new skills and modalities.

On the other hand, maybe you have worked a number of years in a social service agency before returning to school for your graduate degree. Sometimes an agency (Child Protective Services is a good example) will fund a portion of an employee's education in exchange for an agreement to return to the agency for a certain period of time post-degree. If this is the case, there's little choice—you will probably be expected to return to your agency for your internship. What if you've never worked in the field but have made a mid-life career change? Although you won't have hands-on experience in social services, you will have a certain amount of maturity and life experience. Perhaps you've raised children, managed an office, or started a small business. Any experiences like these can be marketed to prospective employers as a strong statement about your capacities. Any experience working with people can only increase your abilities as a therapist.

If your eventual goal is to develop a private practice, you can, more than likely, find a supervisor who will be interested in working out a private practice internship arrangement with you.

Here are some guidelines for obtaining an internship that will offer you a dignified and direct pathway to licensure.

1) Above all else, internship is meant to be a path to licensure: Keep your eye on that main goal.
2) Try to find an internship that is a regular job with decent pay and defined hours that count toward licensure.
3) Private practice internships are usually best as a supplement to the regular job mentioned earlier.
4) Make sure the person who is signing off on your hours is legally entitled to do so by your licensing board.
5) Keep close tabs on tracking your internship hours: Stay in touch with your state licensing board, and make sure to dot all your I's and cross your T's. You are dealing with state

bureaucracies to get your license—they are very rule bound. Respect those rules and pay attention to the details. Nobody cares about your license nearly as much as you do, so make sure to actively shepherd your hours and application through the system!

6) Don't be too prideful in this phase—do your work, however humble it may be, and collect your hours. Soon you will be a licensed clinician and can shape your practice, but first, you need that license.

THE FINANCIAL DIMENSION OF THE INTERNSHIP PHASE

Most interns will do best by landing a regular job at a non-profit agency, school, hospital, and so on. Most such employers will have some sort of retirement plan.

We recommend that you get into the habit of saving into your 410(k), even if it is a small amount. Saving for retirement is a good

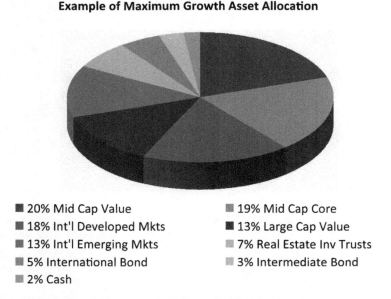

Figure 1 Example of Maximum Growth Asset Allocation[1]

1 Asset allocation does not guarantee a profit or protection from losses in a declining market.

habit to get started early with! Assuming that you are in your Internship Phase, typically a maximum growth portfolio will be appropriate, because you have lots of time before you will actually need the money in retirement.

Health insurance is a must, so buy an Affordable Care Act policy if one is not provided through your employer.

Please see our chapter on student loans if that is an issue for you.

Figure 1 provides an example of a maximum growth asset allocation.

CHAPTER 3

The Launching Phase

You've made up your mind! Maybe you're like the psychiatric residents in my fourth-year seminar—fresh out of training, with all the energy and enthusiasm of youth. On the other hand, maybe you're more like many of our interns—making a mid-life career change or gradually transitioning from agency work to private practice. Whatever your chronological age, your practice is just beginning. So let's take a look at some of the nuts and bolts of establishing a successful therapy practice.

TO SHARE OR NOT TO SHARE—THAT IS THE QUESTION

It may seem like an obvious statement, but before you can see your first client you must have an office in which to do so. Do you want to sublease from another therapist or look for an office that is wholly or primarily yours? The answer to this may also seem obvious—it's a significantly greater financial commitment to lease your own office. But let's consider for a moment. Which feels more comfortable—your own living room or a furnished apartment (even a lavishly appointed one)? Just like your living room, your office expresses who you are. Your books are on the shelves, your pictures on the walls. Along with its effect on you, your office also sends a powerful non-verbal message to your clients. I once had a client "drop by" in hopes of an emergency appointment. She told me: "If you hadn't been here, I would have just sat in the waiting room for a while—that would have been enough." Our bias is clear by now—better a more modest office that's truly "you." If paying rent feels truly not manageable at this point, you might consider finding a colleague who would like to sublease from you.

The "where" of your office is also important. Some things to consider:

- Is the location convenient—easy access to freeways, close to downtown, etc.?
- Is parking available—both for you and your clients?
- Do you need a handicapped accessible space?
- Do you want to be in a building with other therapists for mutual support, consultation, etc.?
- Would you rather be in a building with allied professionals (physicians, attorneys) who could become referral sources?
- Is the building secure and well-lighted for after-hours clients?
- Is the building quiet and conducive to the work you do?

Keep in mind that your first office is the place where you will form some of your first professional connections. Although it's unlikely that you'll stay in the same office over the course of your career, those connections can last a lifetime. I (Daisy) still do much of my cross-referring with my original office mates from 20 years ago.

MANAGED CARE—KEEPING YOUR BALANCE ON THE SLIPPERY SLOPE

Fifteen years ago, when managed care first began making serious inroads into California, I remember frantic conversations with colleagues: How could we get ourselves included on as many panels as possible? Managed care seemed to offer limitless referrals and guaranteed reimbursement. What more could a beginning therapist ask for? Unfortunately, the reality hasn't quite lived up to our expectations. Yes, managed care does offer "ready-made" referrals—sometimes more than you really want. However, reimbursement is invariably lower than standard fees, often substantially lower. Although theoretically guaranteed, reimbursement can be slow in arriving and often requires repeated billings. There is always significant paperwork involved, ranging from annoying to infuriating in its complexity. Most importantly, managed care inserts a third party into the intimate space between therapist and client. No longer are decisions made based on what the therapist considers to be best for the client, but rather on what the insurance company allows or requires.

Does this mean that you should steer clear of managed care altogether? Probably not—at least not early in your practice. Rather, consider managed care to be a temporary measure, providing you with income and a client base to help you develop your skills as you work to establish yourself and build your referral sources.

One caveat: Be sure to read all contracts thoroughly.

- What is the reimbursement schedule?
- What is required for authorization?
- How many visits are typically authorized?
- Once you sign on, are you obligated to see whatever patients are referred to you?
- Is there an obligation to see patients who might be "at risk" even after authorized visits have been exhausted?

Protect yourself in the beginning and you may save yourself a lot of legal and ethical trouble in the long run.

IF NOT MANAGED CARE, THEN WHAT?

If you are not relying solely on managed care, then you will need to develop your marketing skills in order to develop a private pay clientele. You may have become a therapist for any number of idealistic and altruistic reasons. The reality is, however, that you must also make a profit from your therapeutic work. Profit—it's really not a four-letter word. There is nothing shameful or embarrassing about wanting to make a comfortable living from doing the work you love. Simply acknowledging this to yourself is the first step.

COMBINING PASSION WITH NON-ATTACHMENT

As a psychotherapist, rather than selling shoes or books, you are selling your expertise. No one can possibly be interested in your expertise if they don't know about it. This means that you must become comfortable in selling yourself as an expert. You must

THE LAUNCHING PHASE 19

bring your work to the marketplace. You may ask how, in a marketplace that is so vast and so complex, are you going to find a voice that is heard? The answer is by following your passion and bringing to the marketplace a public offering of that which you are passionate about.

A helpful complement to passion is the Buddhist concept of non-attachment. If you present to the marketplace what you love, without attachment to the outcome, you can find yourself reaping rewards in ways you least expect. For a number of years, in the era before online marketing was widespread, we did a huge regional mailing of brochures for our Gestalt training group. For a number of years, we got minimal response! Each spring we would look at each other and question, "Is it worth doing again?" Nevertheless, we kept on, with the faith that we were sowing important seeds even though we couldn't yet see many sprouts. Then some interesting calls began to come in. "I've been saving your brochure for a long time. Now I'm ready to do the training." "I've seen your name around for a long time. You must be pretty well established." By sticking with something that excites and satisfies us and by practicing non-attachment to immediate outcomes, we have succeeded in having our voice heard in the clamorous marketplace.

So where does your passion lie? The answer to this will guide you to the segment of the marketplace that will be responsive to what you have to offer. Your focus may be on a theoretical approach:

- Gestalt
- Psychoanalytic
- Transpersonal
- Jungian
- Cognitive-behavioral
- Emotionally focused therapy
- Mindfulness.

If this is the case, you will want to associate yourself with professional organizations that train and mentor therapists in your chosen particular approach. Many of your referrals will probably come from supervisors and colleagues in these organizations and from networking you are able to do at seminars and conferences.

You may be especially interested in working with specific types of clients:

- Women
- Men
- Adolescents/children
- Gays and lesbians
- Transgender individuals
- Senior citizens
- Couples
- Christian.

If you are interested in a particular client group, it makes sense to go to venues where members of that group congregate. Connecting with counselors and teachers at schools, speaking at a senior citizens' center, making a presentation to your church's Sunday school class for couples—these are examples of possibilities for practicing enlightened self-interest—that is, "doing well by doing good." It's important that your marketing efforts be valid in their own right, rather than merely an advertisement for your practice. If you bring something of value to the community, you will find that the community responds.

Another approach is to focus on specific issues that you would like to work with:

- Anxiety and depression
- Women in the workplace
- Parenting
- Relationships
- Adults abused as children
- Addictions
- Mid-life issues
- Eating disorders.

Focusing on a particular issue can be a way of doing very successful marketing. One of our former interns, "Donna," has chosen to work with eating disorders. She has sent letters to physicians, given presentations at high schools and colleges, listed herself as a referral with the Mental Health Association, and done extensive networking with other therapists. Although she has only been licensed for a few years, she now has a successful practice and is running several eating disorder groups per week. Whenever we need to make a referral for an eating disorder patient, hers is the first name that comes to mind.

KNOWING YOURSELF

Donna is the exception—she feels comfortable with a wide variety of marketing approaches. Most of us are a little less versatile. If you're a person who freezes at the thought of speaking in public, forcing yourself to speak to large groups will be painful and probably non-productive. If you suffer from terminal writer's block, don't offer to write a monthly column for your organization's newsletter. In short, play to your strengths rather than your weaknesses. There are many paths to building a successful practice. The trick is finding the one (or two) that work with who you are.

We have focused much of our practices on training and group work. We're both sociable and we find teaching to be exciting—a great way to keep ourselves and our work fresh. If you're more of an introvert, look for a mentor to work with you one-on-one (a mentor who can also become a referral source). Find websites that cater to people you want to reach and write a column or a blog. If you like to organize and do public presentations, there are innumerable organizations (schools, parent–teacher associations, service clubs, churches and synagogues) that would love to have you volunteer to give a talk or present a workshop for their members. Do you have contacts or interest in the media? Newspapers—yes, newspapers are still part of the media environment!—have a lot of column inches to fill, and radio and TV have a lot of airtime. Contact your local media with ideas for timely topics (e.g., dealing with stress, making your stepfamily work, parenting teenagers) and you may find yourself becoming a minor celebrity—the expert who is called for their thoughts on the topic of the day.

Another, sometimes more sensitive, aspect of knowing yourself is understanding where your wounds and weaknesses lie. Are you tempted to specialize in a problem that you have struggled with yourself? The archetype of the "wounded healer" is a powerful one, and many significant contributions have been made by therapists working in the area that is closest to home for them. However, for this to work well you must have worked with your own issues to a significant extent. If you enter into the area of sexual abuse, for instance, as a "crusader"—determined to rescue victims and right wrongs—you can do a great deal of damage. Through your own therapy and consultation, you must come to a place where you can listen with a "loving neutrality" that allows the client to access her own strengths rather than remaining stuck in victimhood. This loving neutrality will also allow you to take care of yourself in your work—not working more than you can realistically sustain and not forgetting your own interests (including financial) in your zeal to help your clients. One of my early supervisors told me:

> Psychotherapy operates on two levels—the emotional and the financial. If you don't pay attention to both those levels, the therapy can't be effective. It's the tension between the emotional connection and the financial relationship that gives therapy much of its power.

THE RIGHT MARKET MEANS A MARKET THAT CAN AFFORD YOUR SERVICES

I hope my (Peter) former social work professors at Bryn Mawr don't disown me when they read this, but my advice for the beginning private practitioner is to market to people who can afford to pay for therapy out of pocket. It makes sense to direct one's marketing to people who can and will pay for psychotherapy. Most therapists have an altruistic streak, and pro bono work is important for many reasons. However, in order to do pro bono work without becoming resentful and burned out, it's necessary to have a solid base of clients who pay the bills. Before we can care well for others, we must care for ourselves. With a solid base of clients who can pay full fee, you will be in a strong position to provide low-fee and pro bono therapy while taking care of your financial responsibilities to yourself and your family.

Remember the idea of non-attachment, however. If what you are bringing to the marketplace is educational, informative, and useful; if you market to people who understand, appreciate, and are willing to pay for therapy; and if your marketing plan is a comfortable fit with your interests and personality; then you can detach from needing to see immediate results from your efforts. The results will come, but often in roundabout and unexpected ways. Sometimes people show up in your office years after they came to a seminar or class. Sometimes they refer a friend years later. In the meantime, your marketing is a way of bringing an important message to the community.

BEYOND THE CONSULTING ROOM

Erving Polster, one of the leading lights of Gestalt therapy, once said: "Therapy is too good to be limited to the sick." With the tensions and conflicts in the world today, the need for therapists to find a voice in the broader society is greater than ever. Psychological thinking addresses a dimension of human motivation that people in the fields of economics, history, politics, business, and even the arts frequently are not attuned to. For example, we serve on the grants committee of a philanthropic organization that funds visionary ideas, and recently, we were assigned to be the evaluators of a very exciting grant application. We started the evaluation full of enthusiasm. The person applying was clearly brilliant and his project was one we thought could have a huge impact on society. Gradually, however, our enthusiasm faded. Our emails weren't returned, references were lukewarm, and we began hearing distressing stories about the applicant's treatment of people he considered "beneath" him. Because of our psychological backgrounds, we felt confident in saying, "His narcissism is out of control and the chances of his being able to work collaboratively are slim." We were able to take into account not only the intellectual dimension, but also the interpersonal and psychological dimensions and make a decision from a holistic standpoint.

If you decide that the consulting room, working with one individual at a time, doesn't fit for you, your ability to think psychologically can stand you in good stead in a wide variety of arenas. Many therapists are thinking "outside the box" of the traditional consulting room and are bringing psychological understanding and expertise to people and organizations at all levels of society.

Turn your creative mind loose to explore alternatives and you may find yourself working in realms you never could have predicted. Like, for instance:

Mark, a psychologist who works with organizations large and small to do team building.

Jenny, who has built a successful international business working with the hospitality industry on sexual harassment prevention and conflict resolution.

Price, a psychiatrist who serves as a consultant to executives on a broad range of issues.

Michael, who acts as a psychiatric consultant to adolescent treatment facilities.

Jessie, an inheritor herself, who specializes in working with inheritors and works with a major New York brokerage as a "wealth counselor" for their clients.

The rapidly developing technology field can be a tremendous support for alternative forms of therapy. Ours is an era in which communities of interest are arising without regard for geographical proximity. The internet and mass communication have created a global village that allows these communities of interest to thrive. Psychotherapy by Skype and other video-conferencing services is freeing psychotherapy from the consulting room and creating larger markets for psychotherapists.

Some therapists love the 50-minute hour and want a very traditional practice. Others want to teach, consult, write, speak, or market their expertise in creative new ways. The possibilities for expanding a practice beyond the four walls of the consulting room are limited only by the therapist's imagination and willingness to take risks.

THE LAUNCHING PHASE 25

THE FINANCIAL DIMENSION OF THE LAUNCHING PHASE
Practice Management Software and Bookkeeping

If you are just setting up your practice, then you are in an excellent position to set your bookkeeping up correctly. In Chapter 17 we go into detail on getting started with practice management software and bookkeeping software. The main idea we want to convey here is that your practice management software will help you with the day to day tasks of billing, scheduling, note-taking, and other tasks of your practice. Bookkeeping software helps you look at the big picture of your revenues and expenses. A standard bookkeeping program is QuickBooks® by Intuit.

QuickBooks Premiere Health Care version has a mental health setup and template that will take you through all the dimensions of bookkeeping and billing you are likely to need. It is easy to use, and is considered standard among CPAs so that when tax time rolls around, you will likely be able to email your CPA all the information he or she will need to do your practice taxes. You can find Intuit online at www.intuit.com.

Setting Up Your Retirement Plan

Put the time value of money to work for yourself by beginning your retirement plan from your first day of private practice. A good place to start would be to open an individual 401(k) plan. As we discussed earlier, if you are self-employed and organized as a sole proprietorship, the individual 401(k) will allow you to put a maximum amount of pretax retirement money away. Your financial planner will be able to help you with the details of opening and maintaining the retirement plan. If you are in your late twenties or early thirties, you might want to consider a maximum growth asset allocation, meaning that the majority of your asset allocation will go into stocks rather than bonds. At this phase of the game, many investors will trade growth potential for stability because there is a long time horizon before the money will be needed for retirement. A good place to begin is to earmark 15% of your gross (before tax) income for your retirement plan. As your income rises, so will the amount that goes into your 401(k). Also, as we have discussed in earlier sections, you will need to have liability, health, and disability/business overhead insurance.

CONCLUSION

In conclusion, the Launching Phase is a very exciting time for you and your practice. You are getting started on a journey that can sustain you for a lifetime of fascinating and rewarding work. Setting the business and financial aspects of your practice up with careful thought and with robust systems that can sustain you through a lifetime of building wealth will give your practice stability and endurance.

CHAPTER 4

The Establishing Phase

The seeds have been planted and the stage is set. Now comes the sustaining work of managing what you have sown so that you can look forward to a satisfying harvest.

THE IMPORTANCE OF SELF AS INSTRUMENT

"The hardest part for me is balancing my practice and my family. How do I put out emotional energy for my clients all day and still have something left over for my husband and kids?" This is perhaps the central question for therapists at this phase.

Imagine for a moment that you are a concert violinist. You have a beautiful, finely tuned instrument on which you've spent many thousands of dollars. Obviously, you would do everything in your power to protect this violin, giving it all the care and attention it required. As therapists, we have no other instrument but our Selves. We have spent many thousands of dollars on education and training. We have created a beautiful environment in which to work and invested time and energy in our marketing efforts. Doesn't it make sense, then, to treat our Selves with the same respect that a musician would offer her violin?

To function well, we must learn to feed ourselves:

- Physically
- Intellectually
- Emotionally
- Spiritually.

Physical

The physical level is often the most neglected. When it feels that there simply aren't enough hours in a day, our own well-being can easily be squeezed out. Along with paying attention to eating well and getting enough sleep, finding ways to move your body on a daily basis is incredibly important. Can you walk or ride a bike to your office? Is there a gym or health club near where you work? It can feel great to take a 2-hour break in the middle of the day and go to an aerobics or yoga class. How about massage? Giving the gift of a regular massage to yourself once or twice a month is more than a luxury. It's an important piece of "keeping your instrument in tune." What do you do with those 10 minutes between appointments? When I (Daisy) first started practicing, I would routinely let clients run over—often finishing with one just in time to meet the next. A little later on, I started using those 10 minutes to catch up on paperwork or return phone calls. Today I'm much more jealous of this space between one client and the next. I keep a yoga mat in my office and will often sit down for a few stretches in my precious 10-minute break. At other times, I walk outside to reconnect with the larger world. However you choose to do it, it's important to take time throughout the day to refresh yourself— you'll find that this will leave you significantly less exhausted and burned out at the end of the day.

Intellectual

At its best, psychotherapy can be tremendously intellectually challenging. However, this is not automatically true. Do you find yourself feeling bored by the "same old stories"? Is there a sense that you've heard it all before and you find yourself operating by rote? I once had a colleague tell me, "Oh, I can handle most of my cases in my sleep!" If you start to have a similar feeling, it's time for some stimulation. Look for seminars or workshops that excite you. Too often it's easy to focus only on "How many CEUs is this worth?" But your continuing education should do much more than provide you with required continuing education units (CEUs). Find a presentation by someone whose writings interest you and make it a goal to read much of his or her work in preparation. Try a workshop on a topic outside your area of expertise. I personally find that workshops are much more meaningful to me if they include an experiential aspect. Let yourself take some risks and explore an interactive group experience or training that involves personal as well as professional growth.

Consultation is another way to keep yourself intellectually stimulated. Now that you've been in practice for a while, you may have gotten out of the habit of seeking out good supervision. Therapists don't improve their skills through experience alone. Consultation/supervision is important to increasing your skill level. The right consultant can help you sort out difficult cases, better understand your countertransference issues and challenge you to develop your professional self. Over time, he/she can become an important mentor as well a valuable referral source. Peer consult groups also serve an important function. Ideally, they can provide social connection, clinical consultation, and professional networking. Be sure to look for a group that feels friendly, supportive, and also challenging. If you don't find the right group, it's worth taking the trouble to start talking to like-minded colleagues and form your own.

Emotional

As important as keeping yourself well-nourished physically is paying attention to your emotional nourishment. Our clients demand a great deal from us in terms of emotional support and our families and friends expect us to be available at the end of the day. Where does our own emotional sustenance come from? The answer is, it must come from many sources. No one person can provide us with all we need. A spouse or partner can be an important resource. Groups of friends who are willing to really listen and really talk are invaluable. Finding a therapist for yourself (even if you thought you were "finished") may be helpful. Carl Whitaker used to talk about his "cuddle group"—a group of professional colleagues who supported each other through difficult clients and the profession's inevitable ups and downs. There are some things about our profession that no one can understand like another therapist. The energy you put into seeking out and maintaining connection with colleagues you can resonate with will serve you well throughout your career.

Spiritual

What is it that "restoreth your soul"? For some people, traditional religious services are an important aspect of life. For others, spending time in nature is a necessity. Do you love music or art? Concerts, museum exhibits, or joining a choir or an amateur chamber music group may be what you need to feel spiritually fed. Meditation practice, tai chi, or yoga can be both relaxing and centering. It may be that, between the demands of developing your practice and dealing with your personal life, you haven't stopped to consider what your particular spiritual food is. If that's the case, take some time now to experiment. Begin by giving yourself some solitude to tune in to what feels lacking in your life. As you begin to attune yourself to your inner wisdom, that wisdom will begin to speak in an increasingly clear voice. It will be a trustworthy guide as you move through the developmental phases of your practice.

FINDING YOUR POWER—BECOMING AN AUTHORITY

No longer a beginner, in this phase your overall feeling of professional confidence should be growing. In many ways, you are now at the most critical stage of therapist development. It is now that a trajectory is set that will determine the course of your future practice.

Setting Your Fees

One important aspect of setting your trajectory is charging "market value" for your services. Effective psychotherapy can change the course of a person's life. Far from being an optional luxury, it can mean the difference between a life that is productive and satisfying and one that is sterile, disappointing, and destructive. That being said, the person who makes that difference possible (you!) deserves to be well paid for what she provides.

When you're an intern or a newly licensed practitioner, it seems appropriate to charge a lower fee and to be accommodating about providing a sliding scale. However, as one of our Establishing

Phase interviewees said: "I'm at a point now where my fee is my fee. If people can't afford it, I'll be willing to see them less often or provide them with a referral."

The question is, of course, where to set your fee. In most communities there seems to be a fairly wide range of fees charged by experienced therapists. I once got a piece of advice that I found very useful. See if it works as well for you. Begin by finding out what the highest fee is in your community (e.g. $150 per hour). Try saying out loud—maybe in front of a mirror—"I charge $150." If this makes you gulp or stammer, as it very well may, try saying "I charge $140." Continue in this way, working your way downward, until you arrive at the fee that feels like a comfortable fit for you. You may need to repeat this exercise periodically, when it seems like it's time to raise your fees.

WEAVING THE WHOLE CLOTH

In the Establishing Phase, your marketing efforts will take on a different flavor than they had earlier in your practice. You have, by now, developed a niche in which you feel comfortable and in which you are beginning to develop a reputation. Although this niche may change over time, it's probably wise to allow yourself enough time to feel firmly established and become a recognized authority in one or two areas. It can feel exciting and validating to realize that you are well on your way to truly becoming an "expert." As one interviewee in this phase told us:

> I know I do very good work with adolescents. I don't get anxious with them the way I sometimes can with adults. I'm much freer to be myself—to take risks, challenge and tease— and the kids really respond to that.

As patients recognize and appreciate your expertise, you will find them referring others to you. Indeed, in the fee-for-service therapy market, word of mouth is undoubtedly your best referral source.

Another important source of referrals is other professionals. If you are diligent about maintaining your professional connections, you can tap into a rich mine of referrals. When you get a call from a patient who says: "My husband is seeing Dr. Jones and he suggested that I call you," do you immediately make a call to Dr. Jones? It's important to express your appreciation and also (once you have a signed Release of Information) to tap into Dr. Jones's insights about the case. It doesn't even hurt to send a written note occasionally. Let the other professional know that you appreciate his or her referrals and that you're willing to reciprocate. I have been known to cross a therapist off my referral list when neither thanks nor reciprocity have been forthcoming!

Clearly, by the time you reach the Establishing Phase, marketing and networking are threads in the same cloth. Another significant thread is community involvement. One of our interviewees made a most telling comment. When asked about how she decides who to refer to, she replied:

> I tend to refer to people who are active in the community—people I know from committees or who I've worked with in my professional organization. People who are involved in the professional community can usually be relied on to be responsible to the ethical standards of the community. There is a sort of accountability that's missing in people who aren't involved.

If you are willing to work for the advancement of the profession and the well-being of your community, you will find that your fellow therapists tend to trust and respect you. Whether you want to serve on an organizing committee for the Psychological Association, teach a class at your community college, or donate an hour or two a week to the local free clinic, investing in your community is vital to maintaining a successful practice.

INVESTMENT CONSIDERATIONS IN THE ESTABLISHING PHASE
What About Real Estate?
One of the most important investment decisions to make at this phase is whether and how much you want to invest in real estate. Most therapists in private practice will want to own their own homes. How about going further and buying rental property or a

building to house your office? To make the decision about whether this is right for you, the following questions should be helpful:

- Is your credit good enough to obtain a favorable mortgage rate?
- Do you have substantial available cash for a down payment?
- Is your cash flow steady enough to carry the property until you can find appropriate tenants?
- Are you a "handyperson" yourself or do you have someone reliable to help you with repairs and maintenance?
- Are you comfortable maintaining a friendly but businesslike relationship with tenants?
- Is your risk tolerance level such that this kind of investment won't keep you awake at night?

If the answers to all of the above are "yes," our advice is to read the more in-depth discussion on page 168 and then make the leap. We were at a retirement party recently for a very successful therapist who said: "The only regret I have about my career is that I didn't buy the building where I rented my office." Real estate investing can be a challenge, but it can also bring professional, personal, and financial rewards over the long term.

The Establishing Phase is an extremely important time financially. As we have discussed previously, unless you are expecting a source of revenue apart from what your practice provides, it is important that you think like the tortoise, not the hare. With a long time horizon you can provide well for your future self without undue hardship now. As you get older, it gets harder to put enough away for retirement because of a shortened time horizon that diminishes the power of compound interest and the time value of money. In the table below we consider the amount needed to save monthly in order to save $1 million.

MONTHLY SAVINGS NEEDED TO REACH A RETIREMENT SAVINGS GOAL OF $1 MILLION
Assumptions: Rate of return 6% in a tax deferred account. Amounts are invested at the beginning of each month.

Table 4.1 Monthly Savings Toward Goal of $1 Million[1]

Year	Monthly savings toward goal of $1 million
5 years	$14,261.49
10 years	$6,071.69
15 years	$3,421.46
20 years	$2,153.54
25 years	$1,435.83
30 years	$990.55
35 years	$698.41
40 years	$499.64
45 years	$361.04

If you are 35 years old and plan to retire at 70, then you have 35 years to reach your goal. If you average a modest 6% return on your investment over those 35 years, then you could theoretically reach the $1 million goal by putting $698.41 per month into your tax-deferred retirement account until you retire at age 70. On the other hand, if wanted to reach the $1 million retirement goal by age 70, and you are currently age 45 with nothing yet saved for retirement, it would take $2,153.54 per month to reach your goal. This should underscore that if you start in your thirties with retirement investing, it will take a much less aggressive contribution schedule to reach your goals than if you wait until later in life.

The Establishing Phase is also an important time to evaluate your life insurance and disability insurance needs. Clearly, if you have children or other dependents who rely on your income for their well-being, then life insurance should be a consideration for you at this stage of the game. Similarly, if you and your dependents

---

1   The results shown in this table are hypothetical; they do not represent the actual trading of securities. Actual performance will vary from this hypothetical performance due to, but not limited to: (1) advisory fees and other expenses that one would pay; (2) transaction costs; (3) the inability to execute trades at the last published price (the hypothetical returns assume execution at the last closing price); (4) the inability to maintain an equally weighted portfolio in size (the hypothetical returns assume an equal weighting); and (5) market and economic factors will almost certainly cause one to invest differently than projected by the model that simulated the above returns. All returns include the reinvestment of dividends. Past performance, particularly hypothetical performance, cannot be used to predict future performance.

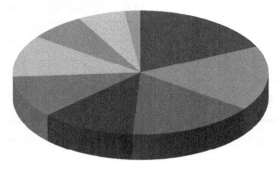

- 18% Mid Cap Value
- 16% Int'l Developed Mkts
- 11% Int'l Emerging Mkts
- 7% Intermediate Bond
- 2% Cash
- 17% Mid Cap Core
- 12% Large Cap Value
- 11% Int'l Bond
- 6% Real Estate Inv Trusts

Figure 2 Example of Growth Asset Allocation[2]

rely on your practice income, disability insurance can make a huge difference in the event that you become ill or injured. Health insurance is necessary at every stage of the game, and you should definitely have coverage in the Establishing Phase as the cost of a major medical condition can devastate your financial life.

Asset allocation at this phase of the game can typically be oriented to growth. With a long time horizon until retirement, many investors feel that they can trade volatility for growth potential in their portfolio of stocks and bonds. A typical growth asset allocation might look something like that in Figure 2.

In every way, the Establishing Phase is full of promise for the private practitioner. It is a time of coming into one's own professionally as well as financially. It is a transitional phase from being a beginner to becoming a seasoned veteran. In the dimensions of professional development, marketing, refining your niche, and investing, the Establishing Phase therapist is laying down the foundations that will make the Prime Phase and Elder Phase successful and fulfilling.

---

2   Asset allocation does not guarantee a profit or protection from losses in a declining market.

CHAPTER 5

The Prime Phase

This is a rewarding time—a time when your practice is firmly established and you are reaching your full professional maturity. Your clinical skills are finely honed; you are recognized and respected in your community and at your peak earning capacity. Financially the stakes are higher than ever. There may well be college tuition or aging parents to provide for, and certainly there is diminishing time to prepare for retirement.

AT THE CROSSROADS

At the Prime Phase, we stand at the crossroads. Looking back, we can take pride in how far we have come and also acknowledge our regrets. My (Daisy's) brother once remarked that the definition of a mid-life crisis is the time when all the stupid mistakes of our youth become unavoidably apparent! No one reaches midlife without a fair share of mistakes, regrets and stupidities, and therapists are no exception. However, to paraphrase Willie Nelson, "There ain't nothing we can do about it now." Will we let ourselves be consumed by the "might have beens" or will we do the developmental work of midlife and move toward integrating all the aspects of ourselves in the effort to become more complete human beings?

Jung said that one could not truly enter into therapy before the age of 40. He was referring, I think, to the individuation process that is lifelong but that reaches a new level of awareness at midlife. By this point, much of the "dragon-slaying" of the younger years has been accomplished and it is time for self-exploration. This may be a time to consider a return to therapy—perhaps with an Intersubjective or Jungian analyst. Working with a dream group or keeping a journal, even if these things have never appealed before, can be important avenues to tapping in to the Self. Some amount of solitude is an important consideration at this phase. In many traditional cultures, women retreat for a time when entering menopause. When they return from retreat, they have assumed the mantle of the wise woman. A lengthy retreat may not be feasible for you, but even a day or two at the ocean or in the mountains can provide a valuable time to pause and reflect.

INTEGRATING THEORY AND AUTHENTICITY

Most of us, in graduate training or sometime early in our careers, embrace a theoretical orientation that feels valid and useful to us. For the theory to sustain us in our work over the long haul, it must also fit our personality style. I (Daisy) often entertain myself by speculating about whether like attracts like in terms of theoretical orientation, or whether opposites attract. For example, is a therapist with a flamboyant, extroverted style likely to become a psychodramatist (like attracts like) or more likely to choose a restrained psychoanalytic approach (opposites attract)? I have yet to arrive at a satisfactory answer to this question, but it does seem clear to me that, over the course of their careers, therapists both shape and are shaped by the orientation they choose.

By the time you have arrived at the Prime Phase, you have gained the wisdom and maturity that allow you to interact with your patients in ways that can be deeply healing and, at times, transformative. The Prime Phase therapist knows that:

- By sitting in the therapist's chair, you automatically assume a significant amount of power. For those of us who came of age in the sixties, this has perhaps been a difficult lesson to assimilate. We haven't wanted to "power-trip" people, after all! However, recognizing that patients inevitably hand you power and authority enables you to handle that power thoughtfully and effectively—using it for the patient's growth rather than denying or abusing it.

- Regardless of theoretical orientation, it is the relationship that heals. It has been said that "therapy is nothing more and nothing less than one human being talking to another." Rather than relying on clever interventions or brilliant interpretations, the Prime Phase therapist values the humanness of the therapeutic relationship.
- The authentic self of the therapist calls to the authentic self of the client. How self-revealing you are as a therapist is an individual decision, but your willingness to be authentically who you are allows your clients to become willing to do the same.
- The "rules" of therapy are important (e.g. no sexual contact with patients) but the rules must serve as a container for the therapy, not define it.

Studies have shown that effective therapists from different theoretical schools are more like each other than are effective and ineffective therapists from the same school (Carkhuff, 1977). The Prime Phase therapist has refined her theory and technique so that she can use them as a bridge between herself and her patients, rather than as a barrier.

Whatever the theoretical orientation of the therapist, in the Prime Phase, the integration of theory is now at a place that is more internalized and expressive of the therapist's authentic life perspective. Theory at this point becomes more of an expression of who the therapist is rather than an intellectualized exercise. The theory that the therapist has lived with over the years has shaped her and now she shapes the theory to reflect her individual style. It has been wisely said that a truly developed therapist is one who has mastered the tools of her trade and can then leave them outside the consulting room door. At the Prime Phase this can become reality.

SHAPING YOUR PRACTICE

Another advantage of being in the Prime Phase of your career is the increased freedom to choose the people you want to work with. When a therapist is first beginning her practice, she is likely to welcome every referral with eager anticipation. The idea of turning down a paying client would never occur to her. Even at later stages of your career, it can seem like tempting fate to say "no." However, if you want a practice that feels truly satisfying—a true reflection of who you are—you will need to shape your practice. And that means, in one way or another, choosing your patients. Certainly, ability to pay your fees is one important criterion. It can be helpful to decide how many spaces in your caseload you are comfortable providing to pro bono or reduced fee clients. Once those slots are filled, you must become willing to provide appropriate referrals to people unable to afford your full fee.

By this time, you probably also want to limit the number of managed care cases you will take. The first time I (Daisy) told a managed care referral that I couldn't see him, my heart was in my mouth. Was this hubris that I would pay for later? Interestingly enough, my willingness to say "no" seems to only have increased the number of calls I get.

So is every full-fee referral a good one? Not necessarily. Pay attention to what interests you and give yourself permission to choose accordingly. I had always enjoyed working with adolescents, but when my children were going through their teens the idea of seeing adolescent clients sounded truly awful. It was important to honor my own limits and focus on adults. One of our interviewees told us that she no longer sees couples. "I found it just too exhausting to be required to maintain neutrality." Many psychoanalytically oriented therapists focus their practice on clients who are interested in working analytically.

We have talked a good deal, earlier in this book, about the freedom of private practice. To truly reap the rewards of your freedom, you must be willing to tolerate the anxiety that can come with open space. If you say "No, I don't have any sliding scale slots right now"; "No, I work only with adults"; "No, I'm not accepting new clients at the moment"; there will inevitably be some empty spaces in your practice periodically. Certainly, this can stir up a lot of anxiety. However, if you can come to consider these spaces as possibilities rather than signs of failure, you will find that your practice will increasingly assume a shape that reflects your individuality.

GENERATIVITY—THE IMPORTANCE OF CONNECTING TO THE LARGER WORLD

Erik Erikson defines the primary developmental task of mid-life as generativity versus stagnation. In the Prime Phase, the therapist finds many opportunities for generativity and it is the seizing of these opportunities that will make the difference between a life well lived and a life of "quiet desperation."

Mentoring

Part of the obligation of each generation is to pass on its knowledge and wisdom to the next. You may find satisfaction in taking on an intern. As one of our interviewees commented: "It's so validating to work with an intern. It helps me recognize how far I've come in my own professional development. Plus, it's a challenge to develop a new way of working—to not just provide answers but to help her arrive at her own answers."

Some of our greatest learning has come from our roles as trainers. Through facilitating training groups for therapists over the last 12 years, we've been challenged to examine our own point of view, look at our blind spots and develop in ways we never could have predicted. You may be interested in putting together a training group of your own, running a consultation group, or teaching some postgraduate courses. Just as our own mentors provided the necessary teaching and support to help us develop in our early years, so by providing the same for younger therapists do we find ourselves developing more fully in the middle years.

Another source of satisfaction during the Prime Phase is recognizing that our work with individual patients often produces wide ripples. Many are the families that have benefited from "therapy by osmosis." Often, too, we find ourselves treating someone—a teacher, a doctor, a judge—who has a wide sphere of influence. If these people find their compassion and self-awareness increased through therapy, they have the potential to make a significant impact on the world.

Prime Phase therapists also provide leadership to professional and community organizations. Among our interviewees, one is chairman of the board of Jewish Family Services; another is active in her Quaker Meeting; another was a founder of the Psychotherapy Institute, a postgraduate training program in Berkeley, California. This sort of activity provides therapists with an opportunity for generativity. At the same time, it raises your profile in the community and allows for marketing through truly enlightened self-interest.

FINANCIAL PLANNING ISSUES IN THE PRIME PHASE
The Prime Phase typically covers the ages from the mid-forties to retirement age. Earning power is at its peak, and this phase represents the last chance to put money away before retirement. The stakes in the retirement savings arena are never higher than they are in the Prime Phase. In all likelihood, if you are to receive an inheritance on the death of a parent, it will come during this phase. If you have a shortfall in your retirement savings now, it becomes vitally important to address the shortfall so that your retirement will not be jeopardized.

Paying for disability income insurance is certainly an important goal in your forties and fifties, but as you get closer to age 65, when most disability policies stop payment, it is frequently sensible to shift the resources you were putting into a disability policy into long-term care insurance. There may be some years in your mid- to late fifties when you will want both, but eventually the long-term care coverage becomes more important. You should have enough in your retirement fund by your late fifties that income replacement becomes less of an issue.

If you are expecting an inheritance, it is important that you go over your parents' finances with them. Although this can be a sensitive area in many older parent–middle-aged child relationships, it is important that you have some idea what to expect with regard to your inheritance so that you can plan accordingly. It may be useful to meet with your parents' financial planner and/or attorney to get a good picture of their finances. One issue that may be appropriate to bring up with older parents is long-term care coverage. This coverage can help to preserve their estate and your inheritance, should the need for long-term care arise.

Remember that long-term care coverage is purchased mostly for the purpose of estate preservation, so if preserving your parents' estate is vital to your financial well-being in retirement, talking with your parents about purchasing such coverage, even if such a conversation is uncomfortable, may be well worth it. Most long-term care policies now offer coverage for home care and assisted living, so that the coverage may be viewed as insurance to stay out of a nursing home rather than coverage for a nursing home.

As with all the other phases, health insurance is of paramount concern. Unless you are very wealthy, you really cannot afford to "go bare" with regard to health insurance in the Prime Phase. As we age, of course, our chances for illness increase, and we have less time to recover from devastating financial loss due to illness than earlier in our careers. Health insurance is simply a must. Don't go without it!

ASSET ALLOCATION IN THE PRIME PHASE

The Prime Phase covers a long period of life—from the mid-forties to retirement age, which for many therapists is well into the seventies. Therefore, we cannot make a sweeping statement about appropriate asset allocation. The closer we get to retirement, the more conservative the asset allocation should be. Some planners suggest that if you subtract your age from 100, you will come up with an appropriate percentage of stocks and alternative securities (with a relatively small percentage in alternatives such as real estate investment trusts) to hold in your portfolio to complement the fixed income securities you hold. So for example at age 30 your portfolio could comprise 70% stocks and alternatives along with 30% bonds and cash. When you are 55, then your portfolio could be 45% in stocks and alternatives with 55% in bonds and cash. At age 70 you would be 30% in stocks and alternatives with 70% in bonds and cash. The point is that the closer you are to retirement, the more weight you should give to fixed securities, as you have less time to make up for losses in the market and usually want decreased volatility.

Example of Growth and Income Asset Allocation With 40% in Bonds and Cash

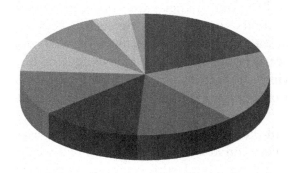

Figure 3 Example of Growth and Income Asset Allocation With 40% in Bonds and Cash[1]

Therapists around age 40 might want to consider an asset allocation such as the example in Figure 3—a growth and income asset allocation with 55% in stocks, 5% in real estate investment trusts and 40% in bonds and cash.

A 50-year-old therapist may choose a growth and income asset allocation with 50% in bonds and cash, such as the model portfolio in Figure 4.

One mistake I have seen Prime Phase therapists make is to try to make up for lost time by being overly aggressive in their investing. As one gets older, and closer to needing one's retirement dollars, it generally makes sense to become more conservative in the asset mix in the retirement account. My advice to Prime Phase therapists whose retirement funds are not fully sufficient is to work

---

1   Asset allocation does not guarantee a profit or protection from losses in a declining market.

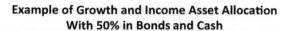

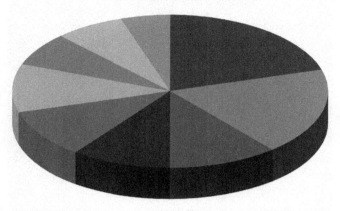

- 20% Intermediate Bond
- 11% Mid Cap Value
- 10% Int'l Developed Markets
- 7.5% Large Cap Value
- 5% Real Estate Inv Trusts
- 20% Short Bond
- 10% Mid Cap Core
- 10% International Bond
- 7% Int'l Emerging Mkts

Figure 4 Example of Growth and Income Asset Allocation With 50% in Bonds and Cash[2]

creatively to find ways to increase regular investments into the retirement fund rather than to invest in ways that are inappropriately risky. In other words, in the Prime Phase it is generally better to *fund* aggressively than to skew your asset allocation aggressively.

Figure 5 shows a model balanced portfolio that might be appropriate for a Prime Phase therapist who is 60 years old. In it, the stocks comprise 37% percent, real estate investment trusts are 3%, bonds are 58%, and cash is 2%.

---

2   Asset allocation does not guarantee a profit or protection from losses in a declining market.

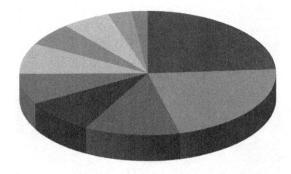

- 24% Intermediate Bond
- 22% Short Bond
- 12% International Bond
- 9% Mid Cap Value
- 8% Mid Cap Core
- 8% Int'l Developed Mkts
- 6% Large Cap Value
- 6% Int'l Emerging Mkts
- 3% Real Estate Inv Trusts
- 2% Cash

Figure 5 Example of Balanced Asset Allocation With 60% in Bonds and Cash[3]

ESTATE PLANNING IN THE PRIME PHASE

In Chapter 26 of this text we cover a variety of basic estate planning issues. In the Prime Phase, it becomes increasingly important to address these issues, as there are important considerations to attend to with regard to the financial well-being of one partner should the other predecease him or her, as well as important issues regarding the passing of assets to the next generation along with advanced medical directives and a will. As we move into middle age and beyond, we come increasingly face-to-face with our mortality and thus with estate planning issues.

FACING LIFELONG PATTERNS IN THE PRIME PHASE

We therapists know all too well that characterological patterns can be incredibly resistant to insight, awareness, and change. Dysfunctional financial behavior often does slow damage to the financial

---

3   Asset allocation does not guarantee a profit or protection from losses in a declining market.

standing of the individual, and by middle age, that slow damage has had time to create a seriously worrisome financial picture. Therapists who find themselves in this position may be well advised to seek out professional psychological and financial help. I have found that many therapists who have thoroughly looked at other of their life issues have not delved very deeply into their financial issues. They have left this dimension of their lives a closed book. In the Prime Phase, it is clearly not in your interest to avoid financial issues that are giving rise to dysfunctional financial behavior. As you face these issues you may well find that the journey of self-discovery is as valuable as the destination of achieving financial stability and well-being.

REFERENCE
Carkhuff, Robert. *Beyond Counseling and Therapy* (Washington, DC: International Thomson Publishing, 1977)

CHAPTER 6

The Elder Phase

What is it about older therapists that is so appealing? Although their bodies inevitably show signs of age, their spirits often maintain a vibrant sense of curiosity and liveliness that many in their twenties might envy. To embark on a career in psychotherapy is to enter into a lifelong journey of self-exploration—an ever-deepening appreciation of one's own humanity and the strengths and vulnerabilities of humankind. Therapists in their elder years have a hard-won wisdom. They have walked with their clients "through the valley of the shadow of death" and arrived at a place where they can truly appreciate life in all its complexity.

AGE AND WISDOM

One of the great rewards of psychotherapy as a profession is the fact that age is an advantage rather than a handicap. My interns often say to me: "I just can't speak with any authority. People tell me I'm too young." It's very satisfying to have reached a position in mid-life where I can speak with authority; and even more satisfying to know that at 75, my authority will have only increased. Because psychotherapy is a field that values wisdom and integration, the position of elder therapist can be rewarding indeed. The integration of skill, life experience, and spirituality—however one might define it—that comes with age finds a particularly complete expression in the Elder Phase.

In looking back on their careers, elder therapists often recognize their own longing for wisdom as a catalyst in their choice of profession. "I considered the law, but that was too dry for me. I needed something that dealt with human beings in a very complicated way—that would really help me understand the human condition."

"Therapy is about a philosophy of life. What we do is work to help people find meaning—not just solve problems, but develop their creativity and begin to live a life that is meaningful to them."

I MIGHT SLOW DOWN—BUT I DON'T WANT TO STOP

A part of wisdom is an increased ability to recognize one's own limitations. It is not possible—nor even desirable—to be all things to all people. Carl Whitaker, one of the great innovators in family therapy, puts it this way:

> Over time you have less and less delusion of grandeur and more and more awareness of the process in which you are invested. As you become less enslaved by your role, you have a greater enjoyment of it and experience an ever-growing inner peace of your own.
>
> (Whitaker, 1989, p. 162)

Aging, of course, brings its own inevitable physical limitations, and the wise elder therapist respects these:

> I'm eighty years old. When I was about seventy-five, I realized that I needed to let my practice slow down, but I didn't want to give it up and I still don't. Right now I'm in my practice about ten hours a week—two of which involve a group I'm leading for the Psychotherapy Institute.

Despite the body's aging, however, even despite struggles with chronic pain or illness, many therapists find their work a source of continued vitality and excitement. One of our interviewees who struggles with fibromyalgia spoke about her feeling that her work is a necessity for her: "I love what I do. It's energizing for me, it keeps my mind going and offers me connection to the therapist community. My whole life is enhanced by my work."

Therapists also keep their youthful spirit alive through cherishing the rebel, the iconoclast in themselves and encouraging it in others. From the days of Sigmund Freud, psychotherapy has challenged the status quo. In the words of one of our interviewees:

> There is a piece in me that rebels against conservative rules. Helping people be more of who they really are and let go of trying to be who they think they ought to be is how I keep the rebel in me alive. There's a lot of possibility for freedom in this world. There are certain constraints, I mean I don't kid myself about that, but in terms of how you do the work, there is tremendous freedom, and you get to be on the side of the underdog.

LIVING WITH AMBIGUITY AND INCOMPLETION

I (Daisy) read a comic strip the other day in which one teenager is saying to another: "I thought for sure by the time I was 16 I'd have it all figured out!" It's easy to chuckle at the innocence of that, but many of us live with the expectation that at some point in our lives—maybe by 60 or 70 (surely by 80!)—we'll have things figured out and feel a sense of completion. The Elder Phase therapists we spoke with certainly have a sense of satisfaction as they look back on their lives and careers, but not necessarily a sense of completion. "One of the developmental issues for me in this phase is coming to terms with the fact that everything is going to be incomplete. We don't complete our lives; they are always a work in progress."

One of the challenges for the elder therapist is coming to terms with the unavoidable regrets and incompletions in her life and allowing herself to appreciate the richness of the present moment. It is this sense of balance and wisdom that allows the elder therapist to serve as an invaluable resource to younger members of the community. Many of us in the psychotherapy field come from families where role models were problematic or absent altogether. It can be both comforting and inspirational to see those on the road ahead of us following that road with courage and grace.

DEALING WITH ISSUES OF MORTALITY

Death is an inescapable fact of life, and during the Elder Phase this becomes an increasingly personal realization. For some Elder Phase therapists, a recognition of personal mortality is nothing new:

> My whole practice has been informed by awareness of the fragility of life. I came very close to dying a few years in a row. So I got it, that I don't have forever and that there are things that I need to continue to integrate while there's still time. I'm interested in the questions of what is wisdom? What is transcendence?

Awareness of mortality frequently leads to life review:

> I'm going back to my roots. . . looking at what I received in childhood—the good and the bad—and how I have made use of what I received and what I missed.

Perhaps above all, awareness of mortality shapes the way the elder therapist lives her life in the present:

> How do you live with yourself and others knowing that you won't be here forever? I'm paying attention to how I can play more, how to give back, how to love people fully and yet be able to let them go.

By the time they have reached the Elder Phase, most therapists have developed a view of life in a larger perspective—whether traditionally religious, spiritual in a mystical sense, or simply a sense of connection to humanity and the greater whole—that allows them to move through their later years with a sense of confidence and equanimity.

FINANCIAL PLANNING IN THE ELDER PHASE
Retirement Age

Of course, a key issue in retirement planning is the age at which you plan to retire. While 65 was, at one time, the magic age for retirement, this is no longer the case. Some therapists retire early,

Table 6.1 Social Security Chart of Retirement Ages With Reductions for Early Retirement[*]

Full Retirement and Age 62 Benefit by Year of Birth

Year of Birth[1]	Full (normal) Retirement Age	Months between age 62 and full retirement age[2]	At Age 62[3]			
			A $1,000 retirement benefit would be reduced to	The retirement benefit is reduced by[4]	A $500 spouse's benefit would be reduced to	The spouse's benefit is reduced by[5]
1937 or earlier	65	36	$800	20.00%	$375	25.00%
1938	65 and 2 months	38	$791	20.83%	$370	25.83%
1939	65 and 4 months	40	$783	21.67%	$366	26.67%
1940	65 and 6 months	42	$775	22.50%	$362	27.50%
1941	65 and 8 months	44	$766	23.33%	$358	28.33%
1942	65 and 10 months	46	$758	24.17%	$354	29.17%
1943–1954	66	48	$750	25.00%	$350	30.00%
1955	66 and 2 months	50	$741	25.83%	$345	30.83%
1956	66 and 4 months	52	$733	26.67%	$341	31.67%

1957	66 and 6 months	54	$725	27.50%	$337	32.50%
1958	66 and 8 months	56	$716	28.33%	$333	33.33%
1959	66 and 10 months	58	$708	29.17%	$329	34.17%
1960 and later	67	60	$700	30.00%	$325	35.00%

[1] If you were born on January 1st, you should refer to the previous year.

[2] If you were born on the 1st of the month, we figure your benefit (and your full retirement age) as if your birthday was in the previous month. If you were born on January 1st, we figure your benefit (and your full retirement age) as if your birthday was in December of the previous year.

[3] You must be at least 62 for the entire month to receive benefits.

[4] Percentages are approximate due to rounding.

[5] The maximum benefit for the spouse is 50% of the benefit the worker would receive at full retirement age. The % reduction for the spouse should be applied after the automatic 50% reduction. Percentages are approximate due to rounding.

Source: Social Security Administration. www.ssa.gov/retirechart.htm

*   Asset allocation does not guarantee a profit or protection from losses in a declining market.

while others enjoy working well beyond age 65. Below is a chart detailing the fact that age 65 is being phased out as the full retirement age by the Social Security Administration in favor of age 67. For people born in 1937 or earlier, the full retirement age for social security remains at 65. For people born in subsequent years, the retirement age gradually rises. For people born in 1960 or later, the full retirement age is 67. Social Security recipients have the option of retiring at 62. However, their benefits are decreased accordingly. In the chart below you will note that taking benefits at age 62 continues to be an option, but the monthly percent reduction increases as the full retirement age increases.

Life Expectancy

The main financial issue surrounding life expectancy is that you not outlive your financial resources. It goes without saying that there is no sure way to know your life expectancy, but because we all took social statistics in grad school, we know that such things can be estimated in terms of statistical probability. If you go to the Social Security Administration's website ssa.gov/planners/lifeexpectancy.html you can pull up a statistical estimate of your expected life span. Once you have estimated your life span, then you are ready to estimate the amount of money you need so that you will not outlive your financial resources.

Estimating Retirement Resources Needed

Estimating the amount of money you need to support yourself in retirement is a complicated calculation taking into account many factors including inflation, rate of return on investments, life expectancy, and so on. To help you make this calculation, I (Peter) have posted a calculator on the Insight Financial Group website. Go to http://insightfinancialgroup.com and then go to the calculators link. From there, go to retirement saving calculator.

To give you an idea of the kind of feedback you will get, I inputted the following information into the retirement saving calculator: A single, 60-year-old person with an annual income of 100,000 who plans to live on $75,000 per year when she retires. Retirement savings are $400,000. Inflation is 4%, and the desired retirement age is 67 years old. The savings are calculated to last for 20 years. The preretirement investment return is 10% per year while the postretirement income is 8% per year. Social Security benefits are figured into the calculation. The calculator then provides the following estimate based on the data we just inputted.

To provide the inflation-adjusted retirement income you desire, you will need to save 9.2% of your yearly income. This year, for example, the amount would be $9,201 or $767 a month. If you wait just one year to start saving for retirement you will need to save 11.5% of your annual income, which amounts to $11,501 in the first year.[2]

If you first work with the life expectancy calculator and then with the retirement saving calculator, you will have some rational numbers to work with around the feasibility of taking your retirement.

Dealing With a Shortfall in Retirement Funds

Many therapists in the Elder Phase see patients part-time. Two primary reasons for this are (1) the continuing need for income to supplement retirement savings, social security, and other pensions, and (2) continued excitement for and commitment to the work. If you find that you need to supplement your income with continued clinical work, and you want to stop working, then you should consider consulting with a financial planner to see if you might be able to devise a retirement plan. There may be creative ways to solve problems of shortfall in the retirement plan.

Here are some ideas for elder therapists who are facing a shortfall of funds:

1) Look into an FHA Reverse Mortgage (HECM) for seniors
2) Take out cash values in life insurance policies

---

2 *The information provided here is to assist you in planning for your future. Any analysis is a result of the information you have provided.* Material discussed is meant for general illustration and/or informational purposes only and it is not to be construed as tax, legal, or investment advice. Although the information has been gathered from sources believed to be reliable, please note that individual situations can vary therefore, the information should be relied upon when coordinated with individual professional advice.

Any rate of return entered into the interactive calculator to project future values should be a reasonable average return for the period. Rates of return will vary over time, and generally the higher the rate of return the higher the degree of risk.

3) Reduce living expenses by simplifying
4) Consider a foreign retirement.

FHA Reverse Mortgages (HECMs) for Seniors

If you are 62 or older, have paid off your mortgage, or have a small balance remaining on your mortgage, you may want to participate in FHA's Home Equity Conversion Mortgage (HECM) program. This program allows you to withdraw a portion of your home's equity. There are many factors to consider before deciding whether an HECM is right for you. You can call 800-569-4287 to find a qualified HECM counselor to learn about the program.

Using Living Benefits From a Permanent Life Insurance Policy

It is not uncommon that therapists will have maintained permanent life insurance while their heirs are still dependent. In some cases, by the time the therapist has reached the Elder Phase, the priority shifts from protecting dependents who are now well on their way, to providing for the elder therapist herself. In such cases it may make sense to explore using living benefits from a permanent life insurance policy.

Surrender for Cash

A permanent life insurance policy may be surrendered for cash. If you have a permanent life insurance policy, you can readily access the surrender value. There will be tax consequences for surrendering your policy, as the value of the policy minus your current basis in the policy is taxable.

Loans on a Permanent Life Insurance Policy

An alternative to surrendering your policy is to take a loan out against the cash value in the policy. Insurance policy loans work very differently from commercial loans. Policy loans will be continued even if no payments are made as long as there is enough cash in the policy to pay the interest. The policy stays in force as long as outstanding loans on the policy are less than the cash value. Many policyholders take loans on their policies and do not intend to pay the loan back in their lifetime. Instead, the death benefit to their heirs will be reduced by the outstanding loan amount at the time of the insured's death. Moreover, there is exceptionally favorable tax treatment for life insurance loans. There is NO CURRENT INCOME TAX due on a policy loan as long as the policy stays in force.

Trading Your Permanent Life Insurance Policy for an Annuity Contract

You may exchange your permanent life insurance policy for an annuity contract tax-free as long as there are no outstanding loans on the life insurance policy. You may take surrender value or maturity of a permanent life insurance policy in the form of an annuity, and defer taxation. Annuity payments may provide you with a guaranteed lifetime of income, or payable over a specific period of time. Annuities are generally difficult for creditors to access, and may be worth considering if you have debtors who may try to come after you.

Living Simply

Some elder therapists have lived their lives in helping others, and have not, for whatever set of reasons, put enough away for retirement to continue with a previously maintained standard of living. If you are in this position, it is important that you work with it creatively. Perhaps there are hidden gifts in your set of circumstances if you work with it. One shift that such a set of circumstances might lead you to, is to work consciously and creatively with simplifying your lifestyle, so that you do not need so much money to be live abundantly.

Many therapists are tuned into the fact that money does not buy happiness. It can be challenging, however, not to let fear take you over if you are older and are facing a financial shortfall. In order to work with these issues, you may want to reach out to others who are working with similar issues. You may find such support in a faith community, or with others who have values similar to yours. Some resources for people who want and need to simplify are:

- Simple Living.com is a company headed by Janet Luhrs. She directs the website (http://simpleliving.com), is the author of several thoughtful books, and puts out a journal on the spirituality and joys of living simply. She provides tools and philosophical inquiry into the enjoyment of life in a slower, more attuned mode. Simple Living has become a movement among people who wish to get off the merry-go-round of American materialism. Even if you have all the financial resources you could wish for, you may find much of value in Janet Luhrs' approach.

- *Your Money or Your Life* is a book by Joe Dominguez and Vicki Robin that has become a bible to many people who want to simplify their lives and live according to ecologically and spiritually sound principles. Dominguez and Robin have developed a nine-step system for achieving a life that is "outwardly simple and inwardly rich."

Choosing simplicity, often difficult in a consumer culture, means readying oneself for a life that is truer to one's gifts, passions and sense of purpose; we have used the term "frugality" to describe this elegant fit between our real needs and how we enjoyably and ethically fill those needs (Dominguez and Robin, 1999, p. xvii).

Foreign Retirement

The key to foreign retirement is the strength of the dollar compared to the strength of the local currency. A Social Security pension that is marginal in the U.S. may buy you a very appealing lifestyle in another country. A solid resource for foreign retirement is www.escapeartist. com, a site devoted to giving realistic information to people who want to retire or move to foreign countries. It has specific information favorite destinations for American retirees: Argentina, Belize, Canada, Costa Rica, Czech Republic, Ecuador, France, Great Britain, Greece, Ireland, Italy, Mexico, Portugal, Spain, and Thailand.

Three useful books are *The World's Top Retirement Havens* by Margaret J. Goldstein (Ed.); *Your Guide to Retiring to Mexico, Costa Rica and Beyond: Finding the Good Life on a Fixed Income* by Shelly Emling; and *The Grown Up's Guide to Retiring Abroad* by Rosanne Knorr. All are available at Amazon.com. There are communities of American retirees living abroad, who love their lives outside of the U.S. This option is clearly not for everybody, but if you find the idea intriguing, perhaps some further research will be of interest.

ASSET ALLOCATION IN THE ELDER PHASE

As we have discussed earlier in the text, asset allocation is of critical importance in all phases of your career. As one gets older, one should generally be more conservative with asset allocation. At the Elder Phase, asset allocation will generally be conservative. A conservative portfolio has a relatively larger position of bonds, with a relatively smaller position in stocks. Some exposure to stocks is usually recommended, even in retirement, in order to allow the portfolio to grow faster than inflation.

Figure 6 shows an example of a conservative asset allocation. Of course the asset allocation that would be best for you is something that you and your financial advisor will need to determine.

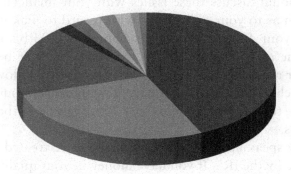

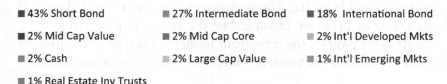

Figure 6 Conservative Model Portfolio[3]

---

3   This model is shown for illustrative purposes only. Please consult an investment advisor before purchasing.

REQUIRED DISTRIBUTIONS IN THE ELDER PHASE

If you have a retirement plan such as an IRA, 403(b), SEP, SIMPLE, or 457 plan you will generally need to start making withdrawals from your plan at age 70½. The reason for this is quite straightforward: The federal government puts a limit amount on the amount of time it will defer taxes on retirement money. This money is tax-deferred, not tax-free. Each year after 70½, you will need to take a minimum amount out of your retirement plan. This money can then go to fund your living expenses, or if you do not need it for living expenses, can be reinvested. If you qualify, it can sometimes make sense to move your distributions into a Roth IRA, which goes in as after-tax money, but subsequently grows tax-free.

Many elder clinicians have 403(b) plans from working in school districts and other qualifying employers. If you have 403(b) retirement dollars that were contributed prior to 1987, you may be able to delay distribution of those dollars until you are 75 years old. You should discuss these issues with your financial advisor to be certain as to your obligations with regard to making distributions on your 403(b). Another exception for 403(b)s is that if you continue to work past age 70, you can defer the beginning date of your required distributions until the April 1 following the year in which you retire. If you have already rolled your 403(b) into an IRA, then you must follow the 70½ age rule for beginning distributions.

Generally speaking, these distributions will be treated as ordinary income by the IRS. If you have money in your qualified plan payable to a beneficiary when you die, that money will be included in your taxable estate. The money going to your beneficiary will be taxed as ordinary income, but the taxes may be reduced by estate taxes paid on the retirement money. This type of taxation to your beneficiary is known as "income in respect to a descendent."

The Form of Your Retirement Distributions

It is often sensible to have a portion of one's distributions annuitized, while another portion is withdrawn as needed. Let's say that Ann Howard, MSW, is 75 years old, has $250,000 in an IRA and $150,000 in a 403(b) from employment with a school district. She has additional assets to help support her retirement. She may want to put her IRA into an annuity contract that will guarantee her income for life while keeping her 403(b) funds in investments that she can draw on as needed. This approach gives her the increased confidence that comes with a lifetime annuity on her IRA along with flexibility of her investments in her 403(b) plan.

If you are wealthier, or if you have other sources of annuitized income such as a defined benefit plan from your own work or from a spouse, then you may choose to not annuitize your retirement dollars and keep the plan as flexible as possible.

For Higher Net Worth Therapists at the Elder Phase: Estate Planning Issues

If you have sufficient assets that the issue is not whether you will outlive your assets, but instead, how much you will leave to your heirs, then there are some important considerations for your retirement accounts to bear in mind that will help you pass on a maximum to your heirs. The estate-planning problem with retirement accounts for high net worth individuals is that the undistributed value in the retirement plan may be taxed after death as part of the estate. If the plan is then distributed to the beneficiary, it is taxable again to the beneficiary as ordinary income. The effect of these two taxes can take quite a toll of the assets you want to pass on.

One solution to this problem is to stretch the payments of the IRA to the lifetime of the beneficiary, and thereby retain the IRA's tax-deferred status over several lifetimes. If, for example, your spouse does not need the income from your IRA on your death, you could make your child the beneficiary of your IRA. The IRA's tax-deferred status stays intact, and minimum distributions are then calculated according to your child's life expectancy. If, for example your child is 30 at the time of your death, her life expectancy is 52.2 years, so the IRA's tax-deferral could be maintained for an additional 52 years while making minimal distributions each year. If you qualify, you may convert your traditional IRA to a Roth IRA, and then stretch the Roth out over more than one lifetime, thereby the minimum distributions may be taken tax-free.

However conversion to a Roth is complicated for the wealthier client by the earnings cap for Roth contributions. If the IRA is used to help pay estate taxes, it may not be stretched out in the ways described earlier.

Another estate planning solution to the taxation of the retirement plan after the death of the retiree is to set up an irrevocable life insurance trust. The life insurance death benefit will not be taxable to the beneficiary. Required distributions from the plan can be used to fund the payment of the premium on the life insurance. The life insurance proceeds can generate money for paying estate taxes as well as providing a tax-free wealth transfer to the beneficiaries of the trust. The irrevocable life insurance trust can be a valuable estate planning tool to ensure that you meet your goals for paying your estate expenses and passing wealth on to the next generation.

Yet another way to reduce taxation of your retirement is to gift the maximum allowable $14,000 to family members without incurring gift or estate taxes. You can use your minimum distributions to fund these gifts, and thereby pass the money on to the next generation in a tax-advantaged way. You can give $28,000 to a married couple in any given year if they "split" the gift between husband and wife. You can gift a child through a 2503(c) trust set up for the benefit of the child. A Uniform Gift to Minors account or Uniform Transfer to Minors account may also be used to make a tax-free gift to a child.

HEALTH INSURANCE IN THE ELDER PHASE

Throughout your career you have been paying taxes in one way or another that go into the Medicare system. As a private practitioner who pays self-employment taxes, you pay a 2.9 percent tax for Medicare. I point this out to bring to remind you that Medicare is a benefit you have been paying for your entire career, and if you are age 65, in all likelihood, you are eligible to receive Medicare benefits. Medicare Part A is available to most older Americans at no cost. Medicare Part B is available in 2017 for a premium ranging from $134 to $428.60.

Table 6.2 Medicare Part B Model[4]

How Much You'll Pay for Medicare Part B in 2016

Single Filer Income	Joint Filer Income	2016 Monthly Premium
Up to $85,000	Up to $170,000	$121.80 or $104.90*
$85,001–$107,000	$170,001–$214,000	$170.50
$107,001–$160,000	$214,001–$320,000	$243.60
$160,001–$214,000	$320,001–$428,000	$316.70
More than $214,000	More than $428,000	$389.80

Source: www.medicare.gov/your-Medicare-costs/costs-at-a-glance/ (accessed 12/10/2016)
* Premium for enrollees who pay through Social Security.

You should contact Medicare about 3 months before your 65th birthday. You can call them directly at 1-800-633-4227 or you can find them online at www.medicare.gov. We have posted links to Social Security and Medicare on www.insightfinancialgroup.com. You can find them in the "Useful Links" section.

Medicare is medical coverage for people 65 and older.

- Medicare Part A is hospital insurance. Most people don't pay a premium for Part A. There are various deductibles and limitations on Medicare Part A.
- Medicare Part B is medical insurance for medically necessary services and preventive services. Most people pay $121.80 monthly for Part B.
- Medicare Prescription Drug Plans (Part D) add drug coverage to Medicare.
- Medicare Advantage Plans (Part C) are another way to receive prescription drug coverage. They combine Medicare Part A, Part B, and Part D.
- Medigap Plans are Medicare supplement insurance, sold by private companies, but highly regulated by the federal government, that fill in costs that are not covered in original Medicare.

---

4   This model is shown for illustrative purposes only. Please consult an investment advisor before purchasing.

Disability and Long-Term Care Coverage

In the Elder Phase, it is likely that you will want to put dollars that previously went to disability insurance into long-term care coverage. We discuss long-term care coverage and disability insurance in Chapter 25, but for the present discussion we will mention that most disability policies stop paying benefits when the insured reaches age 65, so as you approach 65, you should review the actual protection you are receiving from your policy. On the other hand, long-term care coverage usually makes more sense as you age. You may want to pass the risk of devastating long-term care costs on to an insurance company. I often suggest long-term care coverage to my clients in their mid-fifties, but I frequently have recommended policies to clients in their sixties and seventies. When considering long-term care insurance, I suggest that you discuss it with your financial planner, whose interests are aligned with yours and is interested not in selling a policy, but in advocating for your overall financial well-being. There are many circumstances under which long-term care insurance may not be a necessary expense, particularly if you have either a high net worth or low net worth. Long-term care insurance usually makes most sense for people who are neither rich nor poor (the wealthy may self-insure, while low-income seniors may get Medicaid coverage), and who want to save their assets for their heirs.

REFERENCES

Dominguez, Joe and Vicki Robin. *Your Money or Your Life* (New York: Penguin USA, 1999), p. xvii

Emling, Shelly. *Your Guide to Retiring to Mexico, Costa Rica and Beyond: Finding the Good Life on a Fixed Income* (New York: Avery Penguin Putnam, 1996)

Goldstein, Margaret J. (Ed.). *The World's Top Retirement Havens* (Berkeley, CA: Publishers' Group West, 1999)

Knorr, Rosanne. *The Grown Up's Guide to Retiring Abroad* (Berkeley, CA: Ten Speed Press 2001)

Whitaker, Carl. *Midnight Musings of a Family Therapist* (New York: Norton, 1989)

SECTION II

PSYCHOLOGICAL AND THERAPEUTIC CONSIDERATIONS

CHAPTER 7

Raising Your Money Consciousness

An Important Journey of Individuation

What does money mean to you? This may sound like a simplistic question, but actually it's key to establishing a solid financial footing and also to continuing the work of personal development that you began when you embarked on the path of becoming a psychotherapist.

For almost all of us, money carries multiple meanings—both cultural and personal. Culturally, in Western society, money is quite often viewed as an indicator of personal worth. "She's really doing well" means—more often than not—that she's being successful at making money. When the social norms endorse making money as the definition of success, it's easy for those who have chosen a more moderately paid career to feel "less than." If society's yardstick is money, we can forget the importance of less tangible rewards—emotional satisfaction, professional pride, or a sense of fulfilling one's purpose in life.

Of course, there are segments of society where the pursuit of money is frowned upon. In many indigenous cultures the idea of amassing wealth for oneself is quite a foreign one. A high value is placed on community and supporting one another.

But now, let's move to a bit more personal level. Here we'll be looking at your family's values around money and the thoughts and feelings that you absorbed about it growing up. The idea here is not to judge or critique your personal responses to money, but simply to bring them to awareness. The more we understand, the more empowered we become to take actions that will support us.

The more we understand, the freer we are to make choices that are truly our own rather than traveling down a predetermined path.

As you begin to think about money at a personal level you may find yourself having all sorts of emotional reactions—reactions that may surprise you with their intensity. Before we continue, I'd like to ask you to do a little exercise with me. You may want to read this next section aloud into a recorder and then play it back to yourself as you move through the exercise.

Find a place to sit where you can be quiet and undisturbed for about half an hour.

Sit comfortably with your eyes closed and begin to pay attention to your breathing. Without trying to change anything, just let yourself be aware of your breath. Is it fast or slow? Deep or shallow? Ragged or even?

Now, let your attention begin to travel through your body. Starting with your feet, up your legs to your pelvis, belly, chest, shoulders and neck, jaw and head, down your arms to your fingers. As you notice areas of stress or tension, let your breath touch them gently— not trying to "fix" anything, but just breathing into any tight places.

Now pay the same kind of attention to your emotional body. Notice what feelings are arising. Without getting caught in them, just let yourself breathe into any uncomfortable feelings.

Now bring your attention back to your breath. Sit quietly for a moment appreciating your newly heightened awareness. Then let your eyes slowly open and return to the outside world.

You're now (hopefully) feeling a bit more at ease and grounded. If you'll practice some variation of this exercise each time you're preparing to work with money questions, you should find yourself with more self-support and less reactivity to the material.

MOVING INTO THE MEAT OF THE MATTER

Working in your Money Journal or another notebook, begin answering the following questions:

- What was your family's economic status when you were a child?

- Did your family have more, less, or about the same amount of money as your friends' families?
- What was the feeling about money in your family? Did your parents feel comfortable with their financial situation or did they feel they were constantly striving without ever really "making it"?
- What were you taught about money as a child? Was money the "root of all evil"? Was money considered the highest good? Was money something that "nice people" just don't talk about?
- What were your parents' expectations of you? Were you expected to "do good" in the world without caring about financial rewards? Were you supposed to "do well" and bring financial stability to the family?
- What sort of support did you get from your family? Did your parents expect you to work as soon as you could? Was your way through school paid for? Were you given a car? Were you expected to contribute to the family finances?
- Were you emotionally supported in pursuing higher education or other goals for yourself?
- What were the gender messages about money in your family? Were boys expected to grow up and "take care of the little woman"? Were women the ones with "common sense" who were better equipped to handle money?
- Did your family emphasize spending and "enjoying life" or saving to be prepared for the inevitable "rainy day"?

Some of these questions may be easy and comfortable to answer. Others may stir up memories and reactions that are anything but comfortable. Remember the exercise you went through early in this chapter. If the work starts feeling emotionally difficult, take a few moments to just sit quietly and let yourself breathe. You may also want to seek out a trusted companion to walk through this part of the journey with you. If you have a willing partner or understanding friend it can be a tremendous support. A therapist or life coach can offer professional—maybe more objective—support.

Certainly, our ways of responding to and dealing with money are shaped by our family of origin and our early experiences with money. Early on, at an unconscious level, we begin to develop a "money script." This determines our emotional response to money and, by extension, the way we handle (or in some cases don't handle) it.

Here is a brief overview of a couple of money scripts we have found to be most common among therapists. For a more detailed version and an exploration of other money scripts, please go to our book *True Self, True Wealth* (Cole and Reese, 2007).

Many therapists find themselves stuck in the script of the Procrastinator. For this person, money is not a comfortable area of life—rather something to be avoided. After all—we decided to become therapists—not accountants!

Unfortunately, as we move through life procrastination with money begins to cost us—both financially and emotionally. We can't quite get rid of the nagging awareness that we aren't really dealing with a major aspect of life.

We'd like to buy a house for our growing family, but have no idea what our credit score is or how to go about getting a home loan. Retirement is approaching but we've made no preparation for that and our anxiety begins to mount. The good news is that by beginning to work consciously with our money script we can move toward a new maturity and sense of empowerment that will serve us in all areas of our lives.

Another money script all too common for therapists—especially women—is that of the Co-dependent. Like the Procrastinator, this script also has its roots in a discomfort around money. Rather than working to learn about handling money and finding personal power in that, the Co-dependent is all too willing to hand over the reins to his or her partner. Regardless of the partner's competence or reliability, the Co-dependent keeps their eyes tightly closed and relies on the partner to make decisions and carry the burden and the power of making financial decisions. Working successfully with this money script will usually require the help of a couple's therapist, because the pattern is well established and there is significant secondary gain for both partners.

For the Co-dependent, however, opening the eyes and beginning to take more responsibility can be a tremendously freeing experience. No longer at the mercy of the other, he or she can start to assume their rightful place as a grown-up in the world.

Of course, this chapter is a very brief outline of the steps toward increasing your money consciousness and individuating from the money script you inherited. The journey itself is lifelong, but the rewards are manifold.

REFERENCE

Cole, Peter and Daisy Reese. *True Self, True Wealth* (New York: Atria Books, 2007)

RAISING YOUR MONEY CONSCIOUSNESS

CHAPTER 8

The Psychological Dimension

Money—is it the root of all evil or life's highest good? Perhaps it is actually neither of these, but something much more. It is certain that we can't live without money and equally certain that it carries multiple layers of meaning, some conscious and some unconscious.

It has been truly said that most people would much rather reveal their sexual secrets than their financial ones. Why is this? The very question "How much are you worth?" carries a double meaning. While its surface meaning may concern monetary net worth or the bottom line of one's financial statement, at a deeper level the question can resonate with our insecurities, vulnerabilities, fears of being "not quite enough." Are we successful "enough"? Are we measuring up to our peers? To our parents' expectations?

Our attitudes toward money are deeply ingrained and have their roots in our earliest history. Our family of origin sent us many messages, both tacit and overt, about the meaning of money, its proper place in one's life, appropriate ways to use it and talk about it, and so forth. Because they are often so deeply buried, issues about money can be among the most difficult to bring to consciousness. I (Daisy) remember thinking, as I was involved in intensive therapy in my thirties, "If I work to develop myself in every other area, I think it would be okay to just leave money alone." The naiveté of this idea leaves me speechless, now. However, I think it is not too uncommon. Looking at our attitudes toward and wounds around money can be painful and frightening. Nevertheless, it is a vital piece of building a solid financial foundation.

Achieving a level of comfort with money attitudes is equally important for our work with our patients. If we shy away from the topic, we deprive the people we work with a safe space to explore a significant area of their lives. On both a personal and a clinical level, we ignore money issues at our peril.

MONEY—WHAT IS IT REALLY?

As with many of life's fundamental issues, money is both real and symbolic. Although the answer to "what is money?" may seem obvious, the reality is that there are many answers. On a physical level, money is the "greenback dollar." On a social level, money is an agreement between and among people to honor a particular medium of exchange. On a spiritual level, money can be said to be energy made visible. In this discussion, we are particularly interested in the emotional meaning of money—something that can vary widely from one individual to the next.

AN OBJECT RELATIONS PERSPECTIVE

What was the meaning of money in your family of origin? Was there never enough of it so that it took on the aura of the frustrating, unattainable object? Was there too much available, making it into the exciting, overstimulating object? Did your parents treat money as a weapon? As a pacifier? As a substitute for other kinds of nurturing? Almost all of us have feelings of guilt, shame, and anxiety around money. Based on our experience in our family of origin we have developed a particular representation of the self as a financial person, a representation of money as an object, and an affect state linking the two (Kernberg, 1992).

It may be that your father (like mine, Daisy's) was a controller who used money as a way of maintaining his power over family members. Because he had a need to be "the one with the knowledge," it was necessary for the rest of us to assume an ignorant and helpless role in relation to money. I (Daisy) grew into adulthood feeling as if I were totally powerless in money matters. My feelings toward my father had been transferred to money itself. Indeed, just trying to balance a checkbook could send me to bed with a migraine. Needless to say, my feelings of powerlessness were neither realistic nor helpful to me as an adult. However, they were so firmly embedded in my unconscious that it took years of work to see them for what they were. Any efforts to deal with financial issues aroused such negative feelings about myself that I would begin to feel tremendous anxiety and then defend against that anxiety, that is, the migraine.

Contrast this with the experience of a college friend whose father was a high-stakes gambler. He constantly carried her family through wildly fluctuating cycles of "boom and bust." Her mother was passive and co-dependent, either unable or unwilling to confront her father about his lack of responsibility. At an early age, my friend took on the mantle of "the responsible one." She pinched pennies, squirreled away money and never told anyone the full truth about how much was available. Today, she is a physician making a very comfortable living. However, the old habits still hold. She has a separate account that she is unwilling to discuss with her husband and stashes cash in various hiding places around her home and office. She is unable to gain awareness of her relationship to money as something unpredictable and elusive.

Working with the following exercise could be useful in beginning to uncover your underlying feelings about having/not having money.

Take 30 minutes to sit quietly with a journal or notebook. Ask yourself:

- What is my earliest memory concerning money?
- What is a painful memory concerning money? What is the emotion involved?
- What is a pleasant memory around money? What is the emotion involved?
- What do I remember my mother telling me about money?
- How about my father?
- What seemed to be the general feeling in the family when the subject of money came up?

Half an hour may seem like a very short time to work with this material, and indeed it's enough only to make a beginning.

However, once you dip your toe in the water, chances are good that memories will continue to surface and you may find yourself developing a new understanding of how you relate to money and how this impacts your life in the present.

REFERENCE

Kernberg, Otto. *Aggression* (New Haven, CT: Yale University Press, 1992)

CHAPTER 9

Characterological Defenses Around Money Wounds

I think it's safe to say that no one in this culture grows up without some form of wounding around money issues. Money, and the excess or deficiency thereof, is such a powerful force in our society and yet there continues to be so little understanding of and dialogue about its power. The result is that we all develop defenses that prevent us from dealing with money in a healthy, life-affirming way. The following section provides an opportunity for you to reflect on the way you, your clients, and your family members deal with money and financial issues. Remember that—as Peter likes to say to anxious trainees—"everybody's gotta be something." A clearer understanding of where you are now is the first step on the road toward where you'd like to be.

THE NARCISSISTIC DEFENSE

For people with narcissistic wounds around money, money can function as an externalized way of dealing with precarious self-esteem regulation. Money represents the inflated self. This can manifest in two ways. For the Narcissist who identifies with the inflated self, money is a means of winning the admiration and approval of others through the projection of a "larger-than-life" image and thus becomes a manifestation of the false self. This can be expressed through overspending, excessive credit card debt, the "large hat, no cattle" syndrome—in which the appearance of success is maintained at the expense of true financial well-being. For the person with grandiose narcissistic defenses, driving a Honda Civic would produce a sense of shame that would trigger unbearable anxiety. Much better to overextend his credit and buy a Mercedes. As he becomes increasingly overextended, the feelings of worthlessness (deflation) increase, and these feelings must be defended against with ever more frantic overspending. In contrast, the person who is defending from a deflated narcissistic position may pride himself on how well he is able to "do without." In this case, driving a Honda Civic would also be a source of shame. Much more ego-syntonic to buy a 15-year-old clunker that he holds together with baling wire. A narcissistic character may live far above or far below his means. But in either event, money is used more to silence the inner voice ("You'll never really measure up" or "Who do you think you are, anyway?") than to serve his true best interests. Future needs (e.g. retirement planning) are ignored in favor of easing feelings of anxiety and shame in the present.

Malignant Narcissistic Defense

While the both the grandiose and the deflated narcissistic defenses are focused on avoiding shame, the Malignant Narcissistic defense carries this avoidance to a whole new level! In the person of this character type, anger has become rage and anxiety has become terror. There is a deep-seated conviction that others cannot be trusted, and therefore he has to maintain power and control in any way he can. He lives in a hostile world waiting to take away whatever is not well protected, and where there is no justice except for what power provides. Money represents parental power over him in childhood and his power over others in the present. Any vulnerability spells tremendous danger, and the person with a malignant narcissistic defense works tirelessly to make himself financially impregnable. Money is not a means to enjoying luxuries or attaining freedom, but quite simply a way of amassing power in the interests of an ever-elusive sense of safety. As one patient told me: "I keep thinking that the next million will do it, but somehow it's never quite enough."

The internal conflict for the malignant narcissistic character is between his belief in his own "larger-than-life" qualities (reinforced by mother) and his "lower-than-dirt" qualities (attacked by father). Feeling both entitled and under attack, this character can use money as a way to control and intimidate others. Intimacy, or even empathy, are experiences he cannot afford. To fend off his feelings of worthlessness, he must work tirelessly to achieve more and ever more. As he moves toward mid-life, he may well find himself isolated and depressed, having insulated himself so successfully that his human connections have atrophied.

THE ORAL DEFENSE

Stephen Johnson (1994) describes the Oral character as living in the land of "paradise lost." The person with this sort of defense had an experience of being cherished and nurtured and then abruptly lost it. Perhaps a younger sibling was born too soon. Perhaps mother became ill or depressed or absented herself in some way. The Oral carries this sense of having been let down or abandoned into adulthood and develops a sort of chronic, unappeasable neediness. You may have had the experience of sitting with an Oral patient and feeling that nothing you do can possibly be enough.

Because the Oral's needs are so painful and acknowledging them seems hopeless and overwhelming, the Oral defends against them with a sort of counterdependency. "I can take care of everyone. I really need nothing for myself." Unable to meet or even acknowledge her needs in the interpersonal sphere, the Oral will often turn to self-soothing through spending. Fearing that her needs for love and intimacy are doomed to disappointment, she uses the accumulation of material goods as a substitute. After an argument with her husband ("He never listens to what I want!"), she may well visit the mall and max out her credit cards. This, of course, will lead to a feeling of guilt over her "selfishness," so she will spend even more money buying gifts to "take care" of the other.

Like the Narcissistic character, the Oral may spend more than she can afford. But rather than this being an effort to impress others, it is rather an increasingly frantic effort to soothe her own sense of deprivation.

SYMBIOTIC DEFENSE

The central issue for people with a symbiotic defense structure is an abiding fear of abandonment. James Masterson has written eloquently of the anxiety that arises in this character type when they move toward self-activation (Masterson, 1990). In an effort to avoid this anxiety, the Symbiotic character can fall into the trap of allowing herself to be defined by the other. Differentiation can seemingly result only in abandonment. This character type can find herself in serious financial difficulties due to her inability to confront the financial behaviors of those close to her. If the Symbiotic character has a circle of friends who can afford to spend freely on entertainment and travel, she will follow their lead, ignoring the reality of her own more modest means or her need to provide for her future. The trouble is magnified when the Symbiotic character has a partner who is financially irresponsible. I (Daisy) once worked with a patient who had worked hard and lived frugally in order to put aside a substantial sum for retirement. When she was in her fifties, she turned her entire retirement account over to her husband to invest in a "hot stock tip." Within 2 years, he had lost two-thirds of the money, as well as a substantial amount belonging to my patient's elderly mother! Needless to say, my patient was enraged. But it was her own Symbiotic defense that had sabotaged her. Unwilling to "stand apart" from her husband and risk his abandonment, she had turned a blind eye to his financial dealings— never questioning, or even inquiring about, his decisions.

The Symbiotic defense results in an avoidance of confrontation and often an effort to control through manipulation. Rather than look squarely at her own thoughts and feelings, needs and desires, this person will expect the other to "read her mind" and respond to her obliquely expressed wishes. This allows her to maintain the illusion of merger ("it's amazing how we think alike!") and sidestep the difficult and threatening work of understanding and expressing herself as an individual.

MASOCHISTIC DEFENSE

The person with a masochistic defense struggles with a core feeling of being controlled and victimized. Money has come to represent the controlling parent who withholds the nurturing needed for the child to survive and develop. Raised in a family that was both controlling and withholding, the Masochistic character develops a bitter resentment of the world, which "just doesn't treat him right." As a child he felt (and indeed was) helpless in the face of more powerful adults and so learned to turn this resentment inward. As an adult, he may take a certain perverse pride in his own financial suffering, as it demonstrates how poorly he continues to be treated. The Masochistic defense leads to self-defeating behavior around financial matters. He may consistently pay his bills late—racking up late fees and damaging his credit. He may delay routine maintenance on his home until minor repairs become major expenses. He may take a job that is well beneath his abilities and complain bitterly about being underpaid. I (Daisy) see a patient who is a nurse, extremely capable and well able to get an advanced degree or move into management. However, she stays in her staff position, all the while protesting that "it just isn't fair. Floor nurses should get paid better." Because of the secondary gains (proving conclusively that it's all "their" fault), letting go of the Masochistic defense can be difficult. It means shifting one's self-image and one's worldview. Failure to do so, however, can only result in the Masochistic character becoming stuck in a box that grows ever smaller throughout his life cycle.

SCHIZOID DEFENSE

Having been neglected, abandoned, or hated by her parents in early childhood, the person with a Schizoid defense carries a feeling that she deserves none of what money can offer. Her defense is to withdraw both from herself and others. In the extreme, this can become a dissociated state. The Schizoid character typically has trouble accessing her life force. To reach out for anything— food, affection, or material goods—doesn't feel like a possibility. Indeed, this person can be convinced at a very deep level that she does not have a right to take up space or exist at all.

A Schizoid defense doesn't necessarily stem from material deprivation in early life. I (Peter) have treated several Schizoid characters who grew up with considerable wealth. Despite their comfortable environment, self-absorbed, absentee parents left the job of childrearing to hired caretakers, leaving my patients emotionally destitute. As an adult, a person with a Schizoid defense may have trouble holding a job equal to her abilities. She may live in a style so simple as to be almost Spartan, denying herself comfort and sometimes even the basic necessities. The Schizoid defense allows only the most arid of lives, and as the Schizoid character grows older the world appears to be an increasingly frightening, overwhelming place. To begin to move out of this pattern, she will need patient support and a great deal of courage.

REPETITION OR HEALING?

Therapists are only too familiar with the repetitive impulse. Driven by a powerful, unconscious urge to "make it come out different" we replay old patterns from our childhood. The woman with an alcoholic father "somehow" winds up marrying one alcoholic man after another. The man with a cold and distant mother finds himself drawn only to women who cannot return his affection. The same impulse plays itself out in our financial lives. My own mother grew up during the Great Depression and was hard-pressed to throw anything away. Today, I (Daisy) still catch myself saving string and rubber bands far beyond the bounds of common sense.

However, the repetitive impulse is not the only force at work in our unconscious. Equally powerful is the inclination toward growth and healing. Indeed, without this inclination psychotherapy would be a fruitless endeavor. When it comes to working with financial issues, two aspects are equally important. First, it's necessary to develop an understanding of our defenses and the wounds that underlie them. As we begin to work with and resolve our emotional issues, we free ourselves to learn to deal effectively with our finances on a practical level. Allowing yourself to be ruled by the repetitive impulse can be very dangerous to your financial well-being. To avoid this, you must be willing to tolerate a fair amount of anxiety as you explore both the internal and the external dimensions of your financial picture.

It is in taming this anxiety that we can begin to work creatively with money.

Once we have gained insight into money's symbolic meaning in our emotional life, we become more empowered to move toward financial mastery. We learn the "rules of the game"—how money works and how we can make it work for us. As we gain mastery, our old wounds around money become less debilitating and a positive cycle is set in motion.

The key here is maintaining a stance of patience and self-acceptance. Few of us have had good role models or helpful mentors around money matters. Almost all of us struggle with feelings of shame or inadequacy. "Certainly (at my age, with my education, with my years of experience) I 'should' know more than I do." There may be a sense that "I can't possibly get there from here." However, as Gestalt therapists maintain, true change occurs only through first accepting what is. The greater our willingness to learn about ourselves without attacking ourselves, the greater our potential for moving forward.

REFERENCES

Johnson, Stephen M. *Character Styles* (New York: Norton, 1994)

Masterson, James. *The Search for the Real Self* (New York: Touchstone Books, 1990)

CHAPTER 10

What Is Financial Well-Being?

Is it true that "the one who dies with the most toys wins"? Does financial success equal being able to buy whatever you want whenever you want? Most therapists have worked with enough miserably unhappy wealthy people to know that Mom was right: "Money doesn't buy happiness." True financial well-being ultimately depends on being able to answer "yes" (at least most of the time!) to two questions:

1) Are you making conscious choices?
2) Is your life in balance?

Making conscious choices involves defining your values, your goals, and your priorities and living a lifestyle that supports them. One of our daughters is a yoga instructor who lives on a very minimal income. While her friends from college are buying condos and new cars, she lives in a studio apartment and drives a 1989 compact. However, her life is rich in relationships and in a conviction that she is following her spiritual path and making a significant contribution to her community. Certainly, her priorities may shift over the years, but hopefully she will continue to consciously choose a lifestyle that reflects her core values.

At the other end of the spectrum, we have a friend who has decided to work at her maximum capacity, putting away two-thirds of her income for the next 5 years in order to be able to retire at 55. She is sacrificing present comfort and leisure for the promise of a life that she can shape entirely as she chooses. I don't know that I would choose similarly, but she has consciously set her priorities and is living in a way that reflects her values.

Living a life in balance means developing an orientation to money, which is respectful without being overanxious. A respectful attitude toward money allows us to appreciate it as the power that it is. Money can be said to be energy made tangible. We give our time in exchange for it and it provides a necessary foundation for our lives. If we act out around money (through overspending, mismanagement, willful ignorance, etc.), we demonstrate a dangerous lack of respect. On the other hand, too much anxiety around our treatment of money can be equally disastrous. If we save compulsively, without ever spending freely; if we feel compelled to earn more and more because "it's never enough"; then money takes on the role of a tyrant in our lives. Both disrespect and overanxiety prevent us from working creatively with money. Balance allows us to make use of our money to create a life that is whole, in which all the pieces—work, spending, relationships, and values—fit together.

MONEY IN THE FAMILY SYSTEM
Psychological Individuation—Intertwined With Financial Individuation

Financial autonomy is a powerful symbol of adulthood. Nothing signifies individuation more than making one's own way financially, and conversely, nothing keeps families enmeshed quite like money entanglements. As we have seen, our ways of dealing with money frequently represent unresolved issues from childhood. As we move forward on the lifelong journey of individuation, the resolution of the psychological issues are interwoven with learning how to make one's financial life function effectively.

"Pseudo" Financial Individuation

Success at making money does not, in and of itself, demonstrate that one is successfully individuating. Indeed, the drive to make huge sums of money may be more reflective of the person's succumbing to family-of-origin pressures than of having the necessary integration to follow his own path. It is often the case that one will try to resolve emotional issues through financial means. I (Daisy) work with a patient whose father constantly belittled his dreams of becoming a writer. Wealth was the only goal worth pursuing in the father's eyes, and there was no such thing as enough. Today, this man is incredibly successful financially. He has learned to manipulate the economic system most effectively. At mid-life, however, with his relationships in shambles, he is finally face-to-face with the fact that his life has been much more about proving something to his father than about pursuing his own path. A somewhat less extreme example is a colleague with training and interest in Jungian analysis. He, too, comes from a family who values wealth over self-expression. He was able to withstand family pressure and pursue psychological training, but now does psychological evaluations almost exclusively—"because it just pays so much better" than problems whose nature is more emotional. Clearly, wealth and success are no substitute for resolution of the psychological issues of childhood.

At the same time, psychological integration alone is not sufficient. We have a close friend who is, in many ways, one of the most emotionally and spiritually developed people we know. She has a very busy practice and has worked in her own therapy and her spiritual practice toward self-knowledge and integration. However, she has paid little or no attention to the financial realities of life. Her pro bono cases often outnumber her paying clients and she has managed to put away almost nothing toward her retirement. As she enters her sixties, she is faced with the prospect of working to a much older age than she would choose. If she should suffer a debilitating illness, her only choice would be to become dependent on her adult children.

True individuation entails assuming the mantle of adulthood in all areas. We must accept responsibility for ourselves and our lives both emotionally and financially. In doing so, we have the potential to free ourselves from enmeshment—with our families of origin, our partners, or our own children.

FAMILY RULES AROUND MONEY

I (Peter) teach a continuing education class in Sacramento called "Seven Steps to Financial Well Being." In that class I ask people to tell their family stories about money. As they talk, I am listening for examples of their family rules around money. As family therapists know, rules may be either overt (explicitly stated) or covert (never spoken aloud, but everyone shares an understanding). In listening to these family stories over the years, it has become clear to me that rules about money most often fall into the covert category. When something goes unspoken (the elephant in the living room) it tends to assume enormous psychological power. Covert rules become embedded in the psyche and it can be very difficult to even begin to articulate them, let alone think about changing them. Because the couple forms the foundation of the family, understanding how couples communicate about money can be the beginning of understanding how family rules are made. Increased understanding can free the couple and the family to consider what rules they are living by and to make conscious decisions about rules that support the values they want to uphold.

CHAPTER 11

The Couple's Money Dance

Once you become a member of a committed couple, your financial life is no longer yours alone. How successful you will be in living consciously depends, in part, on your partner and the effectiveness of the communication that the two of you establish. Certainly, a saver and a spender who never communicate about money have a partnership in serious trouble. However, trouble can also arise in more subtle forms. Let's take a look at a model, which provides ways for a couple to deepen their communication and become able to effectively address the emotional, interpersonal, and practical dimensions of their financial life together.

MONEY—THE QUINTESSENTIAL INTERPERSONAL ISSUE

Money's very purpose is to serve as a medium of exchange between people. This purpose makes it, perhaps, the quintessential interpersonal issue. Inevitably, then, money reflects both the conscious side and shadow side of human relations. On the conscious side, money can represent generosity, individuation, self-esteem, self-activation, and the ability to care for oneself and one's family. On the shadow, or unconscious side, money can represent social injustice, feelings of deprivation, entitlement, enmeshment, lust for power, and myriad unresolved family of origin issues. Both the conscious and unconscious sides become manifest in our marriages and intimate relationships. Only as we are able to bring the shadow side into awareness and communicate about it with our partners will we be able to shape our financial lives successfully.

Freud taught us long ago that id, ego, and superego make up a dynamic system that is ever-changing and never static. This applies to our money issues no less than to other areas of life. No one can deal with money solely from the ego, or conscious, part of their being. The stakes are too high, anxiety is too great, family history is too compelling, social class issues are too powerful, and primitive feelings of greed, entitlement, and deprivation are too strong for anyone to have a simple, one-dimensional relationship with money.

As individuals we may strive for as much ego-like (as opposed to id-like) orientation to the financial issues as we can muster. As couples, it is communication that allows us to work with the unconscious material productively. It is not some Platonic ideal of perfection that we are after in our communication about finances. Rather, we hope to move toward increasing our conscious awareness, insight, and communication so that we, as a couple, can form an effective partnership. We want to function together in such a way that our money supports our life goals and enhances our relationship.

FOUR LEVELS OF COMMUNICATION
Level 1—Rigid Financial Communication
Level 2—Concrete Financial Communication
Level 3—Emotionally Informed Financial Communication
Level 4—Flexible and Effective Financial Communication

Barbara and Dave are a couple who spent several years with me (Peter) in couples therapy. Because money was a volatile and complicated issue for them, much of our time was spent in working on communication around financial matters. As their work progressed, Barbara and Dave moved through the four levels of communication, away from stereotyped roles and rigid communication toward intimate communication about feelings.

Barbara and Dave
Dave and Barbara are in their early forties with three young children. Barbara is a psychologist in private practice and Dave is a

self-employed carpenter. Their combined annual income is about $160,000, with Barbara making substantially more than Dave. Barbara and Dave fought about money frequently, but had not addressed the underlying emotional issues until they started couples therapy. Barbara felt that Dave overspent on himself. Dave felt that that Barbara was controlling and selfish about money. Their arguments about money felt endless and fruitless to them.

Dave's History

Dave had been very much neglected as a child by parents who lived a high life, but did not attend to his needs. Dave's father was a heavy drinker. He was a lobbyist who spent his high-flying clients' money lavishly on legislators and other influential people, but did not support Dave in his endeavors such as athletics and science. Dave felt himself to be a cast-off, a bum. Although quite intelligent, Dave never went to college. He carried a wad of cash in his pocket that made him feel good, and that he spent rather lavishly, giving financial gifts and bonuses frequently to guys working in his carpentry crew. The wad of cash made Dave feel powerful, was something of an identification with his free-spending father, and served as a transitional object that he could touch and feel, reassuring him that he was not a "loser."

Barbara's History

Barbara was raised by a perfectionist mother while her father was largely absent. Barbara's parents divorced when she was 8, and fought for years over her custody more as a way to stay engaged and enraged at each other than out of a desire to parent her. She specializes in custody evaluations and her professional mission is to help children who are caught in divorcing families. She sees herself very much as the child's advocate. Her self-image was that of the girl who could not do things quite well enough to please her critical mother. Her mother had a perfectionistic approach to finances: She insisted that everything should be highly organized, controlled, and well planned out. While Barbara rebelled against this financial perfectionism (which was part of her attraction to Dave) she had also internalized much of it. So, when Dave walked around with a wad of cash in his pocket and spent, she felt highly critical of him for behaving in such an uncontrolled, imperfect manner.

Difficulties in the Relationship

When Dave overspent, Barbara felt the internalized criticism of her mother for his wastefulness, along with the feeling that she was being neglected by Dave as she was by her absent father. She would lash out at Dave with verbal tirades. When she would rage, all he could hear was that she wanted the financial resources for herself. He felt her to be neglecting his needs and that she was a "controlling bitch." They fought about his spending habits and her controlling perfectionism. Until they were able to address the underlying emotional issues, they were caught in a repetitive, frustrating, destructive conflict.

Rigid Communication

When a couple is caught in rigid communication, they are often living as if they are simply two individuals sharing the same house, but with separate financial lives. Another possibility is that the couple feels that one person can take control and the other does not need to be involved in the finances. Whatever shape the rigidity takes, rigid communication assumes that the financial issues are simple and that an inflexible, non-communicative structure will suffice to take care of the financial issues in a life partnership. Our experience with couples is that this rarely remains the case for very long. Life has a way of complicating the best-laid plans to keep things simple. In our experience, even couples with prenuptial agreements frequently find that finances have a way of becoming commingled and complicated.

Couples using rigid communication are acting on the unspoken assumption that the financial life of a couple can be kept uncomplicated and untouched by the emotional issues that affect the relationship. Not only is this vision of an uncomplicated financial life almost always illusory, it ignores the potential of working with the financial issues to foster intimacy. When the couple realizes that their financial lives are indeed intertwined, then they begin a process of communicating about their financial needs, responsibilities, and difficulties.

Barbara and Dave in Rigid Communication

Barbara and Dave married in their late thirties. Both were established in their work when they married. In the first few years Barbara took control of the family finances. After all, she was organized while he was not. It seemed the obvious and simple way to approach the family finances. Soon, however, certain patterns of behavior on both of their parts began to annoy and anger the other. She disapproved of his wad of cash and wasteful spending, while he found her to be controlling and judgmental. When Barbara became pregnant with their first child, the arguments got worse, and rigid communication gave way to concrete communication.

Concrete Communication

At this level of financial communication, the couple is dealing openly with the external, pragmatic financial issues that face a couple and/or family. This level of communication is some improvement on rigid communication as it does allow for give and take around the practical issues. However, in concrete communication the underlying emotional issues and assumptions are not directly addressed. Because the emotional dimension is not addressed openly, issues tend to get acted out in ways that are indirect and possibly destructive.

Dave and Barbara in Concrete Communication

Dave and Barbara fought constantly. She complained bitterly about his spending habits while he complained that she just wanted control for its own sake. Unaware of any underlying emotional issues, the arguments were a bitter exchange of accusations without any movement toward understanding or resolution. When the arguments seemed to threaten the viability of their relationship, they came in for couples therapy.

Emotionally Informed Financial Communication

At this level, the couple has developed some insight into their emotional issues with money. They have begun to understand how their feelings about money derive from their history, as well as developing some understanding and empathy for the family-of-origin issues that affect their partner's attitudes toward and behaviors around money. At this level, communication is often far less rancorous than at the level of concrete financial communication. To communicate at this level requires the capacity to speak about and listen to the underlying issues. Compassion will often emerge in the couple as the issues are articulated at the emotional level.

Dave and Barbara at the Level of Emotionally Informed Financial Communication

In the therapy sessions, Dave and Barbara learned about each other's history with money in their families of origin. They came to understand where the other was coming from emotionally. For example, Barbara learned that carrying the wad of cash was very reassuring for Dave. Dave learned that just carrying the cash around was enough to make him feel good, and he felt less need to actually spend it. Dave also learned that Barbara's need to keep financial matters under control is more than just a "power trip." As she came to better understand her anxiety around loss of control, she became less apt to lose her temper with Dave. He, in turn, learned that Barbara's mother would shame her when things were not "perfect" and developed a sense of understanding and compassion for her. This allowed him to be patient with her anxiety over his more casual approach to money.

Flexible and Effective Financial Communication

This optimal level of financial communication is achieved when the couple has developed an understanding of each other's emotional issues with money. The couple is now able to deal effectively with the practical financial concerns while at the same time addressing their emotional issues. They are able to plan together, laugh at their foibles, make decisions, and deal with mistakes without undue recrimination. Admittedly no couple can maintain this level all the time, but once a couple has learned to function in this way, they begin to build a foundation of trust and goodwill that will serve them well during the difficult passages that we all inevitably face.

Dave and Barbara at the Level of Flexible Financial Communication
Dave and Barbara struggled diligently in therapy for several years and really learned a lot about themselves and each other. I caught glimpses of flexible financial communication when they were dealing with buying a new house. Although they fought about the old issues, they were rather quickly able to rise out of the old rancor, and deal with some very anxiety-provoking issues with a good deal of awareness and capacity for self-reflection. They did in fact go ahead and buy a house that met their needs quite nicely and did so with a good deal of cooperation and good humor. When Barbara started complaining that the house was not quite good enough and that the deal was less than perfect, Dave suggested to her that her old perfectionism was at work, and she was able to laugh at her own proclivities while moving forward with a deal that was in her self-interest.

THE COUPLE'S MONEY DANCE   93

CHAPTER 12

Complementary Work

Referring to and Working With a Financial Planner

The entire focus of this book has been on examining how money and our responses to money impact our lives. In this section we'd like to explore three very specific ways in which money impacts our clinical work and/or our clinical work impacts our financial decisions.

Do you remember taking your licensing exam? A rhetorical question—I think we all remember that stage of our careers and the anxiety that accompanied it. In my own experience (Daisy), one of the principle things the examiners were interested in was our ability to make appropriate referrals—to a physician, a psychiatrist, 12-step groups, and so on. For many clients, and for ourselves, referral to a financial planner might be most helpful. If you can find a financial planner who understands the emotional dimension of financial work, you might talk with him or her about cross-referring. Working with a psychotherapist around the emotional issues and with a financial planner around the practical issues can provide our clients with the powerful tools they need to get their finances in order.

The therapeutic task is not so much to *change* the meaning and associations our clients have to money as to help bring these feelings, thoughts, and associations to conscious awareness. When brought to awareness, our feelings about money can help us move forward, empowering us to act with conscious motivation in our economic lives, rather than to act out unconscious material. The task of the financial planner, then, is to help the client translate this newly developed consciousness into practical steps designed to create financial security and empowerment.

By way of an example, let me (Peter) present a financial planning client. Sarah is a 60-year-old clinical social worker who grew up in an upper-middle-class Jewish family in Marin County, California. Sarah's father was an attorney and her mother was a homemaker. Her financial issues centered around the fact that her father was authoritarian and controlling about money. Her mother was kept on a tight allowance for family expenses. Money was never discussed, but was nevertheless used as a weapon of paternal power and control. Her father lavished money on her brother's educational expenses for law school, but was tight fisted with Sarah's education expenses. He did not encourage her social work career, viewing social work and psychotherapy as frivolous compared with the practice of law.

Sarah had been self-supporting since completing her MSW. She had lived on a private practice income (supplemented with some agency-based work) while raising her son as a single mother. She frequently felt overwhelmed and anxious about her financial life, but did not receive financial help from her parents as she found asking for money to be shameful and humiliating. When her father died 2 years ago (her mother had died 9 years earlier), her inheritance was sizable. Although she had been looking forward to the financial independence her inheritance would bring, she nevertheless felt a great deal of anxiety about dealing with it.

As the account was in a self-help online brokerage, she was receiving no professional investment advice before she connected with me. She had become immobilized in doing anything with her inheritance, which sat unattended in stock securities, some of which had held ground, and others had lost ground during the recent market decline. When she came for financial consultation, she was feeling scared and immobilized because of the decline in value in her stock portfolio. She was afraid of both taking action to change the portfolio and of inaction. In crafting an investment strategy, we designed a mix of securities and bonds that fit her time horizon and risk tolerance. Concurrently, we discussed the emotional issues that the inheritance brought up for her.

I referred her to a therapist with a psychodynamic orientation. In a rather short amount of time, she gained insight into the sources of her anxiety and was much better able to contain the anxiety in order to work with her portfolio in a rational way. She became aware that her father had humiliated her and had damaged her sense of self as an empowered agent in her financial life. She also became aware of her identification with her mother, who also was subject to her father's authoritarian style. She further worked through some difficult issues with her brother around family history and the inheritance.

In facing her fears, Sarah became able to separate her emotional responses from the investment decisions she needed to make in her own self-interest. It was the *insight* into her own history and growing mastery of her anxiety that gave her the emotional containment she needed to manage her inheritance effectively.

In dealing with money, it is important to honor the feelings and then to act with rational, enlightened self-interest. Honoring and sorting through the feelings can be a difficult and anxiety-provoking journey. When we commit to ourselves to doing the hard work of self-discovery, we are laying important groundwork for our financial success.

HOW TO CHOOSE A HIGHLY QUALIFIED FINANCIAL PLANNER

For most therapists in private practice, it makes good sense to work with a financial planner, as running one's own business necessitates a good many financial decisions, many of which may benefit from professional input. Probably the best way to find a reputable financial planner is to ask people you respect in your personal and professional network if they are working with a financial planner they are happy with, and then interview him or her. If you choose to work with a financial planner, here are some steps to take to help ensure that he or she is highly qualified.

Look for someone with advanced training and qualifications. The ChFC and CFP are the two most widely accepted professional designations for financial planners. ChFC stands for Chartered Financial Consultant. This designation is administered by the American College in Bryn Mawr, Pennsylvania. CFP stands for Certified

Financial Planner. It is administered by the CFP Board of Standards in Denver, Colorado. ChFCs and CFPs have taken a comprehensive curriculum in financial planning and have met specific experience, continuing education, and ethical requirements. Some CPAs have earned a financial planning designation called the PFS (personal financial specialist), which consists of a comprehensive financial planning curriculum on top of the usual CPA requirements. Other qualified financial planners hold MBA or law degrees.

HOW FINANCIAL PLANNERS ARE PAID

Financial planners are paid in one of three ways (often in combination): by commission, fee based on assets under management, or fee-for-service such as a yearly or hourly fee. At our firm, we prefer to work with fees based on assets under management, as we feel that approach aligns our financial interests with our clients and that it provides a sound financial framework for providing our professional services. Too many financial planning clients have no idea how their financial planner is paid. Whatever your financial planner's method of getting paid is, it should be made clear to you. Make sure that your financial planner is willing to discuss how he or she is paid and that the fee is transparent and not made mysterious to you.

Most financial planners are not "stock pickers," nor should they be. Stock brokers or money managers play an extremely important role in your financial plan, but the role of your financial planner should be to find you highly qualified money managers for each asset class you are invested in. If your financial planner is taking the time that he should to consult with you and other clients, then he is not taking the time to research investments as thoroughly as a dedicated money manager should be. Commonly recognized money managers run large mutual funds. With mutual funds and other instruments where many investors' money is pooled, the money manager earns his or her fee by taking a very small percentage of a very large pool of money, so that the cost to the individual investor is kept low.

Be wary of the financial salesman who calls you frequently with stock tips. This may be a sign that he is making transactions to generate commissions that are in his self-interest, but not necessarily in the your best interest. This form of unethical conduct is called "churning" in the industry. Also be wary of the stock tip that is generated by the Wall Street firm that is both performing investment banking services for a given corporation, and then sending its sales force out to sell the company's stock. If you have been reading the papers lately, you know that this type of client abuse has been all too common at some of the major brokerage houses in recent years, and although the brokerage firms have pledged to stop such abuses, it is best for you, the consumer, to be informed that these unethical practices have occurred in the recent past and could well occur again in the present and future. If you are getting frequent calls about hot stock tips from a financial salesman who is managing your money, it may be time to start looking for a professional financial planner who will take a holistic view of your financial well-being and who will not try to ply you with offers that are not in your best interest.

Look for a financial planner who will meet with you regularly, who is willing to take the time to teach and listen, and who has good interpersonal skills. Dealing with the financial dimension of life causes many people a high degree of anxiety. Therefore the ideal financial planner will have the technical facility to give state-of-the-art financial advice along with a capacity for helping clients contain their anxiety so as to make sound financial choices. Ask for references and take the time to call them. Other clients can tell you a lot about your prospective financial planner's interpersonal skills, technical skills, organization, and professional demeanor. Finding a qualified financial planner that you are compatible with is an important step on your path to mastering the financial dimension in your life and in your practice. Take your time in carefully choosing the financial planning professional who feels right for you.

CHAPTER 13

Money as a Transference Object in Therapy

For many patients, the fact of having to pay for the therapist's time and attention is bound to evoke early wounds. We have seen in the previous chapter that money evokes feelings about the self, feelings about money as the object and yokes them affectively. For example, the masochistic defense binds a sense of the self as victim and the money-object as victimizer while the affect that binds them is resentment. When these issues get acted out with money, the money itself comes to represent the control of a domineering parent and self-defeating or passive aggressive financial behavior comes to represent the feeling of resentment. It is no wonder then that the act of paying for therapy may well become fertile ground for acting out. The masochist may for example act out in passive aggressive ways by not paying the bill, forgetting the checkbook, bouncing checks, and so on.

Payment for therapy represents the needs of the therapist in the therapeutic relationship, and thereby frequently evokes ambivalent feelings on the part of the patient. In our earlier discussion about finding your niche, we discussed the inherent tension between the patient's needs in therapy and the therapist's needs. The patient needs to work on his life issues, while the therapist needs to earn a living by providing her expertise and doing work that she finds rewarding. This relationship is by no means equal—the therapist has a great deal more power than the patient. The payment for therapy—representing as it does the reality of the needs of the therapist—is apt to evoke very ambivalent feelings in the patient.

Therapy, by its very nature, evokes to varying degrees the child part of the patient that relates to the therapist as the child does to the parent. However, in the original situation, the child does not need to pay for parenting (at least not with money!). The fact that he must now pay for the therapy with money may bring up many of the feelings connected to the deficits in the original experience of being parented.

If payment for therapy represents the therapist's needs in the relationship, then the therapist should be clear, both in her own mind and with the patient, that her needs are legitimate. The therapist has a legitimate need to be fairly paid for her services. Here it is vital that the therapist be aware of her own money issues so that the patient's financial acting out does not evoke retaliatory or compensatory acting out on the part of the therapist. For example, a borderline patient might fail to pay her therapy bill as an expression of the transference wish that the therapist selflessly mother her. The therapist should not reward this kind of acting out with an overly accommodating stance about prompt payment of the bill. Instead, the issue needs to be discussed in its deeper dimensions while a limit is set around the bill payment. The therapist may open up a dialogue and offer meaningful interpretations about the feelings that the requirement for payment evokes in the patient. This dialogue is essential to sorting through both the emotional and the financial issues. The therapist must be as aware as possible of her own money issues in order to maintain her sense of clarity and her appropriate boundaries.

There are situations in any business when balances due are carried for a variety of reasons and I am not postulating as a "good" that the therapist have inflexible boundaries around the payment of the bill. What I am suggesting instead is that the therapist be clear about her own motivations when she finds that the money boundary seems to be slipping with a given patient (or in her practice in general). It's important to bring these issues to clinical consultation or even personal therapy so that the therapist can sort through the transference and countertransference issues involved.

SECTION III

CURRENT PRACTICE CONSIDERATIONS

SECTION III

CURRENT PRACTICE CONSIDERATIONS

CHAPTER 14

Sustaining Your Prosperous Practice Through Changing Economic Times

The collapse of the housing bubble that occurred in 2008 occasioned a financial crisis that set off the worst recession this country has seen since the Great Depression of the 1930s. Going through this period of economic crisis was, for many psychotherapists in private practice, both a sobering experience and a grounding experience. It was *sobering* in that it brought home the fact that economic conditions can and do change, even in the amazing economic engine that is the U.S. It was *grounding* although in the fact that even though economic conditions had changed, and much wealth had been lost in the U.S., the people's need for psychotherapy was undiminished, even if their capacity to pay for it was more challenged than it had been previously. As one interviewee for this book put it,

> I had to reduce my fee for a number of clients, and some went from every week to every other week. Some people, I put into a group, who I had been seeing individually before. But overall, my clients still needed therapy, and I found ways to accommodate every situation. My overall income went down a bit during the recession, but only by about 15%, and I think I only lost a few clients due to economic hardship.

One of the most important lessons to learn from the recession of 2008 for psychotherapists is that psychotherapy is really not a luxury item for most of our clients. It is a necessity. With almost all of the therapists we interviewed for the book, the story of the recession was the same: Clients found a way to maintain their psychotherapy if they possibly could. This is the *grounding* to which we are referring. As a psychotherapist, you are providing a necessary service, one that your clients will find a way to pay for even when economic times are difficult.

One thing that we have learned from therapists who carried on successfully through the recession of 2008–2009 was that they worked *creatively* with their clients and their practices to maintain success through tough economic times. Let's look at some of the strategies that worked so that you can implement these in good times and bad.

1) Be confident
2) Be flexible
3) Don't be too proud
4) Try new things
5) Focus on your ground game.

BE CONFIDENT

As we discussed earlier, your clients are in psychotherapy because they need the expert care that you offer. Nowhere else in today's society can a person find a trained, skilled professional who will treat them with confidentiality and appropriate boundaries to work with the most intimate and sensitive aspects of their emotional and relational lives. To be in the care of an ethical, skilled psychotherapist is a very precious experience. We encourage you to BE CONFIDENT that this experience is valuable for your clients in good economic times and bad, and that your clients will choose psychotherapy over other spending choices in many circumstances.

BE FLEXIBLE

Given that their psychotherapy is extremely valuable for your clients, when tough economic times hit them, either because of a general economic downturn such as the 2008–2009 recession or because of personal circumstances such as changes in their health or employment, it can be very valuable to be flexible. You can think together about how to keep working together in ways that will be both effective and financially manageable for both of you. Here are a few things that therapists have done to make therapy more affordable:

- Lower the fee
- Go to every other week
- If you lead groups, and have an appropriate one for the client, put the client in a group.

Therapists who do problem solving with the clients around issues of keeping the therapy going despite the client's economic hardship find that involving the client is very helpful. It engages the client's creativity and his sense of agency.

DON'T BE TOO PROUD

We have found some therapists who take a great deal of pride in setting a very high fee and having a very full and "fancy" practice filled with high-end professionals and wealthy people. If you can sustain such a practice, then we applaud you (although we do encourage all therapists to do some pro bono and low fee work). However, we have seen with some private practitioners a "pride problem" sets in. It looks something like this: The therapist lets it be known that he or she has a fancy, high-fee, fee-for-service practice. The therapist was perhaps at one time "riding high" or full, but for one reason or another the practice is much less full, yet the therapist is too proud or stubborn to lower his or her fees.

In these circumstances, we think it best to do one's best to let go of one's attachment to having the "fancy" practice, and to let it be known in the community that you are open to lower-fee clients, or to even sign up with some managed care companies, at least for a limited period of time, to get one's practice back on solid ground. As one therapist who made these adjustments at one in her career explained to us,

> I was embarrassed and thought that my colleagues would think I was a failure. Actually, almost all of the people I reached out to were happy to hear I was lowering my fee, and told me

that they too were making adjustments and taking managed care. I felt very relieved, and ended up getting a bunch of new referrals.

TRY NEW THINGS

If there is an economic slowdown and your practice in turn is slowing down, don't be afraid to try new things. One therapist we spoke with trained in Eye Movement Desensitization and Reprocessing (EMDR) during the recession so that she could attract new clients. EMDR turned out to be an excellent source of referrals for her and she loves the work! Another therapist got training in Dialectical Behavioral Therapy (DBT), and now co-leads several groups using that methodology. Another therapist started an interpersonal therapy group based on Irv Yalom's model of group therapy. Yet another started a men's group based on the work of Robert Bly and James Hillman. The point of all of these is to follow your interest and passion to develop new skills through training and risk-taking so that when things slow down in your practice due to slow economic times, you can respond to that with creativity and trying out new directions in your practice.

FOCUS ON YOUR GROUND GAME

Finally, when tough economic times hit, don't forget to get back to basics. These basics are:

1) Stay in touch with your professional community.
2) Make sure that your colleagues know about the services you are offering.
3) Do some public presenting of your work so that people in the community can be exposed to you and your work.
4) Do some writing so that you can put the word out about your work.
5) Keep your website up to date.

CONCLUSION

Slow economic times remind us of several important things about the profession of psychotherapy. First, what we provide is a necessity for most of our clients and not a luxury. Second, we need to be flexible when dealing with clients in tough economic times—working creatively with them to find solutions to helping them afford to continue to work with us can pay off for both client that therapist. Third, if pride is keeping us from making necessary adjustments to our practice during an economic downturn, then we need to examine this rigidity and make needed adjustments to keep our practices vital and full. Fourth, we need to be open to new skills and new approaches that will both grow our skill set and bring in new clients. Fifth, when the economy slows down, it is smart to refocus on the basics of marketing: getting the word out among your colleagues and in the community about the work you do and the clients you can best serve.

CHAPTER 15

The Affordable Care Act and Beyond

Making Managed Care Work for You

The Affordable Care Act has opened the door to health insurance for millions of Americans who were previously uninsured. Before the ACA, approximately 47 million Americans were uninsured. A RAND Corporation study released in May of 2015 found that since the Affordable Care Act's major provisions took effect, there has been an estimated net increase of 16.9 million people with insurance (Carman et al., 2015). It is estimated by the Centers for Disease Control and Prevention (CDC) and U.S. Census data for the first three months of 2015 that the uninsured rate in the U.S. was down to 9.2% from its rate of 15.7% before the Affordable Care Act was signed into law (http://obamacarefacts.com). Since the adoption and implementation of the ACA, not only are millions more Americans now insured, but mental health care coverage is now required to be included in most health insurance plans as part of the protections built into the Affordable Care Act and the Mental Health Parity and Addiction Equity Act of 2008 (http://mentalhealth.gov).

Clearly, the pool of people that can utilize health insurance to access mental health benefits has increased significantly since the ACA has gone into effect. What does this mean for your practice? Of course the answer depends on many factors, such as the percentages of private pay and managed care you will choose or have chosen for your practice. Most insurance policies procured through the Affordable Care Act make use of in-house or third-party managed care operations to administer their mental health coverage. The days of insurance policies in which the client pays a small co-pay and the insurer pays the rest with minimal paperwork provided by you, the clinician, are mostly ancient history now except for a few "Cadillac" executive policies with exceptional healthcare and mental health coverage. For the most part, a managed care organization will oversee the treatment you provide for your clients utilizing healthcare under the Affordable Care Act.

If you choose to contract with managed care providers, then the ACA makes it possible for you to serve many clients who were previously unable to avail themselves of mental health services. Provision of services to clients who have been hitherto shut out of mental health care can be highly rewarding for personal, ethical, and professional reasons. How the provision of services through managed care can work for you *financially* is a question we will explore in the following sections.

First, let us consider your personal values with regard to working with low-income clients. For many practitioners, and us included, working with a number of lower-fee and pro bono clients is very important from the perspective of maintaining a socially responsible practice. For some psychotherapists, this socially responsible stance translates into contracting with managed care providers, Medicaid, Medicare, or some mix of these. For other practitioners who choose a fee-for-service model, seeing low-income clients can be accomplished through providing a certain percentage of low-fee and pro bono slots in their practice. We have chosen to go with a fee-for-service model for our private practice. This means that we do not contract with managed care, Medicaid or Medicare. We do feel that it is important to work with low-fee clients however, and we each see a number of low-fee and pro bono clients.

For us, and for many of the therapists we have interviewed for this book, there is a give and take with managed care. Managed care *gives* the ability to work with those who cannot afford to pay out of pocket for psychotherapy. However it *takes* away a degree of professional autonomy. While it can be gratifying to work with underserved populations using managed care, Medicaid, or Medicare, it can be aggravating to fill out the paperwork and to fight with managed care representatives about diagnosis, treatment, and prognosis, particularly when it can seem as though the managed care company is rewarding their representatives for keeping psychotherapy as brief and low cost as possible. As one psychologist we interviewed for this book said indignantly,

> I refuse to let some person who has probably never practiced psychology tell me how to do my work. And I don't like being told that CBT is best practice when my training and experience tells me that attachment oriented work will be far more effective.

Managed care companies contain their costs by keeping their reimbursement rates down—meaning that the amount you get paid per therapy hour will typically be significantly less than the amount you would receive on a fee-for-service basis wherein the client writes you a check. Our unscientific survey of therapists in the San Francisco Bay Area revealed that the average reimbursement for master's level clinicians through managed care was $65 per session for master's level and $80 per session for PhDs. Fee-for-service fees varied greatly but averaged $140 for master's level and $165 for PhDs.

AN EMPOWERMENT MODEL

We propose an empowerment model for therapists in private practice who are contracting with managed care companies. With this empowerment model we suggest that you relate to the managed care companies that you contract with as working for you, rather than you working for them. From their perspective you, the therapist, are just one of many contractors who are working for them. You are part of their larger operation, and as such, can be made to jump through their hoops. As one practitioner we interviewed put it, "[the managed care company] puts me on long holds, they frequently reject my paperwork for very small issues, and they often question my treatment plan, always with an eye to reducing the number of sessions." So, our point of view is to make sure that managed care is working for you, and that you are not working for them. Here are some strategies you may want to consider:

1) Contract with a number of managed care companies so that you do not become overly dependent on any one company.

If any of the companies you are working with becomes too demanding or intrusive, let them go! Remember, you are contracting with managed care to support your practice, not the other way around!

2) Contract with managed care for a portion of your practice but not for the whole of your practice. Find the right mix of managed care in proportion to private pay for your practice. The right mix will depend on many factors including the prevalence of managed care in your community and your comfort with marketing your private pay practice. In any event, if you are contracting with managed care, you may well find it empowering to pick up at least a few private pay clients. If you are seeing a few private pay clients, it may feel empowering to tilt the balance a bit more in the direction of private pay. Finding a good balance between managed care and private pay will help you feel that the managed care companies are not running your life!

3) Contract with managed care in the early years of your private practice to get it off the ground, and then let it go over time. Many private practitioners have successfully employed this strategy. Managed care provides a relatively easy way to fill up your practice. Although the managed care companies typically will put restrictions on taking managed care patients to private pay, the rules vary widely, and of course clients change insurance policies and may want to continue with you even if they have left the managed care that you had contracted with. In this strategy, some clients will transfer from managed care to private pay, and the rest of the transition to private pay will happen as a result of the marketing and other sound practices described in this book that will help your private pay practice thrive.

Of course some therapists prefer to work primarily with managed care, Medicare, Medicaid, or some combination of these three throughout their entire careers. Of the therapists we interviewed who make this choice, we found that it was driven by

1) The therapist's social commitment to work with lower income clients;

2) The therapist's preference to not have to actively market their practice and to have their referrals be driven by managed care companies;
3) A greater comfort than private pay therapists with oversight from managed care organizations;
4) A greater comfort with shorter-term therapy than private pay therapists.

So, if this list describes you, then you may be well suited to working primarily with managed care, Medicare, and Medicaid—and that is a wonderful thing, because we as a society will need many thousands of dedicated psychotherapists to work with the millions of people who are finally receiving mental health coverage with the ACA.

SUMMARY

In this chapter we have sought to provide you, the private practitioner, with an empowering model of thinking through the role that managed care will play in your practice. We have sought to help you think through the ethical, financial, and "career satisfaction" aspects of your professional relationship to managed care. We have suggested that each practitioner will need to find his or her own balance point with managed care. Whether you do a fully fee-for-service practice, a fully managed care practice, or anything in between, we encourage you to take charge of your practice. If you work with managed care, we encourage you to assume the attitude that the managed care companies are there to partner with you, to help and serve your practice.

REFERENCES

Carman, Katherine G., Christine Eibner and Susan M. Paddock. "Trends in Health Insurance Enrollment, 2013–15." *Health Affairs*, 34, no. 6 (2015): 1044–1048 (published online May 6, 2015; 10.1377/hlthaff.2015.0266)

"Health Insurance and Mental Health Services." U.S. Department of Health & Human Services. www.mentalhealth.gov/get-help/health-insurance/

"Obamacare: Uninsured Rates." Obamacare Facts. http://obamacarefacts.com/uninsured-rates/

CHAPTER 16

Your Online Presence

In the 12 years since we wrote the first edition of *Mastering the Financial Dimension of Your Psychotherapy Practice*, a website for your practice has gone from being a fancy marketing tool to being a basic necessity. Now your psychotherapy website is really just one of several locations for your online presence. Social media has become a powerful marketing tool for your practice. Additionally, there are third-party providers, notably *Psychology Today*, who provide further online presence for your practice. A modern psychotherapy practice has presence in all of these areas: a website, social media, and third-party web providers. In this chapter we will provide a guide for you to get set up in all of these areas.

Think of your website as the home base of your online presence. This is where potential and current clients will look up basic information about you and your practice. Your social networking presences on Facebook and LinkedIn are there for reaching and connecting with other professionals and potential clients. Here, in your connections with other professionals, centers of influence and potential clients, you will have a chance to put the word out about what you do, who your practice is geared toward, and how you think. Your third-party provider is a quick and easy place for people to find you on the internet—to find out the basics of your practice and to connect with you quickly.

YOUR WEBSITE

Your online presence begins with your website. Here you set the aesthetics and the tone of your online presence. One of the first

113

things you will want to decide is whether to put a picture of yourself on your website. Most therapist websites include a head shot, but a sizable minority choose not to have one. Finding the right picture can be daunting. Aside from body image issues that the picture can bring up for therapists, there is the question of the expression, pose, and mood of the picture. Do you want a big smile? A serious look? An informal shot? An outside shot or a studio shot? We suggest you get on the internet, look at therapist websites, and decide first, whether you prefer websites with a picture of the therapist or ones without a picture, and then decide what kind of a pose seems most appealing.

The next thing you will want to decide is the overall aesthetics of your website. If you work with a web designer, he or she can give you a variety of options. There are also several methods for creating your own website. If you search for "psychotherapy website design" you will see many options for creating your website. They range in cost from a $60 subscription per month to free. If you hire a web designer, make sure that he or she will give you all the information you need to make changes to your website, and that you have all the information about where the website will be housed. This is important, so that if your web designer should move or go out of business, you will be able to make changes to the website and move it to another server should you choose to do so.

If you are reasonably good with computers, you might want to go with a WordPress website that will allow you to edit your website easily and at no cost. Just Google "WordPress website themes for psychotherapists" and you will see a variety of low-cost options for creating a WordPress website. One nice thing about a WordPress website is that generally you will not have ongoing monthly fees to keep it going, except for the fee for the company that is housing your site. Again, a great advantage of a WordPress site is that you can get online at any time and make edits to your site.

The aesthetics of your website are important. Does a practical aesthetic appeal to you? Or a more intellectual tone? Some more erudite therapists and psychoanalysts will feature quite a bit of written material such as PDFs of articles the therapist has written and lists of publications and scholarly presentations. Other therapists such as sex therapists might choose a more lively, sexy tone for their website, with pictures of couples enjoying an innocent yet sensual moment of touch or intimacy. Child therapists might feature pictures of happy families. A Christian therapist might feature inspiring natural scenes. A mindfulness-oriented practice might have pictures of Zen meditation scenes. You get the idea! The aesthetics of your website should reflect the kind of psychotherapy practice that you choose to create. Whether you go with a private web-designer, a subscription service, or a low-cost WordPress site, you will have enough options to choose from so that you can create a website that reflects your practice.

The Various Pages of a Therapist Website

Your website is comprised of a number of *pages*. Each page is a destination that your web visitors will see. A *link* is the word or words you click on to get to the various pages of your website.

Home Page: Your home page is where you have the basic information about your practice. The home page says who you are, what services you offer, and where you are located. If you choose to put a picture of yourself on your website, it will typically be on your home page. Your home page will have links to all of the pages of your website.

Services: This is often a series of links to separate pages detailing the various services you offer. For example, one therapist might have pages for "Individual Psychotherapy," "Couples Therapy," "Adolescents," "Groups," and "Consultation for Psychotherapists." Another therapist might have links to the pages for "Individual Therapy," "Sex Therapy," "Group Therapy and Workshops," and "Supervision and Mentoring." Yet another therapist might have the following links and pages: "Cognitive Retraining," "Neuropsychological Evaluation," and "Cognitive Behavioral Therapy for Anxiety."

About: On this page you will write about yourself. Frequently therapists will put in biographical information, educational background, and areas of particular interest and passion. This is where you get an opportunity to really tell prospective clients about who you are and how you see your work.

Forms: On this page you will have links to PDFs of the various forms your clients will needs such as a new client intake form, a HIPAA-compliant form for consent for treatment, and a form for sharing of confidential case information with other providers.

Contact: On this page you will give clients your email address, phone number, street address, and any other information they will need to reach you. Some websites have a form prospective clients can fill in to inquire about therapy.

Fees and Insurance: Some therapists create this page to state their fees and the insurance companies they are contracted with.

Book an Appointment: Some therapists allow clients to book their own appointments on the therapist's website. The well-reviewed practice management program TherapyNotes (http://therapynotes. com) has a patient portal through which your clients can schedule their own appointments. In our interviews with therapists for this book, we've heard mixed reviews about having clients schedule their own appointments. Some therapists like it, while others lament the control they have ceded over to their clients with this utility.

Useful Links: Therapists' websites often have links to useful public websites to public and non-profit organizations such as the National Institute of Mental Health (NIMH), the American Psychological Association (APA), or Alcoholics Anonymous.

YOUR SOCIAL MEDIA PRESENCE

Your social media presence is distinct from your website, in that you can use social media to connect with other professionals and help prospective clients learn about you and what you do. The two basic platforms for your professional social media presence are Facebook and LinkedIn. You will want to keep your professional Facebook page entirely separate from your individual Facebook page. LinkedIn, on the other hand, is set up for professional networking, so you generally won't have to separate out your individual from your professional LinkedIn presence, as most people will only use LinkedIn professionally.

Facebook: With Facebook you can set up a professional page that is separate from your personal profile. You must have a personal profile set up first, and then you can establish your professional page. Follow the links to set up a professional page, and then go to the "Counseling and Mental Health" heading. Now you can set up a page that is separate from your personal profile, and will not contain the posts you put into your personal profile. You can add information about yourself, your practice, and so forth on your timeline. You have an "About" section that can use much like an "About" page on your website. On the left you can set up contact information. You can set the page up to accept "Reviews" from colleagues or others who have good things to say about your practice. Additionally, your page can be "Liked" by other Facebook members—and your page can "Like" other Facebook pages.

A good way to use your Facebook page is to create buzz or interest for your workshops or public presentations. You can also draw attention to issues that you care about, such as public health issues or other issues of concern for you and your clients.

LinkedIn: With LinkedIn you have a terrific opportunity to highlight your work experience and resume. It is commonplace with LinkedIn to go into a great deal of detail into your work history. A nice feature of LinkedIn is that you connect with your professional community and keep in touch with people you have worked with in the past. This is a nice way to stay in touch with old colleagues who might want to refer to you in the future. Also, through LinkedIn, professionals endorse one another's work. LinkedIn can be especially powerful for you as a therapist if you had a previous career in business or another field and are now in the mental health field. Your old colleagues can keep in touch with you here, and you will be a great resource for them when they need a mental health referral.

Psychology Today: *Psychology Today* has a very simple and easy-to-use format, and while it is not cheap, it is a quick and easy way for clients to find you online. You simply fill out their fill-in form, upload your picture, write a few paragraphs about your practice, upload a link to your website, and you are on your way!

A *Psychology Today* listing is a subscription service, so you will be billed on an ongoing basis. They do a very good job coming to the top of a Google search, so setting up a listing with them can drive business to your practice.

CONCLUSION

Your online presence is a critical part of your practice. Clients expect to find you online and expect to find that you have a good website. Fortunately, there are many good and easy to use tools available to create and maintain your online presence. With a good website and presence with social media and *Psychology Today*, you will have the online presence you need to be found and to be up to date with the tools that today's consumers expect.

CHAPTER 17

Utilizing Practice Management Software Systems for Your Office

Private practitioners utilize practice management software systems to better manage their practices. Approximately 50% of the private practice therapists we interviewed in 2015–2016 for the current edition of this book were using practice management software systems. These software packages generally have functionality for appointment scheduling, maintaining client records, case notes, and billing. As of this writing there are well over 100 such programs on the market.

Luckily, there is a convenient and well organized website to compare and contrast these programs from one another. The website is published by Capterra.com, a company that specializes in providing unbiased information about business software. The following link (www.capterra.com/mental-health-software) will give you a nice list of each of the programs and their capabilities. Even more helpful is the link (www.capterra.com/mental-health-software/system-reviews) that gives you the practice management software packages in rank order based on customer reviews.

Before we dive into practice management software systems, let's first step back and take a look at what a general accounting software accounting package such as QuickBooks can do for you, and then look at how practice management system can complement that. You can think of the practice management software system as the day-to-day tool you use to manage your practice, for scheduling, billing, note writing, taking credit card payments, and interfacing with insurance companies. Let us think of these functions

119

as the micro-economics of your practice. So—your practice management software is your tool chest for running the day-to-day operations of your practice. It represents the micro-economics of your practice because it helps you with all of the details.

QuickBooks or another equivalent small business accounting program such as Freshbooks, Sage 50, or Zoho Books provides a broader look at your practice as a small business. From QuickBooks' perspective, you will see your overall revenue and your expenses and this is an incredibly valuable tool for you to keep track of your profitability. After all, when you subtract your overall expenses from your overall revenues you find your overall profit. To increase profit you can increase revenue or decrease expenses—(in most cases increasing profitability involves a little bit of both!). QuickBooks is your tool for aggregating your revenues and expenses so that you can see and track the big picture in order to increase the profitability of your practice. You can track trends such as expenses that are growing (for example your monthly expenses for bottled water in your waiting room, or your dues for professional organizations) and thereby step back and make decisions about where you might want to make prudent cuts. QuickBooks will also provide your general revenue information.

Your practice management software plays the role of your day-to-day practice tool chest. It will provide you detailed information about the revenue side of the ledger. Here, for example, you can look at which clients are cancelling frequently and possibly costing you valuable time. It allows you to see who are your most financially profitable clients, and who are the least financially rewarding clients. Furthermore, if you are working with managed care, it can provide information about which managed care companies are compensating you more fairly and which ones are paying you less than you deserve. Also, you can track how long it is taking managed care and individuals to pay you. When your analysis of your QuickBooks reports tells you that you need to increase your revenue, then you can dig into your practice management software, and really look at how to better manage your practice so that you can accomplish the goal of increased revenue. Maybe you will take more referrals from the managed care company that pays better, and hold off on the one that pays less well or less reliably. Maybe you will clarify your cancellation policy with a client who cancels a lot and enforce payment for no-show appointments. Much can be done to increase your revenue when you work with the details that a good practice management program can provide.

Practice management software is especially valuable, in fact almost necessary, for your practice if you are actively accepting insurance and working with managed care. Aspects of private practice that in a fee-for-service practice are often handled in a rather casual manner, such as DSM diagnosis, ICD codes and the therapist bill, must be handled with precision in a managed care environment. This is where the practice management software really shines. Billing is usually done electronically. DSM and ICD codes are made easy to check off, and everything is formatted so that even the most bureaucratically minded managed care clerks will be satisfied. Payments are accepted electronically through the practice management software. Your notes can be kept through the software, and everything is set up to be compliant with HIPAA. All of this saves much time and many headaches, especially if you are working with managed care!

Of the people we interviewed for this book, most of the therapists who work heavily with managed care use practice management software. They all reported that it makes their lives much simpler—particularly in the arena of client billing. For therapists who do fee-for-service, a much smaller number use practice management software, but some swear by it! One fee-for-service therapist said that using practice management software (she is using a program called SimplePractice) works very well for her. She uses it for scheduling, billing, and note taking. On the other hand, other fee-for-service practitioners felt no particular need for practice management software. One said, "I have my clients give me a check at the beginning of the session—they don't run a balance, so I rarely give out bills, and I just do my scheduling in an old fashioned calendar, so I just don't see the need."

CONCLUSION

If you are dealing with managed care without using practice management software, we strongly recommend that you try it, unless you are truly computer-phobic. We suspect it will save you much time and aggravation. If you are doing a fee-for-service practice, then the argument for practice management software is less compelling, but many practitioners swear by it, so you might want to give it a try and see if it is helpful for you. Bear in mind that your practice management software does not provide you with the accounting overview that you need to track your expenses and to look at the big picture—it is your tool chest for managing your practice and the revenue you generate with your practice. For the big or macro picture, small business accounting software such as QuickBooks is your best tool.

SECTION IV

A THERAPIST'S MONEY GUIDE

CHAPTER 18

Filling in the Financial Knowledge Gap

We would like to begin this chapter with a case study. Although Dr. Friedlander is a composite of numerous clients, we hope that taking a look at her struggles and successes will put financial planning for private practitioners into a human perspective. Like many therapists we have worked with, Dr. Friedlander has not paid the same quality of serious attention and study to the financial dimension of her practice that she has to the other aspects of her professional life. As a result, her level of financial knowledge is underdeveloped and she feels intimidated by the whole financial arena.

A BRILLIANT CLINICIAN WITH UNDERDEVELOPED FINANCIAL SKILLS

Dr. Rachel Friedlander is a 48-year-old clinical psychologist practicing in Bethesda, Maryland. She is divorced and lives with her 16-year-old daughter, Sarah. Dr. Friedlander has worked diligently to build a highly successful psychotherapy practice. She attended Georgetown University for her undergraduate degree and went on to the University of Michigan where she took her PhD followed by postdoctoral training at the Baltimore-Washington Institute for Psychoanalysis. She is a talented and successful clinician. She has won a respected place in her professional community, with many of her referrals coming from fellow therapists. She nets well over $100,000 per year and lives comfortably. Most of her income has gone toward providing for herself and her daughter. Her ex-husband pays child support in the amount of $1,000 per month, but she will not receive income from his federal government pension at retirement. She maintains a SEP IRA that she has funded sporadically. She is anticipating approximately $200,000 in inheritance if her parents do not eat up their own assets in retirement. She has accumulated a little less than $100,000 in her SEP.

Dr. Friedlander's retirement savings are far below where they will ultimately need to be to fund a comfortable retirement. Moreover, at age 48, she has less time than she once had to make up the difference between where she is and where she will need to be. As Dr. Friedlander moves closer to retirement she is becoming increasingly concerned about what the future holds. She would like to be able to retire in her mid-sixties but is not at all sure that is a realistic possibility. To make her vision of a financially secure retirement a reality, she will have to develop some new skills and begin to view her practice from a more business-like perspective. She will need to reorient herself to the reality that fully funding her retirement is a vitally important life goal. Dr. Friedlander's dilemma is similar to that of many therapists in private practice— she is a highly skilled and successful clinician, but her financial planning and business skills are significantly less developed than her other professional skills. It is for Dr. Friedlander and her peers that this book is intended.

Our goal is to fill in the knowledge gap that many therapists have about the business and financial planning aspects of private practice. While all professional therapists have extensive clinical education and training, few have training of any kind in running the business and financial end of their private practice. With little or no financial training, private practitioners frequently take a "seat of the pants" approach to financial planning, picking up bits and pieces of information along the way from various sources such as money magazines and financial shows on radio or TV. However, just as you didn't learn to practice psychotherapy by reading self-help books, learning to deal effectively with your finances requires more than putting together bits and pieces of (often conflicting) information.

IN AMERICA, A "SEAT OF THE PANTS APPROACH" JUST WON'T DO

A lack of serious attention to the financial dimension might be adaptive if we were Swedish therapists living in a democratic-socialist society rather than Americans living in the individualistic social reality of modern American capitalism. In Sweden, we would have healthcare provided by the state and cradle-to-grave social services—childcare, housing, and college tuition would all be highly subsidized. In America, however, we are expected to fend for ourselves. In particular, private practitioners and entrepreneurs have chosen a high degree of freedom coupled with a high degree of responsibility for our own financial security.

It's true, of course, that at retirement age you will be eligible for Social Security. However, if you do the calculations and take a look at the amount you will actually receive, you will quickly realize that Social Security is merely a supplement to a personal retirement plan—not a substitute. For a detailed explanation of Social Security benefits, see "Social Security and the Private Practitioner" in Chapter 28.

FOUNDATIONS OF PUTTING YOUR FINANCIAL HOUSE IN ORDER

We must put our own financial house in order from the bottom to the top, for if we do not do this for ourselves, who else will? From the perspective of your practice, putting your finances in order begins with effective and accurate bookkeeping. We can think of this as the bookkeeping level of your financially savvy private practice. Getting the bookkeeping level properly organized is foundational to higher-order thinking and action in the financial dimension of your practice. Therefore, it is vital that you get your bookkeeping in good shape.

Have you gone into your dentist's office or your family doctor's office lately? Have you noticed that they have a clerical staff taking care of things like insurance billing, scheduling, ordering supplies, and working the computers? Most therapists do not have that kind of clerical support. Therapists typically rely on themselves, or sometimes a spouse, to deal with the administrative side of their practice. Between seeing clients, paperwork, consultation, and conferences, there is a temptation to procrastinate about bookkeeping chores. Yet this clerical/bookkeeping level of practice management is a vital prerequisite to addressing the broader issues of financial life planning. The clerical/bookkeeping level addresses the nuts and bolts of generating income, while the financial planning level deals with allocating that income into a financial, legal, and tax structure that supports the therapist's long-term needs and goals. Both levels must be addressed and mastered for the financial dimension of a private practice to work successfully.

BOOKKEEPING RESOURCES

One support for mastering this level is to use practice management software as well as bookkeeping software. Please see Chapter 17 for our discussion of practice management software, and Addendum II on QuickBooks to help you get started with accounting. One of the nice things about using a bookkeeping software package like QuickBooks is that it helps you organize your books into appropriate categories. If you are computer phobic or merely computer allergic, you can go to a "one-write" system that was very effective and popular before the PC age. Although providing the nuts and bolts of one-write accounting is beyond the scope of this book, you can find all the one-write resources you need at Safeguard (www.safeguard.com), the venerable producer of non-computerized bookkeeping forms. Once you get organized in your bookkeeping, either by hand or by computer, the more conceptual issues around business and retirement planning will be far easier to deal with.

TREATING YOUR PRACTICE AS A BUSINESS

Sound bookkeeping will allow you to think like a businessperson about your practice. You will know how much money you generate and from what sources. You will understand your expenses better and you will begin to see the big picture of income and outflow in your practice. This is important, because being self-employed is expensive, and you need to be in charge of your cash flow so that you can afford the many expenses involved.

WITH THE FREEDOM OF PRIVATE PRACTICE GOES A RESPONSIBILITY TO YOURSELF

Most private practitioners we know cherish their freedom. We therapists love working for ourselves and doing work that we find deeply meaningful. However, a price we pay for our private practice freedom is that we frequently work outside the formal benefits structure of employment. All those things that an employer would provide for us we must provide for ourselves. We must act both as both employer and employee when we are in private practice. What does this mean in practical terms? It means that our financial self-care must be proactive when we are in private practice. Proactive financial self-care refers to being a good employer to yourself. In the next chapter we will look at five of the most common financial planning mistakes that therapists make. You will notice that one thing all of these mistakes have in common is a failure to treat the practice as a business: to meet the responsibilities of the employer role.

CHAPTER 19

Five Common Financial Mistakes of
Private Practitioners

This chapter covers five common financial mistakes that therapists in private practice make. Notice that they all derive from failing to think about the financial dimension as a good employer would. A good employer would provide a sound retirement package from the business' revenue stream—she would not spend all the business' revenues on salary. She would be prudent in the investment policies of the retirement plan, and would make sure to obtain adequate insurance along with setting up a business structure that minimizes taxation. These considerations would simply be fundamental to doing business in a professional way. Let's look at how we therapists often neglect such fundamentals and look at how such mistakes can be addressed.

FIVE FINANCIAL MISTAKES OF PRIVATE PRACTITIONERS
1) Treating all your income as money you can freely spend
2) Underfunding your retirement plan
3) Inappropriately allocating assets in your retirement plan
4) Failing to obtain adequate insurance
5) Creating excessive tax liability.

Let's take these mistakes one by one and consider appropriate solutions for each.

Mistake #1: Treating All Your Income as Money You Can Freely Spend

Solution

Put Yourself on a Salary

If you begin thinking of your practice as a business, the danger of this mistake becomes clear. Obviously, no business owner could afford to spend all her income on salaries. Overhead expenses, salaries, and benefits must all come out of the revenue coming into the business. Anything left over after all expenses are paid is profit for the business. In the same way, the private practitioner needs to cover all her expenses out of the revenue generated.

Your biggest expense is your salary. A good rule of thumb is that your salary should be about 60% of your target revenue. A percentage of that salary (depending on your tax bracket) will need to be set aside for taxes. About 15% percent of your target revenue should be earmarked for overhead expenses such as rent, continuing education, consultation, furnishings, liability insurance, and so on. That leaves about 25% of your target revenue for funding your benefits package, which includes health insurance, disability insurance, and your retirement plan. Under most circumstances, your benefits and retirement costs as well as your overhead costs will reduce your tax liability.

MARY SMITH'S PRIVATE PRACTICE (ALL NUMBERS ARE APPROXIMATIONS)

Because your revenues minus your expenses equal your profits (revenues − expenses = profits), there are two basic ways to increase your profits:

1) You can increase your revenues. Consider the possibilities of raising your fees, seeing more patients, adding groups to your practice, taking on consulting clients, bringing in passive income from rental property, and so on.
2) You can reduce your expenses. This can be accomplished in myriad ways. Obvious ideas are to shop for a cheaper liability policy (I recently saved several hundred dollars per year by switching carriers), reduce your rent (perhaps by sharing your office), reduce your continuing education expenses, and so on.

Table 19.1 Example of Current Revenues

TARGET REVENUES	
Total client fees with approximately 20 clients per week, an average fee of $100 per session and approximately 2 weeks per year of vacation.	$100,000
TARGET EXPENSES	
Salary (taxes come out of this)	($60,000)
Overhead Expenses	($15,000)
Benefits Package	($25,000)
TARGET PROFITS	
Total Profits	$0

To think creatively about your business means to be constantly reviewing how well your business is working—looking for new ways to increase your revenues and reduce your expenses. This is where your creative imagination becomes an integral part of your dance of prosperity. As you allow your unconscious—your creativity— to inform your thinking, you will be able to shape your practice in ways uniquely suited to you. The result will be a business that is not only more satisfying but also more profitable.

Mary is an example of a therapist who decided to increase her profits by both methods: increasing her revenues and decreasing her expenses. On the revenue side, Mary gave some thought about how to generate more. She enjoys group work, so it seemed like a natural step for her to start two new therapy groups. With two weekly groups of seven members each, she can gross an additional $490 per week (at $35 per session). If the groups meet 50 weeks out of the year, she will bring in an additional $24,500 per year. Mary's efforts to reduce her expenses resulted in less dramatic, but still rewarding improvements. She decided to sublet her office on Saturdays and Wednesday evenings. (Having added two groups to her practice, she was only too pleased to have this time at home!) This reduced her rental expenses by $150 per month or $1,800 per year.

So let's see how Mary's strategies have improved her bottom line:

Table 19.2 Example of Target Revenues

TARGET REVENUES	
Total client fees with approximately 20 clients per week, an average fee of $100 per session and approximately 2 weeks per year of vacation.	$100,000
Additional Revenues (adding two new therapy groups)	$24,500
TARGET EXPENSES	
Salary (taxes come out of this)	($60,000)
Overhead Expenses	($15,000)
Expense Reduction (subletting the office)	$1,800
Benefits Package	($25,000)
PROFITS	
Total Profits	$26,300

Now Mary has a profit. This brings her to a choice point with important implications for her financial well-being, present and future. Has she always wanted a more appealing office? Does she need to increase her advertising in order to boost her practice? Is she long overdue for a vacation? If Mary is like most of us, there will be innumerable opportunities to spend her profits. Before she decides how to spend that money, however, she should consider an important (albeit unsexy) priority: more fully funding her retirement plan.

Mistake #2: Underfunding Your Retirement Plan
Solution
- Develop a realistic projection of your retirement needs.
- Implement a tax-advantaged retirement plan designed to meet your future needs.
- Set realistic funding goals that take into account both your current and future needs.

Choosing a Plan
Before you can fund your retirement plan, you must have one in place. There are a wide variety of retirement plans available, each

with its advantages and limitations. Each has its own set of rules for tax-advantaged investing. Widely used plans are the SEP IRA, the individual 401(k) and the Keogh Profit Sharing Plan. Annuities can also play a useful role in a therapist's retirement planning. Choosing the plan that best fits your situation is a complex and important decision. Throughout this book (see especially Chapter 20: Tax-Advantaged Investing Plans for Self-Employed Psychotherapists) you will find the tools you need to choose the most appropriate plan for you. You would also be well advised to consult with a financial planner and tax advisor before making this important decision.

Taking Care of Your Future Self

No matter what sort of retirement plan you choose, it cannot serve you well unless you fund it at the appropriate level. It is here that your financial advisor can provide crucial advice and support. I once heard Phil Jackson, the legendary basketball coach, say that when the team is behind in crucial situations he simply points out what needs to be done in order to win the game. In the same spirit, your financial advisor's job is to point out to you what you need to do to "win the game" of retirement, that is, to adequately fund your retirement plan. This role of the advisor is seldom a popular one; deferred gratification is no one's favorite pastime. However, your financial advisor can be an advocate for you in your elder years, helping you to keep in mind the long-term goals that you have set. A comfortable retirement at the time you choose to stop working is something you owe to yourself.

Dealing With the Nitty Gritty

Your advisor can help you work out a mathematical projection that will determine the level at which you will need to fund your retirement account.

In brief, the projection should include:

1) Amount you expect to need to live comfortably in retirement;
2) Projected return on your investments;
3) Projected inflation rates;

4) Your current level of funding;
5) Your expected retirement date;
6) Social Security and other retirement benefits (your or your spouse's pension plan, anticipated inheritance, etc.);
7) Other sources of income, if any;
8) Expected healthcare expenses.

A useful way to develop such a projection is to work backwards:

First, estimate at what age you plan on retiring.
Second, estimate your expenses in retirement and make some actuarial assumptions about your estimated life span. These steps will allow you to estimate the ongoing level of funding required to assure that you will have a retirement income sufficient to your needs for as long as you reasonably expect to live. For a rough estimation of your retirement funding needs, we have posted a calculator on our website (www.insightfi nancialgroup.com) that will give you a ballpark idea about how much you need for retirement and how much you need to put away now in order to get there.

When making your projection, there may be other factors unique to your situation that you should also take into account. You may be expecting an inheritance later in life. You may have a partner who is also contributing to your retirement plan. You may have worked for an employer who provided a retirement plan that will kick in later on. You may have other sources of revenue aside from your therapy practice, such as another business or rental property. Your retirement plan should take into account all of these individual factors.

Your gender also impacts your retirement plan. If you are a woman, you face some gender-specific challenges in your financial planning:

1) Statistically, women tend to live longer than men, so the amount needed to fully fund a woman's retirement will, in general, need to be higher than the amount needed to fund the retirement of a man of the same age and lifestyle.

FIVE COMMON FINANCIAL MISTAKES **135**

2) Women tend to be family caretakers, so if a family member develops an illness, it is often the woman who becomes the caregiver. This can result in increased expenses while at the same time reducing the woman's ability to earn.

3) Divorce is another life passage, which tends to take a higher toll on women, often contributing to the phenomenon that sociologists have called "the feminization of poverty." All too often, women wind up with a net reduction in lifestyle and income following divorce, whereas men's income and lifestyle tends to improve after divorce (Feinberg and Knox, 1990).

Once you have considered the variables in your own situation and determined what you need to invest presently to fully fund a reasonable retirement, then your job is to do your very best to assure that your practice supports that level of funding. This may feel overwhelming at first. However, once you recognize the importance of properly preparing for retirement and you begin to "hold the image" of taking care of yourself in this way, you will find yourself thinking creatively. This can take the form of considering either ways to increase income (see more patients, increase fees, add new services such as groups, consultation, and so on) or ways to reduce costs (find less expensive office space, rent out your office part-time, cut back on advertising, and so on).

Mistake #3: Inappropriately Allocating Assets in Your Retirement Plan[1]
Solution
- Calibrate your asset allocation to your needs, goals and time frame for retirement.

This solution sounds so obvious! However, I have worked with many therapists for whom misallocation of assets is a major problem. Most commonly, the issue is one of overly aggressive investing. Sometimes this is a result of poor advice received from

---

1   Asset allocation does not guarantee a profit or protection from losses in a declining market.

unprofessional stockbrokers who allow their self-interest to take precedence over the interests of their client. Misallocation can also be the result of do-it-yourself investing with insufficient information. Without thorough research it is impossible to make wise, informed choices. Anxiety, overexcitement, or greed can also lead to a hyperaggressive approach in the attempt to make "a quick killing." As stock market reversals that accompanied the Great Recession of 2007–2008 revealed, overly aggressive investing can lead to dismaying results.

A PORTFOLIO OUT OF BALANCE (A COMPOSITE EXAMPLE)

John Jefferies, LCSW, and Jennifer Jefferies, PhD, had lost over 50% of their worth over the last 2 years. John had been in full-time private practice for many years and Jennifer had recently left her position with a private psychiatric hospital to open her own practice. Needless to say, they were nervous about the future. At this point, they acknowledged the need to meet with a financial planner. During the real estate boom, they had bought an over-priced house with an adjustable rate mortgage on a low intro-ductory "teaser" rate. When the house price started to fall, and their adjustable teaser rates started to rise, they realized that they were in trouble. They were underwater with their house and were feeling burned and angry when they came for their first financial planning appointment.

Their retirement accounts were far too aggressively invested and had lost almost half their value. Although John and Jennifer were in their early forties, they had what amounted to a maximum growth portfolio.

John and Jennifer knew very well the missteps they had made. They invested far too carelessly in their house. They had also invested far too carelessly and aggressively in their retirement accounts. They had learned a painful lesson and intended to invest more moderately in the future. However, that did not help them in deciding how to move forward. Should they hang on to their house? How should they deal with realigning their investment portfolio? This consultation with a financial planner was the first time they had sought out professional advice.

Their financial planner asked them to consider whether they wanted to stay in their house? Were they willing to cut their losses in their aggressive investment portfolio and invest more appropriately?

John and Jennifer decided to stay in their house, and were ultimately able to participate in the HARP program (the Home Affordable Refinance Program), a federally funded program that allowed them to shift over to a 30-year fixed rate mortgage. Although it took several years for their house to regain its value, it eventually did became an asset for them again.

With regard to their investment portfolio, their financial planner recommended to John and Jennifer that they take some time to analyze where they are in their lives. He asked them to take a look at when they want to retire or at least cut back on work. He also asked them to look at their other financial responsibilities. Further, he asked them to explore how much risk they were willing to tolerate in the market at this juncture in their lives. After exploring these issues, they decided on a moderate asset allocation. This entailed a mix of various categories of stocks, bonds, and cash. Now they had to get from a hyperaggressive portfolio to a moderate one. They made an analysis of the stock portion of the portfolio and kept some of the stronger growth oriented investments while harvesting the losses in others. ("Harvesting losses" refers to reporting securities losses to the IRS in order to take advantage of capital losses, thereby offsetting capital gains.)[2]

They then reinvested in a mix of securities—stocks, alternative investments, bonds, and cash—that provided an appropriate allocation of assets for the Jefferies at their current life stage.

Although John and Jennifer went through a painful period of readjustment, now in 2016, 8 years since the Great Recession, they are on track with their retirement plans and well on the way to getting their home paid off.

Proper asset allocation entails proactive planning, a disciplined investment strategy, and the willingness to hang in there over the long haul.

---

2   It is not intended that any part of this book provide specific tax advice. Please consult with a tax professional about the tax consequences of any actions you may take.

Mistake #4: Failing to Obtain Adequate Insurance[3]
Solution

Make a realistic assessment of your insurance needs. All businesses need insurance, and yours is no exception. The purpose of insurance is the transfer of risk. Rather than assuming an intolerable risk (catastrophic medical expenses, for instance) yourself, you transfer that risk to the insurance company.

Health Insurance

Unless you have sufficient assets to cover your own catastrophic medical expenses, you need health insurance. This may be taken care of through your partner's employer if you can be added to his or her health plan. Failing this, you will need to find a plan—perhaps through your professional organization—that works for you.

How Much? What Type?

Although it's certainly true that no one can entirely avoid the need for health insurance, how much and what sort of insurance you will want is very much a factor of your lifestyle, personal preferences, and risk tolerance. To determine what best fits you, ask yourself the following questions:

- Do I make frequent office visits to my doctor?
- Do I use a lot of prescription drugs?
- Is choice of doctor important to me, or am I OK with whomever the HMO assigns me to?
- Are mental health services something I use or anticipate using?
- Do I have a preference for alternative health practitioners not covered by standard insurance?
- How much could I afford to spend in the event of a major medical problem?
- Would I rather be totally covered for every possible eventuality or pay lower premiums?

The trade-off here is between higher premium payments and comprehensiveness of coverage. Another issue to keep in mind is the

---

3 Asset allocation does not guarantee a profit or protection from losses in a declining market.

importance of obtaining coverage while your health is good. Once a serious or chronic problem develops, it may become well-nigh impossible to find the kind of coverage you need.

Disability Insurance

Disability insurance provides income replacement in the event of debilitating illness or injury. This type of insurance may be unpleasant to think about. After all, no one wants to consider the possibility that they might be disabled to an extent that would make self-support impossible. However, denial or procrastination can result in disaster. There are a number of options in disability insurance and business overhead coverage that your financial planner can help you sort through. A good rule of thumb is to plan on spending 3%–5% of your gross revenue for this coverage. Disability insurance does not come cheap, but insuring that you will have a consistent income flow, even in the case of disability, is an important consideration for almost all therapists.

Liability Insurance

Every practitioner carries professional liability insurance from internship onward. However, have you done any rate comparisons? There can be dramatically differing rates among carriers. Most liability insurance carriers provide continuous insurance—in other words, year 2 of your coverage covers you for acts committed during years 1 and 2; year 3 covers you for years 1, 2, and 3, and so on. For this reason, your premium will probably increase each year until a cap has been reached. It pays to check both the initial premium charged and the cap when you are comparing policies. As with health insurance, give yourself enough coverage to feel well protected.

Life Insurance

The topic of life insurance is a complex one. We will discuss life insurance as an investment vehicle under "Insurance-Based Vehicles" in Chapter 20. We will take an in-depth look at the entire subject of life insurance in Chapter 25. At this point, it is important only to remember that there are two main types of life insurance: term insurance, which provides coverage for a specific period of time; and permanent life insurance, which provides a death benefit as well as tax-deferred growth on cash values in the account. You will be better prepared to answer the questions of how much and which kind is right for you after reading the pertinent chapters. Your financial planner can be a valuable aid in helping you determine which, if any, policy best fits your needs.

Mistake #5: Creating Excessive Tax Liability
Solution
- Year-round tax planning

By this point, you may be gnashing your teeth as you consider all the expenses involved in being your own employer. But don't despair! There is a silver lining. As a self-employed person, practically all of your business-related expenses can be tax-deductible.[4] Make an appointment with your tax advisor. Don't wait until March, when the tax season will make it impossible for you to have his or her full attention. Tell your advisor that you'd like help in organizing your records, keeping track of business expenses, and calculating your estimated quarterly taxes. If you are not paying estimated taxes now, you might be surprised (and dismayed) to see what the IRS charges you in penalties and interest each year. This is another area where your tax advisor will be glad to enlighten you.

Taking advantage of all your potential deductions is important. However, you can realize your greatest tax savings by making use of one or more tax-advantaged investment plans. By investing in a plan that allows you to defer paying taxes—either on the money invested and/or on the money accrued, you reduce your tax liability while at the same time contributing to your retirement.

PAUSE TO REFLECT
This might be a good place to stop for a moment and tune in to how you're feeling. Has the discussion left you feeling excited?

---

4   It is not intended that this book provide specific tax advice. Tax consult with a tax professional.

Anxious? Confused? If you're like most us, the answer is probably "all of the above." Achieving financial mastery is not an overnight event, any more than achieving clinical mastery. If you're feeling a bit overwhelmed, consider a "bite-sized" approach:

1) Decide which issue to work with first. This could be the one that feels most pressing or the one with which you already feel somewhat comfortable.
2) Talk with the appropriate professional (financial planner, tax advisor, insurance agent).
3) Take one concrete step (buy the insurance policy, begin making estimated tax payments, set up a retirement account).
4) Give yourself time to assimilate and take satisfaction in the first step before looking forward to the next one.

A solid financial footing increases the structural integrity of your practice. By dealing with the financial dimension, you are not only providing for the comfort and security of yourself and your family; you are also building a container that will allow you to work with your clients in a way that is deeply supportive and healing.

> Whatever you can do or dream you can, begin it. Boldness has genius, power and magic in it.
>
> (W.H. Murray, 1951)

Target Profitability Worksheet

Use the following worksheets to begin the process of thinking about revenues, expenses, and profitability in your practice. As you work with these issues in your practice, you will develop a more businesslike approach that will help you improve your bottom line.

$$\text{Revenues} - \text{Expenses} = \text{Profit (or Loss)}$$

Figure target revenues and expenses. Projecting these figures gives you something to shoot for. If you are exceeding your targets,

Table 19.3 Target Revenues Worksheet

Approximate number of clients per month	Average fee per session	Average monthly revenue from individuals and couples
A	B $	(A × B) $

Other Sources of Revenue, e.g. groups, consulting, teaching, interns.

Source of Revenue 1 Description	Source of Revenue 2 Description	Source of Revenue 3 Description	
Approximate Monthly Income $	Approximate Monthly Income $	Approximate Monthly Income $	Total Monthly Revenues $

Projected Monthly Expenses

COMPENSATION	
Your Monthly Salary	$
BENEFITS	
Health Insurance	$
Disability Insurance	$
Retirement Investing	$
TAXES	
Federal Taxes	$
State Taxes	$
Local Taxes	$
GENERAL BUSINESS EXPENSES	
Liability Insurance	$
Rent	$
Furnishings	$
Cont. Ed., Consultation	$

PROJECTED PROFIT or LOSS

Projected Revenues	Projected (Expenses)	Profit or (Loss)
$	($)	=

© 2018, *Mastering the Financial Dimension of Your Psychotherapy Practice: The Definitive Resource for Private Practice*, Peter H. Cole and Daisy Reese, Routledge

Table 19.4 Actual Revenues Worksheet

Approximate number of clients per month	Average fee per session	Average monthly revenue from individuals and couples
A	B $	(A × B) $

Other Sources of Revenue, e.g. groups, consultation, teaching, interns etc.

Source of Revenue 1 Description	Source of Revenue 2 Description	Source of Revenue 3 Description	
Approximate Monthly Income $	Approximate Monthly Income $	Approximate Monthly Income $	Total Monthly Revenues $

Actual Monthly Expenses

COMPENSATION	
Your Monthly Salary	$
BENEFITS	
Health Insurance	$
Disability Insurance	$
Retirement Investing	$
TAXES	
Federal Taxes	$
State Taxes	$
Local Taxes	$
GENERAL BUSINESS EXPENSES	
Liability Insurance	$
Rent	$
Furnishings	$
Cont. Ed., Consultation	$

PROFIT or LOSS

Actual Revenues	Actual (Expenses)	Profit or (Loss)
$	$	=

© 2018, *Mastering the Financial Dimension of Your Psychotherapy Practice: The Definitive Resource for Private Practice*, Peter H. Cole and Daisy Reese, Routledge

then you are doing well and heading for a profit for the year. If you are falling short, then you may need to either boost revenues or reduce expenses. A good businessperson is constantly asking herself three questions: How can I increase revenues? How can I reduce expenses? How can I reduce my tax liability?

REFERENCE

Feinberg, Rene and Kathleen E. Knox (Eds.). *The Feminization of Poverty in the United States: A Selected, Annotated Bibliography of the Issues, 1978–1989* (New York: Garland, 1990)

Murray, W.H. (1951). *The Scottish Himalayan Expedition*. London: JM Dent & Sons.

CHAPTER 20

Tax-Advantaged Investing Plans for Self-Employed Psychotherapists

In this chapter we will explore selected retirement vehicles in greater depth. First, we will look at employment-based retirement vehicles: the SEP IRA, the 401(k) for individuals, and the SIMPLE IRA. Next we will discuss the Traditional IRA and the Roth IRA. Next, we will take a look at insurance-based vehicles: variable universal life insurance and variable annuities. Finally, we will consider two tax advantaged education savings plans: the Education IRA and 529 plans.

A thoroughly comprehensive discussion of retirement vehicles is beyond the scope of this book, as they constitute a complicated area of tax and employment law. Instead, we have tried to sift out the information that you need as a solo practitioner to make informed choices as to the retirement plan you might choose. We strongly recommend that you seek professional advice in putting together your retirement plan. Please bear in mind that if you have employees, you must follow very strict guidelines for funding the SIMPLE and SEP IRAs. As a sole proprietor in solo practice, these plans can be significantly less complicated.

EMPLOYMENT-BASED VEHICLES

The following information is derived from the IRS website, which has lots of good information that is easy to access and easy to understand (www.irs.gov/Retirement-Plans/Retirement-Plans-for-Self-Employed-People).

401(k) for Individuals

- You must have no employees to be eligible for the individual 401(k) plan. This plan works very well many therapists in private practice. You are allowed to:
  - Make salary deferrals up to $18,000 in 2015 and 2016 (plus an additional $6,000 if you're 50 or older) either on a pretax basis or as designated Roth contributions.
  - Contribute up to an additional 25% of your net earnings from self-employment for total contributions of $53,000 for 2015 and 2016, including salary deferrals.
  - Tailor your plan to allow access to your account balance through loans and hardship distributions.

A SEP IRA or Simplified Employee Pension plan is probably the most popular retirement savings vehicle for therapists in private practice. If you have employees, you can utilize the SEP IRA as a retirement vehicle for yourself and for them. You can also utilize the SEP IRA if you have no employees. I won't go into the rules you must follow for the SEP if you have employees, just please note here that you should consult your CPA or financial advisor if you have employees and you are setting up a SEP so that you follow the rules correctly. If you have no employees, in 2016 you can contribute as much as 25% of your net earnings from self-employment up to $53,000.

Savings Incentive Match Plan for Employees (SIMPLE IRA Plan)
You can put all your net earnings from self-employment in the plan: up to $12,500 in 2015 and 2016 (plus an additional $3,000 if you're 50 or older) plus either a 2% fixed contribution or a 3% matching contribution.

Traditional IRA and Roth IRA
Traditional and Roth IRAs represent two different approaches to individual tax-advantaged investing. With the Traditional IRA, contributions are tax-deductible and taxes are collected when distributions are made. With the Roth IRA, contributions are made

in after-tax dollars but distributions are non-taxable. In 2016 both Roth and Traditional IRA contributions are capped at $5,500 or your taxable compensation for the year if it was less than this dollar amount. Certain qualifications apply to the tax advantages on both the Traditional and Roth IRA, so please consult with a tax professional before investing.

Many financial advisors think that the Roth IRA has advantages. If you qualify, your Roth contributions can grow tax-free and qualified withdrawals can be made tax-free. Your Roth IRA contribution might be limited based on your filing state and income. Please consult your financial advisor or tax advisor to make sure you qualify.

If you are investing in another retirement vehicle such as a SEP IRA or individual 401(k), this may affect the tax deductibility of your Traditional IRA, so again, it is important to get tax advice before you invest.

Catch-Up Contributions to IRAs

If you have reached age 50 and you meet the law's adjusted gross income limits for making IRA contributions, you may invest an additional $1,000 per year in your Roth or Traditional IRA.

Current Information on IRS Funding Limits and Income Restrictions

The IRS limits the amount you can put into any tax advantaged plan. These restrictions relate to how much income you can have and still be eligible, along with maximum amounts you can put into such plans. We keep current information on these issues posted on our website. Please go to www.insightfinancialgroup. com and click through to the Tax Center. There you will find updated information on eligibility and restrictions on tax-advantaged investing plans.

INSURANCE-BASED VEHICLES
Variable Universal Life Insurance

Common wisdom about life insurance used to be "buy term and invest the rest." The idea was that you should buy low-cost term insurance and invest the difference between the cost of the term insurance and the cost of higher-priced whole life insurance. There are instances when this wisdom may still hold true. Life insurance can be used for a variety of purposes, and we will take an in-depth look at the various types of life insurance and the purposes best served by each type in Chapter 25. Here, however, we'll examine a type of life insurance that is well designed for both investment and death benefit purposes: variable universal life insurance.[1] Here's how it works.

The policy allows you to invest in separate accounts that consist of a variety of underlying investments such as various classes of stocks and bonds. You can invest in a variety of these separate accounts, many of which are typically managed by well-known money management firms. Investments can range from very conservative bond and money market investments to very aggressive growth investments. This product is known as variable life insurance because the value in the separate accounts will vary with the market. Part of the premium you pay goes to cover the cost of the life insurance death benefit, part of it goes to paying various expenses, and part of it goes to fund the separate accounts. The contract is treated by the IRS as a life insurance policy as long as it is funded within certain parameters, which your investment advisor and insurance company will inform you about. You pay the premiums with after-tax dollars, but the money grows tax-deferred within the separate accounts. You may borrow against the cash value in the separate accounts and will not be taxed on the loan. When you die, the death benefit is treated as life insurance and therefore will generally pass directly to your heirs without having to go through probate and is generally not taxable to the beneficiary.

As you can see, the variable universal life insurance (VUL) concept allows the investor to both save for retirement and create an estate for her family in the event of her death with the life insurance death benefit. This vehicle allows the investor with

---

1   Variable life insurance policies are not short-term investments and are offered by prospectus only. An investment in a variable life product involves investment risk, including the possible loss of principal. Investment return and principal value will fluctuate, so your shares when redeemed may be worth more or less than the original cost. Read the prospectus carefully before investing or sending money. An investment in the securities underlying the policy is not guaranteed or endorsed by any bank, is not a deposit or obligation of any bank, and is not federally insured by any government agency.

dependents to create an instant estate via the death benefit, and to fund a retirement nest egg through tax-deferred growth in the separate accounts. Of course the separate accounts can lose value just as any market-based investment can. The VUL is most appropriate for investors who really need the life insurance aspect of the policy. If you have dependents or a spouse who will need significant resources in the event of your death, and you also want to put money away that can grow tax-deferred, then variable universal life may be worth investigating.

Variable Annuities

A variable annuity is a contract with an insurance company. As in variable universal life insurance, variable annuity investments are made in separate accounts that are frequently managed by leading money management firms. Also, like variable universal life insurance, the variable annuity is usually funded with after-tax dollars (although annuities can be used inside a tax-deferred vehicle such as a SEP IRA and funded with pretax dollars).[2] In the variable annuity (as in variable universal life insurance), the separate account investments grow tax-deferred. You pay tax on the growth in the investment when money is taken out at retirement.

Although the variable annuity has some features in common with variable universal life insurance, it is not life insurance. Death benefits do not transfer to the next generation with the same favorable rules that apply to life insurance.[3] It does have one unique feature, however: The annuity is the only vehicle that can offer the retiree a guaranteed lifetime income. The guaranteed

2   Because tax-qualified retirement plans are already tax-deferred, there are no additional tax benefits when purchasing an annuity. Other benefits such as lifetime income payments and protection of principal through death benefits may make such a purchase suitable for some investors.

3   Variable annuities are sold by prospectus only. Investors should read the prospectus carefully before investing. Annuities are long-term investments designed for retirement purposes. Withdrawals of taxable amounts are subject to income tax and, if taken prior to age 59½, a 10% federal tax penalty may apply. Early withdrawals may be subject to withdrawal charges. An investment in the securities underlying a variable annuity involves investment risk, including possible loss of principal. The contract, when redeemed, may be worth more or less than the original investment. The purchase of a variable annuity is not required for, and is not a term of, the provision of any banking service or activity. Guarantees are backed by the claims-paying ability of the issuer.

lifetime feature of annuities along with the tax deferral of growth in the separate accounts can make the variable annuity an attractive, integral part of the private practitioner's retirement plan. There are two distinct phases in the life of an annuity. The first phase is the funding phase. This phase occurs when you are working and putting money into the annuity. The second phase occurs when you retire and "annuitize" the contract. When the contract is annuitized, payments are made from the insurance company to the annuitant according to the terms of the annuitization. Commonly, the annuity is set up to pay until the death of the annuitant. Sometimes the contract stipulates that it will pay for a certain period of years to the annuitant's beneficiary, even if the annuitant dies prematurely during the annuitization period.

TAX-ADVANTAGED EDUCATION SAVING PLANS

If you have children or grandchildren, you are undoubtedly aware of the high cost of a college education. The bad news is that college is very expensive, and is becoming more so with each passing year. The good news is that the Economic Growth and Tax Relief Reconciliation Act of 2001 has created some significant enhancements to existing programs that provide for federally tax-advantaged college savings.

Education IRAs

You may make a non-deductible contribution to an Education IRA for a designated beneficiary. That money will grow free of federal taxes on capital gains and distributions. If distributions are used for qualified educational expenses, they are not taxed as income. Beginning in tax year 2002, the new law increased the maximum annual contribution from $500 to $2,000 per beneficiary. Under the old law, qualified expenses were limited to postsecondary educational expenses, but under the new law some expenses such as uniforms, computers, and room and board expenses are allowable for students enrolled in private K–12 schools. The new law allows corporations and non-profit organizations to make contributions. Also, the new law eliminates the 6% penalty tax on contributions to an Education IRA made in the same years that contributions are made to a 529 plan.

As you can see, there are many enhancements to the Education IRA under the new tax law. Of course you should talk with your professional tax advisor and financial planning professional before you invest.

529 Plans[4]

These plans are paid for with after-tax dollars and are allowed to grow, federally tax-deferred, until the funds are used for qualified higher education expenses. Under the new law, when distributions are used for qualified expenses they are not taxed as income. This represents a very substantial benefit for your college savings. The new law allows for tuition credits or other amounts to be transferred tax-free from one 529 plan to another for the same beneficiary. Additionally, the new law allows institutions of higher learning to create 529 plans for prepaid tuition to that institution. You can make a yearly contribution of up to $14,000 into a 529 plan, and may contribute up to $70,000 in a given year as long as you do not make further contributions for the following 5 years. As with the Education IRA, there are many advantages to the 529 plans, and you should seek professional tax and investment advice before investing.

There are many new opportunities for therapists to help our children and grandchildren pay for higher education expenses. Planning early is important, so that you are prepared when the time comes to pay the high cost of tuition, room and board, and other expenses.

CONCLUSION

This section is a brief overview of your many options to save on taxes and prepare for three important financial issues: retirement, protection for your dependent survivors, and college funding. Which

---

4 Investments in 529 plans involve risks to principal and may involve additional fees such as enrollment charges and annual maintenance fees. These plans offer no guarantees. Depending on your state of residence and the state of residence of the beneficiary, the plan may or may not be eligible for state tax benefits. There are exceptions to the gift tax and estate tax exemptions; please contact a qualified tax, legal, or financial advisor for more information prior to investing.

vehicles to use will depend upon your individual circumstances. An investment professional can help you tailor a plan to your needs. Many roads lead to Rome, and there is no one correct way to set up your investment plan. In choosing your tax-advantaged vehicles, here are some issues to bear in mind:

1) Reducing your tax burden through tax advantages while investing for your future makes a lot of sense.
2) Keep your plan flexible, so that in good years you can put in more money and in less profitable years you are free to put in less.
3) Direct your investment choices with an asset allocation mix that is right for you.
4) You can address the needs of your dependent survivors in the case of your death with life insurance.

Once you have designed an investment plan that fits your needs and circumstances, the next step is to implement your plan. You will need to build the funding of your retirement plan into the financial structure of your practice. You can then settle into a routine of funding your retirement in a consistent and disciplined way.

CHAPTER 21

A Therapist's Guide to Fundamental Investing Concepts

DOLLAR COST AVERAGING: A PRESCRIPTION FOR THE FLUCTUATING MARKET BLUES

While most everyone loves a strong bull market, bear markets are an inevitable part of the cycle, and investors must learn to deal with the bad times along with the good. The stock market is in constant motion, responding to an ever-changing set of conditions. Economic and political factors such as interest rates, taxation policies, and the business cycle all influence the stock market along with international political factors and intangibles such as the psychology of investors.

I advise against trying to "time the market"; that is, waiting to invest until you feel that market conditions are ideal. Instead, you might want to consider a time-tested approach known as "dollar cost averaging." With dollar cost averaging, you invest a given dollar amount each month into your portfolio of securities regardless of current stock market conditions.

To illustrate: Let us suppose you invest $1,000 a month into a given security within your individual 401(k). This way you will automatically buy more shares when the price is low, fewer when the share price is high. Because you accumulate more shares for your money when the market is down, your average cost per share will be less than the average market price per share in fluctuating markets. Dollar cost averaging involves continuous investment in securities, regardless of fluctuation in price levels.[1]

---

1   Dollar cost averaging involves continuous investment in securities, regardless of the fluctuating price levels. Investors should consider their ability to continue purchases through periods

No plan can assure a profit or protect against a loss in a declining market. However, if you can continue to invest regularly through changing market conditions, dollar cost averaging can be an effective way to accumulate assets to meet your long-term goals. It can make sense to make the *accumulation* of securities a goal, because now you have an advantage in a market downturn—your automatic investment is going to buy you more shares when the price of shares is down. Those same shares will be more valuable when the market has its next upswing!

Like our emotional lives, the stock market has sometimes unpredictable cycles—periods during which they are generally up and periods during which they are generally down, with variations on a daily basis. Psychotherapists are trained to help our clients develop resilience to weather life's inevitable ups and downs. To be successful investors, we must develop resilience to deal with the inevitable ups and downs of the marketplace. Just as anger, sadness, loneliness, and other feelings are as much a normal part of life as feelings of joy and satisfaction, so too are bear markets as normal and inevitable as bull markets. Moreover, in the stock market, as in a functional person's life, the good has historically outweighed the bad.

A quick review of the S&P 500, a broad index of the stock market, will reveal that overall, stocks as an asset class have historically had a positive trend. I (Peter) am writing this on March 3, 2016. To illustrate the overall long-term trend in stocks, I have looked up this date at 10-year intervals and looked at the closing value of the S&P 500 on each of those dates. The following table shows the S&P on this date in 10-year intervals starting in 1953. If you look at the Closing Quote column you will see a consistent, long-term, positive general trend in stock prices.

Remembering the stock market's long history of upward movement can give you the confidence you need to invest wisely in your future.

of low price levels or changing economic conditions. Such a plan does not assure a profit and does not protect against loss in declining markets. Regular investing does not ensure a profit and does not protect against loss in declining markets. Investors should consider their ability to invest continuously during periods of fluctuating price levels.

ASSET ALLOCATION[3]

Asset allocation is the investment strategy of diversifying your investments among a variety of investment classes. Broad categories of investment classes include stocks, bonds, and cash. Within these three categories are a great many subcategories. A typical asset allocation model will frequently include the following categories.

Table 21.1 S&P 500 Selected Dates[2]

Date	Closing Quote
3–23–1956	48.83
3–23–1966	89.29
3–23–1976	103.42
3–23–1986	235.33
3–23–1996	650.62
3–23–2006	1302.95
3–23–2016	2036.71

Table 21.2 Asset Classes

STOCKS	BONDS	CASH	SPECIALTY
Value Stocks	Government Bonds	Money Market	Real Estate
Growth Stocks	Corporate Bonds	Certificates of Deposit	
Foreign Stocks	Government Agency Bonds	Bank Accounts	
Large Cap Stocks	Junk Bonds		
Mid-Cap Stocks	Municipal Bonds		
Small Cap Stocks			

2   An investor cannot invest directly in an index. Past performance does not guarantee future results. The Standard & Poor's 500 (S&P 500) is an unmanaged group of securities considered to be representative of the stock market in general.

3   Asset allocation does not guarantee a profit or protection from losses in a declining market.

The essential idea behind asset allocation is to align your investment portfolio with your investment goals while avoiding two traps:

1) Trying to time the market
2) Putting all your eggs into one basket.

Your financial advisor should be well versed in asset allocation strategies designed to meet your goals. He or she can help you design and implement a rational strategy.

Steady as You Go
Combining Dollar Cost Averaging With Asset Allocation[4]

A strategy therapists commonly use in their retirement plans is that of combining dollar cost averaging with an asset allocation strategy. This combination can be used in any qualified or individual retirement plan. As we have discussed, dollar cost averaging involves investing the same amount of money on a regular basis (usually monthly) into a given investment. Combining dollar cost averaging with asset allocation involves investing a fixed amount of money each month into a variety of investments that comprise a particular asset allocation mix. For example, Mary Smith, LCSW, invests $1,500 per month into her individual 401(k) plan. She has established an asset allocation model with her financial advisor that includes 70% into a mix of equities-based securities, 20% into bonds, and 10% into cash equivalents. Each month, $1,050 goes into her equities securities, $300 into her bond securities, and $150 into her money market fund.

The combination of asset allocation and dollar cost averaging combines two well-established approaches to investing. The whole process can be automated with scheduled bank deductions that

---

4   Dollar cost averaging involves continuous investment in securities, regardless of the fluctuating price levels. Investors should consider their ability to continue purchases through periods of low price levels or changing economic conditions. Such a plan does not ensure a profit and does not protect against loss in declining markets. Asset allocation does not guarantee a profit or protection from losses in a declining market.

go toward the purchasing of the securities in the asset allocation model. The regularity of the investing helps to put the investor in a more proactive and disciplined frame of mind.

Fluctuations in the market can be compared to fluctuations in weather conditions. Just as you wouldn't close down your office during cold weather or cancel a client because it looked like rain, so is it important not to allow changes in the market "weather" to dictate your investment activity. Dollar cost averaging plus asset allocation provides you a disciplined, consistent way to structure your investing on your path toward establishing a sound financial footing.

MODERN PORTFOLIO THEORY

In the 1950s economist Harry Markowitz wrote about optimizing a portfolio through diversification. Markowitz looked beyond the picking of individual stocks and considered the issue of creating overall portfolios that are efficient in terms of generating maximum return for a given degree of risk. His innovative approach to stock market investing won Markowitz the Nobel Prize in Economics. His approach is known as Modern Portfolio Theory. This theory has been highly influential among investment professionals and is a widely respected approach to investing.

Markowitz noted that certain stocks have an inverse correlation to each other in terms of price. For a simplified, hypothetical example, let's say that low fuel prices are good for the airlines and bad for the oil companies. Conversely, high fuel prices are bad for the airlines and good for oil companies. If the stock prices of ABC Oil Company and XYZ Airlines reflect these issues, than the prices of these stocks may exhibit a history of low correlation with each other. A correlation coefficient of 1 means that the prices of two securities move in lock step. A correlation coefficient of 0 means that two securities move totally independently of each other. A correlation coefficient of –1 means that two securities move simultaneously in opposite directions. You would attain better diversification if you invested in ABC Oil and XYZ Airlines than if you invested in ABC Oil and DEF Oil. Diversification lends stability to a portfolio.

Markowitz and his colleagues quantified a series of observations about risk, return, correlation coefficients, and portfolio efficiency. The process of establishing an efficient portfolio involves asset allocation among individual securities or asset classes that are chosen in part for diversification purposes. An efficient portfolio maximizes total return for a given risk level.

The Importance of Modern Portfolio Theory to You

Although a discussion about the correlation coefficients of various asset classes may not be scintillating to many therapists, it is in fact important for you to consider your overall portfolio and its asset allocation in making your investment decisions. It is very difficult for even the most experienced professional to consistently pick winning individual stocks. It is even harder for people outside of Wall Street to pick winners. If you orient yourself to proper asset allocation based on Modern Portfolio Theory, you do not need to "pick a winner." Instead, you can put together an asset allocation, based on your risk tolerance and life circumstances, that makes sense and that makes up an efficient portfolio. Your financial planning professional should be able to help you assemble a portfolio that is appropriate for your needs.

TIME VALUE OF MONEY AND TAX-DEFERRED INVESTING

Anybody would prefer to have $10,000 given to her today than $10,000 given to her a year from now. There are two basic reasons for this: The first is that the sooner you have the money in hand, the sooner you have an opportunity to make money with your money. The second reason is that inflation decreases the value of your money, so that $10,000 a year from now will in all likelihood buy you fewer goods and services than it does today. A familiar example of the time value of money is a job bonus, where your boss gives you two options: You can receive a $10,000 bonus now, or a $10,800 bonus after 1 year.

How does the time value of money relate to your financial life? Let's look at the issue of tax-deferred savings versus taxable savings. With tax-deferred savings, you have the opportunity to hang on to more of your money, because you are deferring the payment of taxes on capital gains and dividends that you would pay with a taxable account. The fact that you can defer the payment of taxes allows for the possibility of amplifying the time value of your retirement money, and represents the chief advantage of tax-deferred investing for retirement.

Let us consider the case of Joseph Sanders, MD, a psychiatrist in private practice who earns $175,000 per year, and the money he earns beyond $91,150 is taxed in federal income taxes at the rate of 28%. Dr. Sanders has just completed a course of treatment with a patient suffering from depression. He bills her insurer and receives a payment of $7,500. Because this income is federally taxed at the rate of 28%, he must pay $2,100 of his fee in taxes, leaving him with $5,400. If he were to invest that money in a portfolio of securities for 1 year and achieve a gain of 10%, he would add $540 of gain to his $5,400, giving him $5,940. However, when he sells that security after 1 year, his gain is taxed at the long-term capital gains rate of 15% (if he sells before 1 year, his capital gains are taxed at his income tax rate of 28%), thereby reducing his gain by $81 leaving him with the amount saved after 1 year of $5,859.

On the other hand, if Dr. Sanders had put that $7,500 into his qualified retirement plan, then he could avoid all of the aforementioned taxes. If he were achieving a 10% return, after 1 year he would have made $750 in interest and the $7,500 would now be worth $8,250. This is quite a contrast with the $5,859.

Now consider the time value of Dr. Sanders's investment in his tax-deferred account. Again, bear in mind that he is not paying taxes on capital gains or dividends on his investments, thereby amplifying the effect of compounding. Let us assume that Dr. Sanders is 40 years old at the 1-year mark when his $7,500 has grown to $8,250 and that he has invested it in his SEP IRA, that he holds the money until age 65, and that his average annual rate of return is 7%. At age 65, that pot of money will have grown to $44,776. Of course Dr. Sanders will need to pay ordinary income tax on the money when he takes it out of his SEP in retirement.

We could also have figured out this whole payment scheme and looked at what how Dr. Sanders would have come out if he had

Table 21.3 Taxable vs. Tax-Deferred on $7,500 in Income—Year One

	Taxable Account	Tax-Deferred Account
Amount of Insurance Payment	$7,500	$7,500
Subtract 28% for Federal Tax	$2,100	No Taxes Due
After-Tax Amount Saved	$5,400	$7,500
Earn 10% Return on Investment	$540	$750
Subtotal	$5,940	$8,250
Deduct Long-Term Capital Gains Rate of 15% after 1 Year When Security Is Sold	$81	No Taxes Due on Interest Earned
Total After 1 Year	$5,859	$8,250

put his original $7,500 into a Roth contribution into his individual 401(k). In that case, he would have paid all of his taxes up front, but would not have to pay ordinary income taxes when he took the money out in retirement. Either way, Roth or Traditional, tax-advantaged savings is a good thing for helping you build wealth!

When taxation is deferred, the time value of money can be higher, because gains in your account will only be taxed when you withdraw the money in retirement. In the meantime, the power of compounding is not reduced by taxation. This explains the popularity of tax-qualified retirement accounts among therapists in private practice. It also provides a strong argument for starting your saving program as early as possible so that you have time to put the time value of money to work for you.

CHAPTER 22

Securities That Therapists Commonly Invest In

STOCKS

Stocks are classified as equity instruments, because they provide the stockholder with ownership or equity in a corporation. Common stocks are the most widely held type of equity security. As an investor, you can own common stocks directly or through a variety of instruments such as mutual funds or separate accounts in variable annuities and variable universal life insurance. Common stocks are initially issued by the corporation in a stock offering for investors; this offering raises money for the corporation. Thereafter, common stocks are traded in the various stock markets from one investor to another.

Corporations are owned by their stockholders, and the stockowners elect a board of directors who in turn appoint upper management. Many common stocks pay dividends out of the corporation's profits, but corporations are under no legal obligation to pay dividends to common stockholders. Some stocks pay low or no dividends, but are attractive to investors because the company has growth potential that will hopefully be reflected in rising stock prices. A typical dividend-paying stock might be a well-established utility company that is not likely to grow a great deal, but has healthy profits from which to pay dividends to stockholders. A typical growth stock that does not pay dividends might be a relatively new high-tech firm that has the potential to grow. Such a firm may well use its profits to invest in its future growth rather than to pay profits to shareholders.

Stock investing inherently involves risk. Investments in stocks are not guaranteed to grow in value, or even to have any future value whatsoever. If an investor bought stock in the XYZ Internet Firm at the height of the early 2000s tech bubble and the firm subsequently failed (as many did), the stock value may well have gone to zero, leaving that investor with worthless equity in a non-existent company. On the other hand, many intelligent and prudent people are heavily invested in common stocks. The reason that many investors assume the risks of stock ownership is the possibility of financial rewards. I am writing this in March 2016, and so I have plugged in average returns on an S&P 500 calculator for the last 100 years—from February 1916 to February 2016—and the average returns come to 9.877% when the dividends are reinvested (http://dqydj.net). Historically, stocks have provided returns higher than inflation, and many investors value stocks as a fundamental component of their investment portfolio.

BONDS

Bonds are debt securities or IOUs issued by governments, government agencies, and corporations. Bonds are usually purchased at face value. The bond issuer pays the bondholder regular interest payments until the bond matures. At that time, the bond issuer pays back the face value of the bond. Bonds are initially purchased by investors from representatives of the issuing entity. They can then be sold to other investors on the secondary market. Bond prices on the secondary market fluctuate inversely with interest rates. When interest rates go up, bond prices decline. When interest rates go down, bond prices rise. Overall, bond prices will fluctuate less than stock prices (although a bond could become worthless if the issuing entity goes bankrupt). Investors typically purchase bonds for their income potential and to diversify their investment portfolio. As a general rule, more conservative portfolios will have a higher percentage of bonds relative to stocks in the asset allocation. More aggressive portfolios will have a higher percentage of stocks.

Bonds issued by corporations usually have a $1,000 face or par value. An intermediate term bond has a maturity of 2–10 years and is usually called a "note." Long-term bonds have maturities over 10 years. Corporate bonds have a periodic interest payment rate called the "coupon rate." Interest is paid twice a year to the owner of the bond. Corporate bonds mature at a specified date, at which time the issuer pays the owner the face value of the bond. Corporate bonds are rated by independent rating companies for the financial strength of the issuer. Moody's, Standard & Poor's, and Fitch are the major bond rating companies. Bonds with strong ratings are considered "investment grade." Bonds with lower ratings are known as "junk bonds" and of course are riskier than investment grade bonds. Investors will take on more risk if they can achieve a higher reward, so the more risk inherent in a bond, the higher the coupon rate that will be offered.

Bonds issued by municipalities are called "munis." Munis pay interest that is federally tax-free. Because of the federal tax-free status of the interest payments, munis have lower coupon rates than other bonds. Therefore, you should avoid buying munis inside a tax-deferred retirement account because taxes are already deferred in these accounts. You are better off with higher-yielding taxable bonds in your retirement account.

The federal government is a major issuer of bonds. The Treasury Department issues treasury bills (T-bills) that have a maturity of less than one year, notes that range from 1 to 10 years, and bonds that reach maturity in more than 10 years. Federally issued bonds pay less than bonds issued by corporations, because the default risk on a federally issued bond is considered to be negligible. Because T-bills are short-term securities that mature in one year or less, they do not pay interest semi-annually. Instead, the investor buys T-bills for a price less than their face value. When they mature, the U.S. government pays their face value. The interest paid is the difference between the purchase price of the T-bill and what the U.S. government pays out at maturity. For example, if you bought a $10,000 26-week Treasury bill for $9,800 and held it until maturity, your interest would be $200. Treasury notes and bonds, being longer term, pay a fixed rate of interest every 6 months until they mature, at which time the U.S. government pays their face value. The difference between a treasury note and a treasury bond is the length of time until maturity. You can usually buy notes and bonds for a price close to their face value.

The U.S. government sells two kinds of treasury notes: fixed-principal and inflation-indexed. Both pay interest twice a year, but the principal value of inflation-indexed securities is adjusted to reflect inflation as measured by the Consumer Price Index. The U.S. Treasury calculates the semi-annual interest payments and maturity payment based on the inflation-adjusted principal value of the inflation-indexed note. Inflation-indexed securities have the advantage of removing the risk that inflation will outpace the coupon rate of the bond.

As with the purchasing of stocks, many investors leave the purchasing of bonds to professional money managers just as they do the purchasing of individual stocks. Bond mutual funds are often a convenient and prudent way for the average investor to get involved in the bond market. We will discuss mutual funds in more detail later.

CASH INSTRUMENTS
Savings Accounts, Bank CDs, and Money Market Deposit Accounts
Depository institutions such as banks, savings and loan institutions, and credit unions offer savings accounts that are insured up to a maximum of $250,000 by the Federal Deposit Insurance Corporation (FDIC). Such institutions also offer certificates of deposit (CDs). CD maturities range from 30 days to 10 years. Banks also may offer what is called a money market deposit account, which earns interest at a rate set by the bank and usually limits the customer to a certain number of transactions within a stated time period. Money market deposit accounts and CDs are insured by the FDIC for up to $250,000.

Money Market Mutual Funds
The money market mutual funds (please note that a money market **mutual fund** is not FDIC insured, whereas the money market **deposit account** *is* FDIC insured) consists of very short-term debt securities issued by the federal government, banks, corporations, and other financial institutions. Money market mutual funds use

the interest payments they receive on such securities to provide interest payments to investors in the money market fund. Money market mutual funds attempt to maintain a stable price of $1 per share. The money market is very liquid. Most money market funds provide checking features with no sales charge for early withdrawal of funds.[1] Money market instruments such as Treasury bills, commercial paper, and large bank CDs are considered very secure. Investors participate in the money market for stability of their principal and liquidity. Money market instruments are often referred to as cash.

Mutual Funds

A mutual fund pools the resources of many investors into a professionally managed portfolio of securities.[2] Each share represents a proportional ownership of the mutual fund's portfolio. Funds may invest in a variety of securities, but most invest in stocks and/or bonds. Mutual funds are commonly held by large and small investors alike. They allow investors to pool the cost of stock transactions with other investors. Also, they allow smaller investors access to professional money management and diversified holdings. Mutual funds offer instant diversification, in that one share of a mutual fund represents your proportional ownership in all of the stocks underlying a particular fund. Further diversification occurs when the investor participates in a variety of mutual funds, each focusing on a different asset class.

Mutual funds are a fundamental tool for investing in today's financial marketplace and are commonly held by therapists. They

---

1 An investment in a money market mutual fund is not insured or guaranteed by the FDIC or any other government agency. Although a money market mutual fund seeks to preserve the value of your investment at $1 per share, it is possible to lose money by investing in these funds. CDs are FDIC-insured up to $250,000 as to timely payment of principal and interest if held to maturity. Do not confuse a money market mutual fund with an FDIC-insured money market deposit account that earns interest in an amount determined by, and paid by, the financial institution where your funds are deposited.
2 Mutual funds are an investment that fluctuates with market conditions, and do involve risk. Investment return and principal value will fluctuate so that when redeemed, an investor's shares may be worth more or less than original cost. Mutual funds are sold by prospectus only. Please read the prospectus carefully before investing or sending money.

may be an appropriate investment vehicle for therapists who do not have the time, expertise, or inclination to pick their own stocks. There are a great many mutual funds to choose from. Many mutual funds are very specialized, focusing on a specific type of investment or asset class. This specialization of mutual funds allows you and your financial advisor to create a well-diversified portfolio.

In our earlier discussion of asset allocation, we mentioned a variety of asset classes that typically constitute the elements of a diversified portfolio of securities. In the following table, we provide a brief definition of major asset classes that are commonly held in mutual funds.

Table 22.1 Major Asset Classes Defined

Stock Funds	
Value Funds	Stocks that are considered a good buy primarily because analysis of the stock indicates that it is underpriced in relation to the earnings and overall health of the issuing corporation.
Growth Funds	Stocks of corporations that are poised to grow. Typically, growth funds will invest in corporations with higher risk and higher potential for growth, with dividend payments being a secondary consideration.
Foreign Stock Funds	Stocks of non-U.S. corporations diversify a portfolio to temper the risk of macro-economic factors affecting the entire U.S. stock market.
Large-Cap Funds	These funds invest companies with large capitalization, many of which are household names such as GE, GM, IBM, Coca-Cola, Microsoft, and so on. These funds provide the stability of highly established corporations in a portfolio. Such funds are likely to pay more in dividends than growth funds.
Mid-Cap Funds	These funds invest in companies with medium capitalization. These funds tend to be more volatile than large-cap funds.
Small-Cap Funds	These funds invest in companies with relatively small capitalization. These funds tend to be more volatile than large- or mid-cap funds.

(Continued)

Table 22.1 (*Continued*)

Bond Funds	
Government Bond Funds	These funds provide investors with a variety of issues of the U.S. Treasury. These funds are considered conservative investments that provide stability to a portfolio. The interest from U.S. government bonds are not subject to state and local taxes.
Corporate Bond Funds	Corporate bond funds generally focus on high quality, investment grade corporate bonds. Make sure to read the prospectus, because some corporate bond funds invest in below–investment grade securities (junk bonds), which are of course more risky than investment grade securities.
Junk Bond Funds	These funds focus on high-paying bonds of entities with below–investment grade ratings. Such funds can play a useful role in a given portfolio, but should not be confused with more secure bond funds of higher rated bonds. These funds are sometimes called High Yield Bond Funds.
Municipal Bond Funds	These funds comprise municipal bonds that are issued by entities such as states, cities, and counties. These funds are usually exempt from federal income taxes. They are not appropriate investments in a tax-deferred account.
Specialty	
Real Estate	These funds invest in real estate–related securities such as real estate investment trusts and companies in the real estate and construction businesses.
Cash	
Money Market Funds	Money market funds are the most conservative element in a mutual fund portfolio. Comprised of secure, short-term securities, money market funds attempt to keep the value of a single share at $1. Most mutual fund companies and brokerage houses allow investors to write checks against their money market funds, as they are highly liquid.

REAL ESTATE

Although real estate can be a profitable investment, investing in real estate beyond your own home is not suitable for all investors. Many therapists would be better advised to invest in real estate–related securities as part of a well-diversified portfolio rather than to buy property directly. Without the ability to invest a fairly significant amount of capital and without disposable income to devote to the "care and feeding" of property in the early stages, investing in real estate is not a wise option. If you are considering a real estate investment, you should consider the following issues:

1) Investment in real estate inevitably entails risk. You will need to take out a substantial loan and make a down payment. The capital you invest will be "illiquid"—not easily converted to cash. When looking for property to buy, many investors look for a "desperate seller." This is something you don't want to be. You must be able to hold your real estate until market conditions are favorable and you are able to find a qualified buyer willing to pay an acceptable price.

2) There will inevitably be a vacancy factor—the period between when one tenant moves out and the time you are able to find another suitable tenant. Real estate investors typically calculate the vacancy factor as 5% of their total rents. In a "down" market, it could climb as high as 10%, putting a significant dent in your cash flow.

3) You will need funds for emergencies, maintenance, taxes, covering the vacancy factor, and so on. A wise real estate investor maintains a "slush fund" for unexpected expenses. You should plan to put a percentage of each month's rental income (typically 3%–5%) into this fund.

4) Real estate investments require regular supervision and attention. If you do not live nearby, or for some reason are unable to provide this attention yourself, the property must pay enough of a return to cover hiring a property manager.

5) Investment property can be quite time-consuming. The property must be kept clean and in good repair, rents must be collected, tenants kept satisfied, and proper bookkeeping maintained. These tasks require time and a certain degree of skill. Unless you can afford the services of a property manager, bear in mind that each hour spent on property management is an hour in which you are not managing your practice.

6) A good credit rating is vital in order to obtain favorable mortgage rates and terms of a loan.

We don't want to discourage you from considering real estate investments. Certainly, many fortunes have been made in real estate. We simply want to be clear that real estate investing requires four things:

1) Sufficient capital;
2) The time and skill necessary to manage and maintain the property;
3) Willingness to tolerate a fair amount of risk;
4) The ability to be comfortable with the prospect of having your money tied up for an indefinite period of time.

If you have these attributes and investing in real estate appeals to you, it may be an excellent alternative for you. Regardless, you will want to maintain a diversity of investments to provide yourself with a balanced portfolio.

Buying the Building You Practice In

If, having considered the issues listed earlier, you feel ready to make the leap into real estate investing, you might want to consider buying a building for your practice. Many therapists (including your authors) have found owning the building they practice in to be good both as an income-producing investment and as a practice-building venture.

Owning the building you practice in and renting space to other professionals can have a number of benefits:

1) Rather than spending money each month on renting an office, you are building capital.
2) Your tenants will (at least theoretically!) cover your mortgage, providing you with rent-free office space.
3) You will have the freedom to shape your space to suit your own tastes rather than adapting to a landlord's.
4) You will have control over the people with whom you share your space. You have the authority to screen and select tenants.

5) Because you will be at your office on a regular basis, supervision and maintenance of the property can be more easily accomplished.
6) Your investment should decrease your tax liability.[3]
7) Becoming a landlord is another way to become known in your professional community.

If you own a well-kept and well-run office building and lease space to fellow therapists, your name will become increasingly familiar to others in the community. Gaining respect as a landlord can be a form of indirect marketing for your practice, just as becoming more established in your practice can make a building you own more appealing when other therapists are seeking office space. The downside of renting to colleagues is that you may be tempted to be less than businesslike in your dealings with them. If you find yourself offering people "special deals" or overlooking past due rent because they are friends, you will quickly discover that your investment has become a liability. In our experience, most therapists are cooperative, responsible tenants. You must do your part by being clear about expectations and living up to your part of the bargain—that is, providing a well-maintained space with a pleasant, professional atmosphere.

Buying a professional building need not be a grandiose undertaking. Many therapists work in older homes that have been converted for professional use. This type of arrangement can be quite congenial for the therapist/landlord, in that owning this type of building has much in common with owning one's own home and may be less intimidating, and more financially feasible than buying a building that was originally designed for commercial use. An older home often has the kind of comfortable feeling that can be quite appealing to therapists and clients alike.

Real Estate–Related Securities

If investing directly in real estate is not for you, you might want to consider the possibility of participating in the real estate market

---

3   This is not intended as specific tax advice. Please consult your professional tax advisor for information suited to your individual situation.

indirectly through real estate stocks or other real estate related securities. There are several types of indirect real estate investments that may be suitable for you.

REITs

A real estate investment trust (REIT) is a company that owns, operates, and in some cases finances commercial real estate such as apartment buildings, shopping malls, warehouses, or hotels. REITs were created by an Act of Congress in 1960. There are three kinds of REITs: Equity REITs invest in commercial property; Mortgage REITs make construction and mortgage loans; Hybrid REITs do both. The majority of REITS are Equity REITs. In creating the legal structure for REITs, Congress's purpose was to make available to the *small* investor the many financial benefits that accrue to the well-capitalized commercial real estate investor. This is accomplished by pooling the financial resources of many small investors whose combined capital is put in commercial real estate ownership and financing. REITs are required by law to pay 90% of their taxable income each year to their shareholders.

As a shareholder in a REIT you are paid a dividend. REIT dividends are partly taxable (part of the dividend is a return of capital that is not taxable). So, a good place to own a REIT is inside your retirement account, where the taxation will be deferred. Illiquidity has traditionally been the bane of real estate investors. However, with a REIT that is publicly traded on a major stock exchange, you can turn your investment into cash immediately. A list of stock exchange–traded REITs is available at www.investinreits.com.

Another attractive feature of REITs is that they have a low correlation to other stocks and bonds, so they can help with the diversification of your portfolio. Whether stocks go up or down, REIT prices tend to act independently, giving your portfolio balance. A report from Ibbotson Associates, a leader in asset allocation strategies, "show(s) that, given their low correlation (to the price of stocks) real estate stocks are an important and effective source of diversification" (Natl. Association of Real Estate Investment Trusts, 2001).

Mutual Funds That Hold REITs

Buying into a REIT is not unlike buying an individual stock. You should do a good deal of research and due diligence before you buy. Of course the problem is that most therapists have neither the time nor the expertise to do the necessary research. If you have a financial advisor, he or she may guide you in finding a REIT that is reputable and appropriate for you. Otherwise, you might consider investing in a mutual fund that invests in REITs. These funds are professionally managed and offer a diversity of REITs so that your risk is spread out. An online resource for learning about REITs and REIT mutual funds is www.reit.com, which contains a comprehensive list of REIT mutual funds and allows you to sort by various factors such as net asset value and return. REIT mutual funds also offer the advantage of liquidity, allowing you to turn your investment into cash at your convenience.

Limited Partnerships

Real estate limited partnerships (RELPs) were quite popular as a tax shelter until 1986, when the U.S. Congress changed the rules as part of the Tax Reform Act of 1986. I have worked with many psychiatrists and other mental health professionals who were heavily invested in RELPs, which turned significantly downward after the tax rules changed in '86. RELPs can work successfully if you know well the track record of the general partners and have fully vetted every aspect of the deal. However, for most therapists who probably lack the resources to fully vet such partnerships, it is usually best to steer clear of these investments. One of the principle problems with RELPs is a lack of liquidity—they are usually difficult to sell and frequently cannot be liquidated until the general partners liquidate the entire limited partnership. Therefore, the limited partner has little control over when she can get her principal out.

REFERENCES

DQYDJ. http://dqydj.net/sp-500-return-calculator/

"REITs' Low Correlation to Other Stocks and Bonds is Key Factor for Portfolio Diversification." Natl. Association of Real Estate Investment Trusts, May 29, 2001

CHAPTER 23

Socially Responsible Investing

Most therapists are, by nature and training, attuned to the social dimension of life. After all, we have chosen work that is deeply human. We care about people. Remembering that money is a powerful energy that can have both positive and negative effects upon our world, it may become important for you to align how you invest with the values you hold. There are socially screened investment options available for mutual funds, annuities, variable universal life insurance, and individually managed accounts. A good resource for socially responsible investing is USSIF (www.ussif.org/), a clearinghouse of information on all aspects of socially responsible investments. Socially responsible investing involves making a social analysis of the companies that you are considering investing in. Perhaps you do not want your money going to a tobacco-producing company. Perhaps you are concerned about ecological issues and do not want to invest in companies that have a poor environmental record. Perhaps you are concerned with children's issues and do not want your money invested in companies that hire child labor in underdeveloped countries. Perhaps you are tuned in to women's issues and want to avoid companies with poor conditions for women. Perhaps you do not want to invest in arms manufacturing. Socially responsible investing is the practice of taking these kinds of issues into account when determining the companies one will invest in.

Socially responsible investing can work in a number of ways. The first way is by avoiding companies with poor records for social responsibility. Another way is by advocating for corporate change with shareholder resolutions. This means that the socially responsible money management firm may stay invested in a corporation with practices that it considers less than fully responsible. Shareholder resolutions are then used as a leverage to create dialogue with the company about the practice in question. Common shareholder resolutions deal with environmental and workplace practices of the corporation. If your social concerns are being addressed in your investment portfolio, it may help you feel better about investing, and therefore help you to more actively integrate your financial thinking into your life.

SOCIALLY RESPONSIBLE INVESTING   **175**

CHAPTER 24

Debt and Credit Issues

Backpackers who want to pack lightly have an apt saying: "take care of the ounces, and the pounds will take care of themselves." So it goes in our financial lives: Wasted dollars lead to wasted thousands of dollars, and so on, until we are talking about real money. On the other hand, staying conscious and conservative with small expenses can lead to surprisingly significant improvements in the bigger picture. We therapists typically cannot look forward to "a big deal": a sale or transaction that can bail us out. Just by the nature of our profession and the regularity (hopefully) with which we generate our income, we are the financial "tortoise" rather than the "hare." Therefore, we need to constantly bear in mind the overall trajectory of our financial lives. It is important for us to be conscious of our spending habits while attending to the profitability of our professional practices. If we can do these two things consistently, we will, over time, build a strong financial structure for our lives.

Choices we make about debt are particularly important in determining the direction our financial trajectory will take. Debt is, by design, easy to get into and difficult to get out of. The credit industry is huge and extremely sophisticated, and it stays in business by making a profit on your debt. It is the industry's right to make legal profits off of the uninformed consumer. Accordingly, it is your responsibility to become an informed consumer in order to act in your own long-term self-interest. Let's take a look at some ways in which you can use credit wisely—increasing your financial well-being rather than undermining it.

KEEPING ON TOP OF YOUR CREDIT

Your credit report is significant, as it can impact the cost of a number of your business and personal expenses. Whenever you apply for credit of any kind, a good credit rating can result in your being offered more favorable rates and terms. It can even be the deciding factor in whether or not you're able to move forward with a particular transaction. Your credit rating impacts:

- Your office lease
- The mortgage rate on your home
- The availability of a home equity loan
- Rates on your car loan
- The availability and desirability of credit cards
- Rates on life and homeowners insurance.

So—what *is* your credit rating? It's actually quite easy to find out. All consumers are given a FICO score, which is a numerical evaluation of your overall credit. This score is the criterion on which most creditors base their lending decisions. Scores range from 300 to 850. A variety of factors go into generating your FICO score, including your financial stability, your outstanding balances, and your past payment history. You can go on line at Equifax.com or MyFICO.com to find your FICO score. The report will inform you about your scores, compare them with national averages, and give you information about how to improve them.

Getting Help for Debt and Credit Problems

Once you have checked your FICO score, you have an idea of how well you are doing in managing debt and credit in your life. At this point, it's important to be honest with yourself. Issues around debt and credit can loom large, and many of us experience a good deal of shame if we get into difficulty in these areas. For most of us who struggle with credit issues, it is credit cards that present the biggest temptation and the biggest problem. We will look specifically at the question of credit cards shortly. For the moment, however, here are some general guidelines for working through difficulties with debt and credit:

- Come clean with your spouse or partner. In Chapter 11, we address the importance of open, flexible communication around finances. If you are hiding details about your credit history or your financial dealings from your partner, you are creating a recipe for disaster. Have a frank discussion and enlist your partner's aid in working through whatever problems you're struggling with.
- Consider accessing professional financial help. You may need to talk with an attorney, a tax advisor, a financial planner, or all of these. There is help available to sort through legal tangles and put you back on course.
- Consider professional psychological help. Chapter 8, explores the powerful unconscious forces that underlie the ways we deal with money. Working with your own therapist to come to a better understanding of how these forces impact your financial decisions can be enlightening and liberating.
- Pay careful attention to the discussion of credit cards that follows.

Credit Cards—Nine Steps to Debt Reduction

Credit cards can be to personal finance what cigarettes are to your health. Daisy smokes one cigarette a day at most. Many days she goes without any cigarettes at all. The five cigarettes she has per week are (so she assures me) not excessively harmful. I (Peter) in contrast, used to be a pack-a-day Camel Filters man. Today, I smoke not at all, because I know that moderation is not possible for me. Daisy is able to use tobacco without becoming addicted, whereas I am a tobacco addict. There is a corollary in the way in which people use credit cards. If you are a person who can pay off your credit cards each month without carrying a balance, they can be useful and convenient. However, if you are carrying thousands of dollars of credit card debt and making the minimum payments each month, you may consider looking at your use of credit as a form of addiction.

How serious is this addiction? In researching this chapter, we found some quite sobering statistics:

- The average American carries a credit card balance of $15,762 (http://nerdwallet.com).
- The average American spends $2,630 per year on credit card interest payments at an average APR of 18% (http://nerdwallet.com).
- You are more than likely paying occasional late fees and perhaps an annual fee in addition.

Now let's look at what you could do with the money rather than paying off credit card debt:

- Beginning at age 40 you invest that $2,630 into an IRA each year.
- You receive a hypothetical return of 8%.
- You retire at age 65.

At retirement time you would have over $210,280.11 in your IRA. When you carry credit card debt, not only are you paying out exorbitant fees but also you are paying a lot in lost opportunity. You are losing opportunities to invest in yourself—your own retirement, your children's education, your professional development, or other life goals.

Like the cigarette companies, the credit card companies are simply offering you the right as an American to exercise your freedom to choose. Fair enough. But (also like the cigarette companies) they target young people and manipulate the consumer with sophisticated and misleading marketing. To put it bluntly, the credit card companies are not your friends. They make money by seducing consumers into overspending and then charging exorbitant interest and fees.

In my view, the credit card industry along with the advertising industry has played on the susceptibility of consumers. The message to buy is ubiquitous—now advertisers are even spreading their message in schools. Credit card offers start coming in before a young person has even graduated from high school. Kicking the credit card habit is a little like quitting junk food: Everywhere you turn, you are invited to spend impulsively, just as the innumerable junk food outlets you encounter daily invite you to eat impulsively and without thought.

When I was a smoker, I used think of my familiar Camel Filters as a friend. Now, I recognize them as an adversary. This kind of cognitive reframing may be useful with regard to credit card use. In modern America, it is just about impossible not to use plastic. But thinking of consumer credit as your adversary rather than your friend will begin to put you in a more realistic frame of mind about your spending. When you use plastic, it is best to have a debit card arrangement where you are limited to the funds you have available. If you are using credit to get airline miles, be sure to pay those balances off each month. It will be a lot cheaper for you to buy your tickets online than it will be to pay 15%–25% on revolving credit.

If you have a problem and have determined that you want to work on your credit card spending, here are some practical steps you can take.

1) Make a "fearless and searching inventory" of your credit card debt. Study your balances along with the interest and fees you are paying. To help contain the anxiety, it can be helpful to have a trusted friend simply sit with you while you look carefully over your balances.
2) Resolve that you will only use your credit for emergencies. If you can't afford it, then don't buy it. Save money until you can pay for it in cash.
3) List the cards by the interest rates they charge, ranking them from lowest to highest.
4) If you have a credit card with an interest rate of 14% or less, move your balances to that card. If you don't have a card with a low rate and you have a good credit standing, go to www.cardweb.com for comparison card shopping. Get a lower interest rate card and transfer your higher interest card balances to that card.
5) Many cards have low introductory fees. Move the balances to one of these cards, and pay aggressively for those first six months.

6) Determine the maximum you can to afford to pay each month in order to pay off your balances. Remember: "No pain, no gain." Make a pledge to yourself to pay off at least 2.5% of the balance each month. If you make only the minimum payments, it will take you a very long time, and a great deal in interest payments to get down to a zero balance. How much could you pay if you absolutely had to? $500? $750? $1,000?
7) When paying off credit card debt, pay off your highest interest rate cards first.
8) Refinancing your home will usually give you a more favorable interest rate plus possibly some tax benefits. Refinancing or a home equity loan may be a good alternative for paying off credit card debt. But beware . . . do not then run the credit cards up again!
9) Hang in there! Credit cards are seductive and the ensuing debt can be seriously damaging—do not give up.

I (Peter) lost count of the number of times I "quit smoking for good." However, I refused to get discouraged and today have been a non-smoker for 15 years! You can get the credit card monkey off your back! Don't give up until you succeed!

HOME MORTGAGE—TERMINABLE AND INTERMINABLE

The housing bubble bust, credit crisis, and Great Recession of 2007–2009 was a sobering reminder to stay grounded with sound financial principals regarding the financing of one's home. Consumers got seduced into homes they could not afford by unscrupulous mortgage lenders, and people with good home equity frequently took out unwise second and third mortgages. In this discussion we will cover sound financial principals for financing your home.

As we begin this discussion, remember your ultimate financial planning goal: a financially secure and financially low-stress retirement. A cornerstone of such a retirement is a paid-off mortgage. There are just a few obvious points that I would like to make in order to frame this discussion. Most people, and therapists are generally no exception to this, will have less income in retirement than they had during the heyday of their income-earning years. It is common practice in financial planning to project reduced income and expenses in retirement. Factors in reduced expenses in retirement include: The children's education has been paid for, office expenses are reduced or eliminated, and wardrobe expenses are lessened. The most significant factor in reduced expenses in retirement, however, is a paid-up mortgage. Paying off the mortgage is an important goal in most people's retirement planning.

Let's take a look at home mortgages and the pros and cons of refinancing.

At the time of this writing, interest rates are at historic lows, and refinancing one's mortgage is currently a very popular strategy with homeowners. While it may make sense to refinance your home when rates go down, there is another side of the story. The amount of equity one has in one's home represents an important asset. While it is difficult for many people to save, building equity in one's home is a kind of forced savings, in that we must pay the mortgage or else we will lose the house. While many people invest less than they should in their qualified retirement plan, it is not an option to miss payments on the home mortgage.

The issue at hand is that every time you refinance, you start a new mortgage. If interest rates have gone down, then the good news is that your monthly payment should be lower. However, if the overall period of time that you are paying the new lower rates extends your mortgage over many additional years, then you may well be paying more for the new loan over the course of time.

Not All Mortgage Payments Are Created Equal

Amortization is the process of gradually reducing the debt owed on your mortgage. It occurs over the lifetime of a mortgage loan. In the early years of a mortgage, the great majority of your payment goes to paying interest, while in the later years, increasing percentages of the payment go to paying down principal. Let's look at a 30-year, $350,000 loan at a fixed rate of 4%. This 30-year loan has 360 payments. The chart below shows the 1st, 90th, 180th, 270th and final payments on the loan. Please observe how much

Table 24.1 Amortization

Year	Payment Number	Payment Amount	Interest Paid	Principal Applied	New Balance
1	1	$1,432.25	$1,000	$432.23	$299,567.75
7	90	$1,432.25	$860.59	$571.65	$257,606.76
15	180	$1,432.25	$786.72	$645.43	$192,841.58
22	270	$1,432.25	$391.67	$1,040.58	$116,459.92
30	360	$1,432.25	$4.76	$1,427.49	$0

goes to paying interest in the early years of the loan. Even in the fifteenth year, at the halfway point of the life of the loan, well over half of the total payment amount goes to interest.

If you continually refinance your home, you start at the beginning of the amortization process over and over again, never really gaining on your equity. If, for example, you purchased your home in the year 2010 with a 30-year loan, and then refinance in the year 2015 with another 30-year loan, you have extended the life of your mortgage payment to 35 years. Do it again in the year 2020 and you will have extended the life of your mortgage to 40 years. If on the other hand, you stick with your loan over the years, you are gradually paying off more and more principle and thereby increasing your equity in your home. In making a decision about whether to refinance, a balance must be struck between the desirability of reducing the interest rate and the goal of paying off the mortgage in the shortest number of years.

If current rates are sufficiently lower than the rate you are paying on your mortgage, you may well want to consider refinancing. Do not just look at your reduced monthly payments, however. You should also look at the amount you will be paying over the life of the loan and compare that number with the amount you will pay over the life of the loan with your current loan. Try to avoid the interminable home mortgage. It is a declining principal balance that will eventually lead to a home owned free and clear, and a free and clear home is a great thing to have in retirement.

Prepayment of Your Principal

Whether or not you refinance, making prepayments on your principal balance due can often be a good strategy. However, there are some words of caution here as well. First off, whenever you refinance, be certain that the loan does not have prepayment penalties. You do not want to have to pay the bank a fee every time you prepay. Second, make certain that the bank will recompute the interest that you owe when you pay off principal early. Some lenders do not recompute the interest owed and simply follow their set amortization schedule, thereby disallowing the main advantage you gain through prepayment: speeding up the amortization of the loan. If the bank is not reducing your interest due, you are in effect loaning your bank interest free money every time you make a prepayment! If your lender *does* recompute the interest owed with prepayment, then you can speed up the paying off of your principal by making 13 payments over the course of the year (i.e. one extra payment per year). Such a strategy will reduce a 30-year mortgage by at least 8 years. Another approach is to simply pick a fixed amount of money that you add to your monthly payment that goes directly to the reduction of principal. Yet another approach is to get an amortization schedule from your lender, and pay the amount that is due on the following month's principal payment with this month's payment.

If your lender will not recompute the interest you owe when you pay off principal early, there is an alternative that can work very nicely for you. Instead of making the extra payment to your bank, consider opening an account that is specifically earmarked to invest the money you would have used to pay off your mortgage early. A Roth IRA might work very well for this purpose.

Let's say you are 40 years old and that you are just starting out on a 30-year mortgage. You do not have a prepayment penalty, but when you call up the bank you find that the fine print of your loan states that the bank will not recompute the interest you owe if you pay off principal early, but instead, the amortization table applies and the bank simply takes your prepayment as an interest free loan from you to them. You decide that prepayment is not in your best interest and instead you open an investment account. Let's call this account your Mortgage Empowerment Account. Your mortgage is a 30-year 6% fixed rate on $225,000. Each monthly payment is $1,649. In order to save the equivalent of approximately 10% of your monthly payment, you invest $165 per month into your Mortgage Empowerment Account (you have it automatically deducted from your checking account so that you don't miss any payments). Under certain circumstances, it might make sense to invest your Mortgage Empowerment Account in a Roth IRA. In any event, this money is invested in a mix of stock and bond investments that earn you a hypothetical return of 8% per annum. Let's skip forward 22 years. Now you are age 62 and you would like the freedom to retire, or at least cut back your practice. Your biggest expense item is your mortgage payment. You are about to make your 270th mortgage payment and you have a principal balance on your mortgage of $120,304. You take a look at your Mortgage Empowerment Account and find that you have a balance now of $124,914. You can simply pay off the mortgage or follow the following strategy. Up until this point you have been reinvesting your earnings in the Mortgage Empowerment Account and have been investing in a combination of growth and income securities. Now you reallocate your portfolio primarily for income (please see the conservative model portfolio in Chapter 6). You have the interest payments sent to you, which fund about half of your mortgage payment, thereby significantly reducing your biggest monthly expense. In eight more years, at age 70, your mortgage is fully paid off, and you still have the entire principal from your Mortgage Empowerment Account.

STUDENT LOANS

If you carry student loans from your undergraduate or graduate school days, you may want to consider consolidating them. The U.S. Department of Education maintains a very informative website (https://studentaid.ed.gov/sa/repay-loans/consolidation) that has many tools, calculators, and comprehensive information about student loan consolidation. The Direct Consolidation Loan program consolidates multiple federal education loans into a single monthly payment. The U.S. Department of Education has contracted with consolidation servicers who do not charge a fee for consolidating your loans.

You can consolidate Direct Subsidized Loans, Direct Unsubsidized Loans, Subsidized Federal Stafford Loans, Unsubsidized Federal Stafford Loans, Direct Plus Loans, PLUS loans from FFEL, SLS Loans, Federal Perkins Loans, Federal Nursing Loans, Health Education Loans, and some existing consolidation loans.

As with credit card debt and mortgages, the principle to keep in mind is that you want to pay off maximum principal so that you pay off the loan in its entirety in a reasonable amount of time. Debt consolidation can help you to simplify the process of paying your student loans. You may consolidate several types of student loans, possibly lower your interest rate, and restructure your repayment to more favorable terms.

Table 24.2 Loan Repayment Plans

Overview of Direct Loan and FFEL Program Repayment Plans			
Repayment Plan	*Eligible Loans*	*Monthly Payment and Time Frame*	*Eligibility and Other Information*
Standard Repayment Plan	• Direct Subsidized and Unsubsidized Loans • Subsidized and Unsubsidized Federal Stafford Loans • all PLUS loans • all *Consolidation* Loans (Direct or FFEL)	Payments are a fixed amount. Up to 10 years (up to 30 years for Consolidation Loans).	All borrowers are eligible for this plan. You'll pay less over time than under other plans.
Graduated Repayment Plan	• Direct Subsidized and Unsubsidized Loans • Subsidized and Unsubsidized Federal Stafford Loans • all PLUS loans • all Consolidation Loans (Direct or FFEL)	Payments are lower at first and then increase, usually every two years. Up to 10 years (up to 30 years for Consolidation Loans).	All borrowers are eligible for this plan. You'll pay more over time than under the 10-year Standard Plan.

Overview of Direct Loan and FFEL Program Repayment Plans

Repayment Plan	Eligible Loans	Monthly Payment and Time Frame	Eligibility and Other Information
Extended Repayment Plan	• Direct Subsidized and Unsubsidized Loans • Subsidized and Unsubsidized Federal Stafford Loans • all PLUS loans • all Consolidation Loans (Direct or FFEL)	Payments may be fixed or graduated. Up to 25 years.	• If you're a Direct Loan borrower, you must have more than $30,000 in outstanding Direct Loans. • If you're a FFEL borrower, you must have more than $30,000 in outstanding FFEL Program loans. • Your monthly payments will be lower than under the 10-year Standard Plan or the Graduated Repayment Plan. • You'll pay more over time than under the 10-year Standard Plan.
Revised Pay As You Earn Repayment Plan (REPAYE)	• Direct Subsidized and Unsubsidized Loans • Direct PLUS loans made to students • Direct Consolidation Loans that do not include PLUS loans (Direct or FFEL) made to parents	• Your monthly payments will be 10 percent of *discretionary income*. • Payments are recalculated each year and are based on your updated income and family size. • If you're married, both your and your spouse's income or loan debt will be considered, whether taxes	• Any Direct Loan borrower with an eligible loan type may choose this plan. • Your monthly payment can be more than the 10-year Standard Plan amount. • You may have to pay income tax on any amount that is forgiven. • Good option for those seeking Public Service *Loan Forgiveness* (PSLF).

(Continued)

Table 24.2 (*Continued*)

Overview of Direct Loan and FFEL Program Repayment Plans

Repayment Plan	Eligible Loans	Monthly Payment and Time Frame	Eligibility and Other Information
		are filed jointly or separately (with limited exceptions). • Any outstanding balance on your loan will be forgiven if you haven't repaid your loan in full after 20 or 25 years.	
Pay As You Earn Repayment Plan (PAYE)	• Direct Subsidized and Unsubsidized Loans • Direct PLUS loans made to students • Direct Consolidation Loans that do not include (Direct or FFEL) PLUS loans made to parents	• Your maximum monthly payments will be 10 percent of discretionary income. • Payments are recalculated each year and are based on your updated income and family size. • If you're married, your spouse's income or loan debt will be considered only if you file a joint tax return. • Any outstanding balance on your loan will be forgiven if you haven't repaid your loan in full after 20 years.	• You must be a *new borrower* on or after Oct. 1, 2007, and must have received a *disbursement* of a Direct Loan on or after Oct. 1, 2011. • You must have a high debt relative to your income. • Your monthly payment will never be more than the 10-year Standard Plan amount. • You'll pay more over time than under the 10-year Standard Plan. • You may have to pay income tax on any amount that is forgiven. • Good option for those seeking Public Service Loan Forgiveness (PSLF).

There are eight types of repayment plans: Standard, Extended, Graduated Extended, Revised Pay as You Earn Repayment, Pay As You Earn Repayment, Income-Based Repayment, Income-Contingent Repayment, and Income Sensitive Repayment.

Because a great many of our readers have student loans, we display table 24.2 that reproduces an informational grid from the Department of Education's website, with detailed information about each of these loan repayment plans as of March 2016.

AUTOS AND AUTO LOANS

I would venture to guess that we therapists are a bit less image-conscious about our cars than the general American population. Nevertheless, we therapists need to drive ourselves and our kids around just like all other red-blooded Americans. The questions that I want to address are the financial issues around car ownership. If you are not particularly image-conscious about your car, then you can focus on safety and your budget with regard to auto ownership. If car image is important to you for personal or professional reasons, then you will probably need to support higher auto expenses in your budget. In either case, there are always ways to save money.

All other things being equal, you are almost always better off buying a used car than a new one. You can save thousands by buying used, and you can usually do better buying from a private party than from a dealership or used car lot. Check out Consumer Reports' online site (www.consumerreports.org) for rankings of used cars, and buy one ranked high for safety and low for rate of repairs. Your authors' last car purchase was a 4-year-old Toyota Prius, which had the safety and reliability and gas mileage rankings we were looking for. From a financial perspective, the best bet is to save up and to buy a used car with cash. If you need to finance your car, shop around. You might be surprised at the amount you can save by taking a little extra time to shop a loan. Even if your credit is less than perfect, you may have more leverage then you think, so take the time to shop for the best car loan you can find. Bankrate.com has excellent tools and resources for shopping a car loan.

If, for whatever reason you choose to get a new car, then you will be faced with the decision to lease or to buy. If I were writing this book for real estate agents, who really do need a good-looking car as a tool of their trade, I might recommend leasing under certain circumstances. The one true advantage of a lease over ownership is that you can drive around in a nicer car for fewer dollars up front. However, for most therapists, we need not go in over our heads for our cars, and purchasing is almost always a better choice than leasing from a purely financial point of view.

When you purchase with a traditional auto loan, you are building equity in the car. If you keep the car, you will eventually, own it free and clear. On the other hand, leasing a car is analogous to renting a house rather than buying it. The leasing agent will take possession of the car after your contract is up. The lure is usually low up-front costs and the opportunity to drive an upscale car for a manageable monthly payment. However, before you sign on the dotted line of a lease agreement, please consider the following words of caution:

1) You are building no ownership in the car.
2) Getting out of a lease prior to its termination date can be very expensive, as leases are usually written to levy heavy fees on early returns.
3) Leases commonly charge fees if you put on more than the specified number of miles.
4) You will need to return the car in clean shape, as the leasing agency will likely charge a hefty fee for any cosmetic or mechanical damage.
5) Leases are written by lawyers who work for the leasing agency. The fine print of the contract may favor the leasing agency in ways that are not immediately apparent.

You may do well to shop for auto insurance also. There is a wide range of premiums available for similar coverages. The internet is a fantastic medium for doing this kind of comparison shopping. To compare auto insurance premiums simply search on "compare auto insurance premiums" and you will find a plethora of sites. Insure.com's auto section will generate quote comparisons for you.

REFERENCES

"2016 American Household Credit Card Deb Study." Nerdwallet. www.nerdwallet.com/blog/credit-card-data/average-credit-card-debt-household/

"Repayment Plans." Federal Student Aid. https://studentaid.ed.gov/sa/repay-loans/understand/plans

CHAPTER 25

An Insurance Primer

LIFE INSURANCE

Life insurance can be a confusing subject in that there are many varieties of it, the products can be complicated, and your needs will necessarily change in relation to your life phase and circumstances. The purpose of this chapter is to help you clarify your needs and to provide you with consumer information that will help you make sound choices.

Who Needs It?

If someone is dependent upon you for income, you wish to continue to provide for that person in the event of your death, and if there are not sufficient assets in your estate to provide for that person, then you probably need life insurance. The classic case for life insurance is the young family, where the children will need continued support in the event of the death of one or both parents. This is all the more true when the surviving parent is a clinician in private practice, because the increased parental responsibilities may well decrease the surviving parent's availability to work clinical hours. Another issue for therapist families is that we therapists often have a moderate income, but are highly educated, with high hopes and expectations for our children's higher education: a major life expense.

How Much Do You Need?

There are a variety of ways to calculate your life insurance needs. Feedback from your financial planner may in fact be the best way for you to arrive at a figure, as he or she should know your financial situation in detail. However, we have posted a life insurance calculator on the calculators sections of our website (http:// insightfinancialgroup.com) to give you a starting place to figure out how much you need. Alternatively, you can utilize the life insurance calculator on bankrate.com (www.bankrate.com/calcu lators/insurance/life-insurance-calculator.aspx).

What Kind of Life Insurance Is Right for You?

There are two basic types of life insurance: temporary and permanent. Temporary, or term insurance, does not build up a cash value, and simply provides a death benefit for a given period of time. Permanent insurance, on the other hand, is designed to last until the death of the insured, and does build up a cash value. Varieties of permanent insurance include whole life insurance, universal life insurance, and variable universal life insurance. For the present discussion, let us focus first on whether term insurance or permanent insurance is right for you. Next, we will go on to consider the question of which type of term or permanent insurance you may find most advantageous.

The rule of thumb for going with term insurance is that if your need is temporary, then temporary life insurance should do the trick. A case where this might apply would be a family with two working parents and young kids. Should one or both die, the children will need additional support. However, unless the parents feel it is necessary to support the children into adulthood, that need might fall off when the children finish college—say at age 25. If the youngest child were 15, then perhaps a 10-year term policy might be sufficient to meet the temporary need of supporting that child.

The rule of thumb for permanent insurance is a permanent need for insurance. A case where this might apply would be a situation where there is an ongoing need for income for the surviving partner. This kind of situation is very common for private practitioners because we are self-employed and therefore not usually part of a traditional pension plan that pays lifetime benefits. An example of a situation with permanent need is Dave and Alice. Dave is an LCSW and Alice is an MFT. Alice works for a family service agency with a very minimal 403(b) plan. Dave is in private practice. They have not built up sufficient retirement funds, and neither can make it financially without the income of both. In this case, both Alice and Dave would be better off with a death benefit in the event of the death of the other.

Another example of a couple who chose permanent insurance is Michael and Clarissa. Michael is an attorney making $500,000+ per year. Clarissa is a psychiatrist making $200,000+ per year. They have extensive securities investments, real estate holdings, and expect to inherit several million more when Clarissa's mother dies. Their need for insurance is driven by the fact they will owe extensive estate taxes, and do not want to put their children in a position to have to come up with a large amount of money to pay taxes when they die.

If you determine that permanent life insurance is right for you, then you will need to decide which kind to use. Whole life insurance gives you a fixed rate of return on the savings portion of your insurance and has a fixed premium. Ordinary whole life insurance gives you reasonable payments on the assumption that you pay the premiums until you die. However, as you pay into the policy over the years, you may have options other than retaining the policy until you die. For example you may be able to use dividends to pay the policy off in a shorter amount of time, surrender the policy in favor of an annuity, or trade the policy in for a smaller amount of paid up insurance. Whole life insurance provides permanent insurance for the lowest premium dollar and has limited but important flexibility as your life circumstances change.

Another approach to permanent life insurance is universal life insurance. Universal life insurance offers flexible premiums and allows the policy owner to take money out of the account without taking a loan. With universal life, you do not direct the investments in your cash value. Instead the insurance company gives you a fixed rate of return. With universal life, you can choose a level death benefit or an increasing death benefit. The level death benefit maintains the same death benefit while the amount owned in the cash value increases. Therefore, as you own more and more in the cash value, the amount that the insurance company has put at risk decreases. Your other choice is an increasing death benefit. Under this scenario, the death benefit rises as the amount you own in the cash value rises. If you are looking for more flexibility than a whole life policy offers, but want a fixed rate of return on your cash value, then universal life insurance may work well for you.

Yet another approach to permanent insurance is variable universal life insurance.[1] Variable universal life (VUL) provides permanent insurance along with cash value like whole life or universal life. A unique feature of variable universal life is that you direct investments in the cash balance with stock and bond investments in separate accounts that pool the resources of many investors and are professionally managed. The money management firms that run many of these separate accounts are leading investment companies that are well known names. Most VUL policies offer a fairly wide range of investment choices, typically with a variety of familiar money management firms, there are even VULs that have a variety of socially responsible investment choices available in the subaccounts. If you are looking for maximum flexibility in permanent insurance, a VUL policy may be an investment to consider.

With any permanent insurance, it is very important that you make a serious commitment to staying with the policy over the long haul. Canceling these policies out after just a few years can be quite costly as the money in the cash value or separate account typically has steep surrender charges, meaning that if you close out the policy in the early years, the insurer will likely hit you with charges that will reduce the value of what you can cash your policy out for. If permanent insurance helps you meet your financial planning and/or estate planning goals and you plan on sticking with it over the long haul, then permanent insurance may play in important role in financial life. If on the other hand, you have only a limited need for life insurance, say for example insuring your life until your children

---

1 Variable life insurance policies are not short-term investments and are offered by prospectus only. An investment in a variable life product involves investment risk, including the possible loss of principal. Investment return and principal value will fluctuate so your share when redeemed may be worth more or less than original cost. Read the prospectus carefully before investing or sending money. An investment in the securities underlying the policy is not guaranteed or endorsed by any bank, is not a deposit obligation of any bank and is not federally insured by any government agency.

are of an age where you expect them to support themselves, then relatively inexpensive term insurance is probably right for you.

Good health and life insurance can have a problematical relationship to each other. If you are in good health, then you might feel as though life insurance is an unnecessary expenditure. On the other hand, once your health fails, it may be prohibitively expensive or impossible to get the coverage you need. Try to think of your need for life insurance dispassionately. Is there someone or more than one person who will be in bad financial shape if you die? How long do you want to provide protection for him or her? Permanently or temporarily? Think these issues out while you have good health, for if you wait too long, you may close out options for yourself.

LONG-TERM CARE INSURANCE

The very reputable insurance company Genworth does an annual survey of long-term care costs. In 2015 they state that the average annual cost of a semi-private nursing home stay is $80,300. The California Department of Health Services reports that "Of those who enter nursing homes, 55% will have a lifetime use of at least one year, 24% will stay between one and five years, and 21% will have a total lifetime use of five years or more."

Clearly, the danger of a devastatingly expensive stay in a long-term care facility is a real one. Long-term care insurance (LTC) can be sensible and even extremely important for many therapists in private practice, but it is not for everyone. Many in the psychotherapy professions fit into the income category of people who may benefit from long-term care insurance; people with a middle range of assets—between $150,000 and $1.5 million. A little background will explain that people with a middle range of assets are best suited to long-term care insurance.

You cannot rely on Medicare for your long-term care coverage. Medicaid (Medi-Cal in California), on the other hand *currently* pays for long-term care, but only if you have extremely limited assets. Think of long-term care insurance as insurance for your assets, so that you do not have to spend your assets down in order to qualify for a Medicaid/Medi-Cal to pay for your long-term care bed.

Long-term care insurance may not be necessary if you have a high net worth, but if your assets are less than $1.5 million and more than $150,000, you might want to consider this kind of insurance. If your assets are high enough, then you probably will not need the coverage as you could pay for it yourself, out of pocket and still protect sufficient assets for your heirs. If your net worth is low enough, then you may be able to spend down your assets and Medicaid/Medi-Cal can kick in.

Here are some long-term care guidelines. The younger you are, and the better your health, the lower your premiums will be. On the other hand, these same favorable health conditions mean that you may well be paying into your policy for many years and never need it. I sometimes counsel my clients to purchase long-term care insurance in their mid-fifties. Another issue is home care and assisted living care. Make sure that if you would prefer these options, that they are written into your policy. Some policies only cover skilled nursing facilities, which for many consumers is their last choice.

You may save money if you do not buy your policy too early in life. Most consumers should wait until their fifties to buy LTC insurance. Another sensible way to save money can be to increase your elimination period, which is a waiting period before your benefits kick in. Do not save money on your policy by eliminating the inflation coverage. I recommend to all of my clients that they choose a 5% compound inflation coverage so that spiraling healthcare costs do not overtake the coverage in the LTC policy. Make a few calls to the better LTC facilities in the area where you would want to be should you need long-term care. Then design your policy around what you will need. With the 5% compound inflation rider, today's coverages should keep pace with inflation. A client of mine knows that if she were ever to need coverage, it would be at the finest facility in New York City, the same facility her mother was in for 7 years. We called up their intake worker to find out cost: The facility charges a whopping $600 per day, or $219,000 per year! As you can imagine, we designed a very high-end policy for her. On the other hand, if you are in a lower cost part of the country, don't base your coverage on the crazy prices we pay in California or New York. Your costs will be lower and your premiums should be too.

A source of independent insurance ratings is available through Standard and Poor's (www.standardandpoors.com). Standard and Poor's will give you financial solvency information that is very important in choosing an insurer. You obviously want your insurer to be around and able to pay claims if and when the time comes, so do your research!

DISABILITY INSURANCE AND BUSINESS OVERHEAD INSURANCE

A common financial mistake of therapists in private practice is lack of adequate disability insurance. If you have money in your family of origin that you can call upon, if you have significant investments that generate income, or if your spouse or domestic partner can support your household, then you may be able to do without replacing your practice income in the event of disability. However, if you cannot manage, over the long haul, to live without the revenue that your practice pulls in, then disability and business overhead insurance may be a very important investment to make.

If you are dependent on your practice income, and will be for the foreseeable future, disability insurance is usually more important to your financial well-being than long-term care insurance. Think of disability insurance as a basic coverage for your private practice working years, and long-term care insurance as a basic coverage for the years when you are transitioning to retirement and in retirement. If you can afford both when you are in your mid-fifties and beyond, that is best, because both kinds of coverages are important. But again, if the money you generate from your practice cannot be replaced from some other source, you should strongly consider investing in disability and business overhead insurance.

I have had a number of clients confuse disability and long-term care insurance, so let me take a moment to discuss what each is. Long-term care insurance covers the cost of your care if you become unable to take care of your activities of daily living such as bathing, dressing, and ambulating. The classic case for long-term care is a scenario where Alzheimer's disease renders the individual unable to care for himself or herself, and that person lives on for many years. Disability insurance, on the other hand, is income replacement insurance for people who had been working, and cannot now return to work. The classic disability case is the private practitioner who has a stroke and cannot return to work for a number of years while she is rehabilitating.

Disability insurance is very complicated in its underwriting and policy provisions. I suggest that you work with a financial planner who has experience in designing these policies, as they vary widely in their quality. Here are some things to look for in a disability policy.

Definition of Disability

Some policies use a definition of disability as restrictive as Social Security: The insured cannot work at any occupation. This restrictive definition of disability would be problematic for the therapist in private practice. Say you had a stroke and needed to rehabilitate your speech before you could function again in your practice, but could do some other kind of work. You would likely want disability insurance that defines disability as the ability to function in your "own occupation." In recent years, most disability carriers have stopped offering long-benefit duration periods for "own occupation" disability, and have shifted to a dual definition of disability wherein the insured is covered for 2–5 years in his or her "own occupation" and then shifts to "any occupation."

Partial Disability Benefits

Say you had a heart attack and were rehabilitating. Furthermore, you have a small number of long-term patients who simply must continue to see you if they are to function, but you cannot work more than a few hours a day. Partial disability benefits cover either partial or residual disability following a total disability. Such benefits may be desirable for the private practitioner. Residual disability benefits are designed to make up the difference between income prior to disability and income earned during disability. Look for a policy that allows the definition of prior income to be the greater of two base periods so that you are not penalized by a single base period during a slump in your practice.

Guaranteed Renewability

You do not want a policy that will weed you out if you begin to develop a medical problem that could result in disability, so avoid disability contracts that are not either guaranteed renewable or non-cancellable. Also, avoid policies that can raise your premium on an individual rather than a class basis. Some companies will offer guaranteed renewability to age 65 and then conditional renewability to age 75. Many therapists continue to work into their seventies, so this feature may be worth looking for.

Elimination Period

Disability policies usually have an elimination period, or waiting period before benefits kick in. Of course you can save on premium with a longer elimination period. Typical options are 30, 60, 90, and 120 days. If you have savings or other sources of short-term income, you can save some premium dollars with a longer elimination period.

Duration of Disability

How long your policy pays for disability is of course a key provision. Obviously the longer your benefit duration, the higher your premium will be. Many policies will offer duration periods ranging from 2 years to age 65. Some companies offer a lifetime duration period. I suggest that you consult with your financial planner on this issue, as the choices you make with this provision of your policy may have a lasting impact on the financial health of yourself and your family.

Cost-of-Living Adjustments

Many insurers offer cost-of-living adjustments as an option, and also allow you to decide the percentage rate used to calculate the adjustment. As with other features in your disability policy, there is a trade-off between level of benefit and premium. As with other features of your disability policy I suggest you consult with your financial planner on this issue, as there is a trade-off between premium dollars spent and potential benefit derived that depends on many individual factors such as your age, present and future financial responsibilities, and your state of health.

Business Overhead Insurance

Should you become temporarily disabled, you will likely have ongoing expenses associated with keeping the infrastructure of your private practice in place while you recover. Business overhead insurance is designed to cover your fixed practice expenses such as rent, secretarial services, utilities, and so on in the case of short-term disability. Business overhead insurance is commonly written in conjunction with disability insurance and can be a cost effective adjunct to it. It is usually written for a benefit period of 1 or 2 years with a short elimination period. Because a private practitioner's fixed cost of doing business is relatively low, business overhead insurance can be quite affordable as an adjunct to your disability income insurance.

REFERENCE

"Genworth 2015 Cost of Care Survey California." Genworth. www.genworth.com/dam/Americas/US/PDFs/Consumer/corporate/cost-of-care/118928CA_040115_gnw.pdf (accessed December 12, 2016)

CHAPTER 26

Estate Planning

Financial Planning for After a Death

Dealing with issues of one's own mortality inevitably arouses many feelings, one of the foremost being anxiety. This sense of anxiety can be even greater when we consider the possibility that our partner may predecease us. Therapists are no different from our clients in our wish to avoid anxiety. Understandable though this may be, it is imperative that we make thoughtful, practical decisions about end-of-life issues. Whatever your net worth, estate planning is a vital piece of a well-thought-out financial plan. The last gift we can offer our loved ones is an estate plan, which protects them after our death. Likewise, we owe it ourselves to ensure that our own financial well-being is protected should our partner predecease us.

Estate planning is a very complex area of law and financial planning. I strongly recommend that you implement your estate plan with the help of a qualified financial planner and attorney. The purpose of this chapter is not to replace professional help, but rather to give you a general orientation to some basic estate planning issues and techniques.

The first step in making an estate plan is to establish your overarching estate planning goals. You can then begin to work with your attorney and financial planner on implementing strategies designed to accomplish your goals. Following are some common estate planning goals. Hopefully, the list will serve as a trigger to help you think more specifically about your personal goals.

COMMON ESTATE PLANNING GOALS

1) Providing for your children and partner;
2) Protecting your assets from creditors;
3) Making plans for your practice and other businesses;
4) Minimizing estate and income taxes;
5) Minimizing or bypassing the probate process;
6) Assuring that your home will be available to your partner during his or her lifetime and then pass to your children;
7) Providing for bequests of special items for specific people;
8) Assuring that assets are divided fairly, thus minimizing animosity among surviving family members;
9) Providing for children and/or grandchildren's higher education;
10) Putting advanced medical directives in place;
11) Making provision for guardianship of minor children;
12) Providing direction should you become incompetent;
13) Protecting your own financial security should your partner die before you.

Take a moment if you would to think about your own estate planning goals. What are your concerns? What are your hopes and dreams? What are your core responsibilities? The answers to these questions will give you the beginning of your estate plan. You can then bring this to your attorney and financial planner. They will use what you bring as a starting point to begin the process of setting up a formal estate plan that reflects your priorities.

Estate planning is a dynamic and changeable topic because as tax laws change, the strategies you use to minimize the tax burden on your estate must necessarily change in response.

The following list consists of estate planning *techniques* that are typically used to accomplish the goals you identified earlier in this section. Let's consider each one in turn in order for you to become familiar with basic estate planning terms and techniques. Once you have developed some familiarity with the basics of estate planning, you will be able to begin to think creatively about your personal estate planning goals and how to best accomplish them.

COMMON ESTATE PLANNING TECHNIQUES

1) Living trust
2) Pour-over will
3) Choosing the best methods of ownership
4) Credit shelter trusts
5) QTIP/marital trust
6) Durable power of attorney for healthcare
7) Living will
8) Life insurance.

LIVING TRUSTS

The living trust is an effective method of efficiently passing on many assets according to your wishes. A living trust is established and operates while the creator of the trust is still alive. In most cases, the living trust is revocable, meaning that it can be rescinded, amended, or terminated by the person who created the trust. The most typical arrangement is that you create the trust and appoint yourself to be the holder of the property, or the trustee. Once you have created the trust, you change the title of the property from your own name to the name of the trust. Within the trust, you appoint a trustee who will take over in the event of your death or incompetence. Please note that living trusts do not change the tax picture for the grantor or for the estate. By moving the property to a living trust, you are not changing your present tax picture.

For an example of retitling property in the name of the trust, let's say Jane Simon, PhD, has a brokerage account in her own name. She establishes the Jane Simon PhD Revocable Living Trust Dated April 25, 2015 and subsequently changes the registration of her brokerage account to Jane Simon PhD Revocable Lvg Trst Dtd 4-25-15. She also changes the title of her house and vacation home and car to the living trust.

The arguments in favor of a living trust include the following:

1) Property passes from the grantor to the beneficiary without the need for probate. Probate is the process of proving a will's validity in court and executing the provisions of the will under the guidance of the court. Probate can be costly and time-consuming.

Even uncomplicated estates can take 6 months or more to sort through. The living trust allows you to bypass the probate process, as the property in the trust passes by operation of law to the beneficiary.

2) If you operate your practice as a sole proprietorship, you may pass your practice through a revocable trust to avoid termination of the practice. Let's say for example that you are a psychologist in private practice and so is your partner. You may leave the practice to your partner so that she can either continue to treat your patients or at least wrap up the billing and other loose ends prior to closing your practice.

3) If you own property in more than one state, you can avoid having to go through probate in two or more states by putting the property in your living trust in the state where you reside. You avoid ancillary jurisdiction of out-of-state property by titling it in your living trust.

4) When property goes through probate, the records are made public. With a living trust you avoid probate and the public record of private financial information.

5) A living trust is relatively easy to set up and change. There are self-help books (notably from Nolo Press), but I strongly recommend that you use an attorney. There are many nuances to estate planning, and tax laws are a constantly moving target.

6) Living trusts are difficult to contest, whereas, in general, wills are more vulnerable to being contested.

7) Living trusts may help you to consolidate your assets and get better organized. As you add property to the trust, you must think about its disposition and management.

The types of property that are commonly transferred into the living trust include:

Real Estate
Bank Accounts
Brokerage Accounts
Stock and Bond Certificates
Vehicles and Boats

POUR-OVER WILL

The revocable living trust allows you to detail the disposition of property that is titled in the name of the trust. However property that is not specifically owned by the trust is not included in the trust. Therefore, you will need a will to direct property not already owned by your living trust to either be bequeathed to the trust or to the individuals you want the property to go to. This is where the "pour-over" will comes into play. A pour-over will is so named because the will instructs your executor to place into the trust the assets that are not yet titled in the trust at your death.

It is virtually impossible to title everything you own in the name of your living trust. Much property such as jewelry, clothes, your favorite lamp or vase, or that special book of poetry are quite difficult to title at all. You may detail in the pour-over will who gets what is not titled in the name of the trust. All items that are not otherwise named in the pour-over will or titled in the name of the trust can be directed to pour into the trust, to be divided among your heirs according to its provisions.

Probably the most important issue in any will is the appointment of guardianship for your minor children. This issue can be addressed in your pour-over will. I suggest that you discuss the matter of guardianship with the future guardian, and have a frank discussion about the emotional and financial issues involved. It is easy to dismiss the possibility that death or incompetency may take you away from your children, but we know that such scenarios are being played out each and every day. It is best to prepare for these unwanted and unforeseen circumstances so that your children are well taken care of. If the best people to care for the children will need financial help to do so, then life insurance held by a trust for the benefit of the children may well come into the picture as a way to finance their future needs.

CHOOSING THE BEST METHOD OF OWNERSHIP

There are a variety of ways to title property. Each has a different legal definition that affects the disposition of your property after your death. Let's take a look at the advantages and disadvantages of several methods of ownership.

Table 26.1 Fee Simple Ownership

Advantages of Fee Simple Ownership	Disadvantages of Fee Simple Ownership
◆ Easy to establish. ◆ Absolute ownership and control. ◆ Appreciation of real estate and individual securities are generally untaxed and may receive a step-up at death, meaning that the appreciation in the property is untaxed to inheriting party.	◆ Property is subject to probate. ◆ Property held fee simple in your name will be included in your estate and subject to estate taxes. ◆ If not specified in a will, property is passed by the rules of state law at the time of your death. ◆ If you become incompetent, a court could decide who will control the property.

Fee Simple Estate

A fee simple estate or fee simple ownership of property is an interest in property that belongs simply to one individual. Most property is owned in this way. The owner has individual and absolute ownership of the property. He or she can give the property to another person, persons, or entity during his or her lifetime or bequeath it to anyone at death.

Joint Tenancy With Right of Survivorship (JTWRS)

When your property is held in "joint tenancy with right of survivorship," it is held by two or more people, most commonly a couple. When one of the people dies, the survivor or survivors take the entire property by operation of law. Real estate, bank, and brokerage accounts are commonly held in this manner.

Although JTWRS ownership is very common in the U.S., it has many drawbacks, and should be carefully considered as a form of ownership. One problem is that JTWRS ownership supersedes a will. An example from my practice is Lisa, a social worker in Sacramento. Lisa's father was a self-made man, an immigrant who arrived from penniless from Russia and did well in the plumbing business through dedication and hard work. His dream was to leave a legacy for Lisa that she would use to give her children the finest education money can buy. Lisa's parents owned a valuable home and a substantial stock portfolio held in JTWRS. When her father died suddenly of a heart attack, her mother became sole owner of the home and stock portfolio.

ESTATE PLANNING **207**

Table 26.2 Joint Tenancy With Right of Survivorship

Advantages of Joint Tenancy With Right of Survivorship	Disadvantages of Joint Tenancy With Right of Survivorship
◆ Not subject to probate until the death of the second joint tenant. ◆ Easy to set up.	◆ Property could pass to unintended heirs as in the case of Lisa. ◆ There is a variety of estate tax and income tax pitfalls. ◆ Loss of control in your lifetime. If your joint tenant becomes incompetent, you could end up with a court appointed conservator as your join tenant. ◆ Precludes having property pass to a QTIP or credit shelter trust (we will discuss these later in the chapter).

A few years later, Lisa's mother remarried a man with two children of his own. Having been accustomed to JTWRS ownership, the mother put the house and stock portfolio in JTWRS with her new husband. She specified in her will that the house and stock portfolio should pass to Lisa. Lisa's mother died in the aftermath of a stroke 2 years later. Although the will specified that the house and stock portfolio should pass to Lisa, the property went to the new husband instead. This was because JTWRS ownership supersedes a will and the husband was the joint tenant. The stepfather, whom Lisa has never gotten along with, will not return her calls. Lisa feels certain that the property her father worked so hard to accumulate will now pass to her mother's second husband's two children. She is distraught about this turn of events.

Tenancy in Common

Tenancy in common is the holding of property by two or more people, usually a couple, each of whom has an undivided interest in their portion of the property. A brokerage account, for example, could be registered as "Douglas Jones and Janet Jones, Tenants in Common." With this form of ownership, neither Douglas nor Janet owns 100% of the property. They each have an undivided interest in 50% of the property. Either Douglas or Janet can sell or gift their portion of the property at any time. Property does not pass automatically to the tenant in common as it does with

Table 26.3 Tenancy in Common

Advantages of Tenancy in Common	Disadvantages of Tenancy in Common
◆ Easy method of titling property. ◆ Each co-owner has control of his or her portion of the property. Each owner's portion can be sold or gifted to another without the co-owner's permission.	◆ If your co-tenant passes her portion to someone else, you may not be well suited to share property with the new person. ◆ You never have full control of the entire property, just your portion of it. ◆ If your co-tenant becomes incompetent, and has a court ordered conservator appointed, you could end up owning property with a conservator. ◆ Your interest in the property becomes part of your estate at your death and could be subject to estate taxes.

joint tenancy with rights of survivorship. In the case of tenancy in common, the property is passed according to the deceased tenant's will or if there is no will, by state law. There are no survivorship rights for the remaining co-tenant when one tenant dies.

Community Property

Community property law recognizes property ownership by a husband and wife. There are currently nine community property states: Arizona, California, Idaho, Louisiana, Nevada, New Mexico, Texas, Washington, and Wisconsin (Wisconsin uses a different terminology than community property). Alaska is an opt-in community property state that gives both parties the option to make their property community property. Each state is somewhat different, but the essential idea is that in a marriage, some property is considered *separately owned*, while other property is considered *community owned*. Community property is property that was purchased after the marriage or owned by husband or wife before the marriage but retitled after the marriage. Your portion of community property passes to whomever you wish when you die. It does not automatically pass, as joint tenants with rights of survivorship property does, to the co-tenant. When the husband or wife dies, the tax basis of the property is "stepped up" to its current value. This can save on taxes for the surviving spouse if she sells the property.

ESTATE PLANNING **209**

Table 26.4 Community Property

Advantages of Community Property	Disadvantages of Community Property
◆ You may will your portion of your property to whomever you choose. Your portion does not have to be left to your spouse. ◆ You receive a step up in basis of the entire property when your spouse dies and leaves you his half of the property. In JTWRS title, the deceased's portion is stepped up, but the survivor's basis remains the same. "Basis" refers to the value used to calculate the capital gain on the sale of property.	◆ The property belongs half to the husband and half to the wife. The decedent's half must pass through probate. ◆ Property owned by one party before the marriage and then retitled in community property is now half owned by the new spouse. This may look appealing in the honeymoon period of a marriage, but less appealing if the marriage seems to be heading for divorce.

Portability

When you die, a tax is imposed on all of the property you are passing on to your loved ones. The value of all of your property is added up. This includes the value of your home, accounts, personal property, and so on. You then have an exclusion amount, which is an amount that you do not have to pay taxes on. I am writing this in March of 2016, and currently, the estate and gift tax exemption is $5.45 million per individual, which means that an individual can leave $5.45 million to heirs and pay no federal estate or gift tax, while a married couple will be able to exclude $10.9 million.

When the first spouse dies and has an unused portion of their $5.45 million exclusion, it is "portable" and can be carried over to the surviving spouse.

ADVANCED MEDICAL DIRECTIVES

I worked for several years at the University of California Davis Medical Center as a social worker in the hospice program. Here is just one story of many that underline the importance of setting up advanced medical directives. The patient was a 40-year-old man with Lou Gehrig's disease. He was gradually losing motor control in his body, but he was quite intact cognitively. I discussed on several occasions the importance of clarifying his wishes, should he need to be put on life support. He told his family and me that he did not want extraordinary measures taken if there was no chance of recovery, but he avoided putting his wishes into a legal document. Sadly, he was rushed, semi-conscious, to the hospital at one point where he was eventually put on life support, even though his treating physicians all agreed that there was no chance of recovery, his family did not want him to suffer further, and even his minister asked that no heroic medical measures be taken. He died 4 months later, but his family was hit hard by the medical bills and by the emotional toll of this unnecessary prolonging of his suffering.

Advanced medical directives are your chance to give instruction about the level of treatment you want in case you are rendered unconscious or incompetent but could be kept alive by modern medical technology. Say for example you were in a car crash and were brought to the emergency room brain-dead with no chance of recovery. I know this is a gruesome thought, but of course these situations occur every day. Would you want to be kept alive indefinitely with machines without regard to the cost to your family? Would you want to appoint someone to act as your agent? These are the questions you address in your advanced medical directives so that your family can have the peace of mind and legal standing they will need to carry out your wishes.

Living Will

The living will addresses your wishes should you become terminally incapacitated or unconscious. In such a situation there can be a conflict between the physician's oath to preserve life and your right to self-determination. Your living will provides legal protection for your physician to carry out your wishes. In many states, the law requires that one or two physicians certify that death is imminent as the living will is only applicable when the patient's condition is terminal. The living will usually states in legal language that you do not want to prolong a dying process that is painful, fruitless, and financially devastating for your family.

Durable Power of Attorney for Healthcare

While the living will is limited to terminal medical conditions, the durable power of attorney for healthcare is applicable under broader medical circumstances. You appoint an agent to carry out your wishes. You may also appoint a co-agent and/or a successor agent. Choose an agent whose judgment and good will you really trust, as he or she will have a great deal of power and responsibility over life and death decisions.

When I worked in the hospice at UC Davis Medical Center, I had a patient who was diagnosed with terminal cancer. Her husband was pushing hard for information on euthanasia and assisted suicide, which I did not provide, as providing such information was outside of our code of ethics. He wanted to be appointed as her agent as well, but she instead appointed her sister to act as her healthcare agent. As the social work unfolded with this couple, it turned out that before she was diagnosed with cancer, she was involved in an extramarital affair that he was absolutely enraged about. He wanted her dead—not out of compassion but out of a jealous rage!

I share the above cautionary tale to emphasize that your agent should be a person who you deeply trust to act in your best interest. A durable power of attorney may also provide direction in medical issues other than those involving terminal illness such as incompetence due to dementia or psychiatric disability.

A living will and durable power of attorney are by no means mutually exclusive. Many estate-planning attorneys suggest that both be implemented.

LIFE INSURANCE IN ESTATE PLANNING

One of the principal goals of estate planning is to limit the amount money in your taxable estate so as to assure that a maximum of your hard-earned dollars go to your loved ones rather than to the

Table 26.5 Living Will and Durable Power of Attorney

Living Will	Durable Power of Attorney
♦ Applicable only in terminal illness. ♦ Involves only the author of the living will and his or her physician.	♦ Addresses broader medical decisions including incompetence due to dementia or psychiatric illness. ♦ Involves a third party who acts as agent for the patient.

IRS. Life insurance policies have an owner, a beneficiary(s), and of course the insured party. If you have a life insurance policy that pays on your death, then you are the insured party. Just because it is your life that is insured does not mean that you are necessarily the owner of the policy. For example, you, your spouse, or anyone with an insurable interest in you could conceivably own a policy that pays upon your death. If there is an insurance policy that pays on your death, it will be included in your taxable estate if you are the owner of the policy. It will also be included in the taxable estate if the estate itself is the designated beneficiary of the policy or if the beneficiary is a person whose charge it is to use the proceeds for the benefit of the estate. One way to avoid inclusion of your life insurance proceeds in your taxable estate is to have someone else own the policy (usually a spouse or adult child) and make certain that the policy proceeds are not earmarked to pay for any estate-related obligations including the payment of estate taxes.

If you are married, it can make sense to have cross-ownership of your life insurance policies. For example, Steve and Jessica Smith are both in private practice. Steve is a psychiatrist who makes a higher income than Jessica, who is a social worker. Steve makes $160,000 per year and Jessica makes $65,000. They have two dependent children. They have a strong need for life insurance, as they depend upon two incomes and two parents to take care of the kids. If one were to die, not only would a large chunk of income be lost, but there would be a loss of available time to generate new income as the parenting responsibilities would greatly increase. In this circumstance it might make sense for Mary to own a policy on Steve's life and for Steve to own a policy on Mary's life. Let's say that Steve dies. The general rule of life insurance death benefits is that they are excluded from the gross income of the beneficiary. Therefore when Steve dies, and Mary receives the life insurance proceeds, they will be excluded from Mary's income tax. Furthermore, if Mary is the owner of the policy on Steve, then the death benefit is also excluded from his taxable estate.

Another method of avoiding the inclusion of your life insurance proceeds into your estate is to establish an irrevocable life insurance trust (ILIT). The ILIT can be established so that the income is for the benefit of your spouse, with the corpus (principal) to go to your children. You will need an attorney to draw up the trust. You will then fund the trust with money to make premium payments. An ILIT is irrevocable and a complex financial instrument, so make sure to get good professional advice before proceeding.

Planning for Your Practice

What if you became incapacitated suddenly or died suddenly? What would your clients do? Have you thought about this? Have you made contingency plans? It is a good idea to make preparations for the possibility of a sudden transition from working to either disability or death. A well-known authority on this subject is Ann Steiner, PhD, who suggests that psychotherapists create a professional will. Her website (www.psychotherapytools.com) has plenty of handy resources for putting together a professional will and a plethora of resources on preparing for a sudden transition out of your psychotherapy practice.

CONCLUSION

Covering the issues in this chapter is not easy—nobody likes to think about one's own death or disability—but thoughtful planning of one's estate is an important gift to give to your family. It allows them to know that you have thought of their well-being when after you die. With proper planning, you can leave maximum assets to them and minimize your estate's tax burden. Advanced medical directives are of course a must so that your wishes can be carried out should you become incapacitated, and so that your family members can be sure they are carrying out your wishes. Having created wealth with your private practice, it creates a good feeling to pass it on according to your wishes in an orderly way.

SECTION V

YOUR MONEY PAGES

CHAPTER 27

Introduction to a Lifetime Plan for Your Financial Well-Being

We have looked at emotional issues, clinical issues, the therapist life cycle, and some practical financial steps you can take. This section offers you an opportunity to put together your own personal financial plan.

To do this you will need to bring together:

- Your rational thinking function
- Your creative imagination
- The courage to contain your anxiety
- A willingness to look at your shadow.

The thought of going through the worksheets in this chapter may stir up a lot of unpleasant feelings—impatience, anxiety, perhaps even dread. However, we think that you actually *can* have an interesting time with this material. The trick is having a willingness to activate your creative imagination around the issues in your financial life. If you can move into a creative space, you may well find yourself enjoying the exercise and experience surprising pathways to resolution emerging. You will notice that we have provided a "Process Page" facing each worksheet. We hope you will use these pages for a journal of your feelings, reactions, and images as you complete the worksheets. By integrating your "right brain" process responses with the "left brain" financial information you are compiling, you will be doing the "integrative money

217

work" that will allow you to move toward a new sense of financial mastery and empowerment.

Each person's financial plan must reflect the particular and complex realities of their individual situation. There really is no substitute for sitting down with a qualified financial planner who can help you shape a plan that is right for you. Our goal in this chapter, however, is to provide you with useful tools that are designed to give you an in-depth analysis of where you are and where you are heading financially. The worksheets offer you a structured framework to help you conceptualize your financial situation and goals.

We start with the gathering of personal financial information.

- The first set of worksheets is aimed at clarifying your financial objectives.
- Then we take a snapshot of your private practice with the Psychotherapy Practice Basic Worksheet.
- Next, we take a broader look at your total family income.
- Our next task is to help you make an analysis of your net worth by completing a balance sheet of your assets and liabilities.
- Next, we provide you with some tools to take charge of your cash flow, with a detailed expenses worksheet as well as a cash flow worksheet.

The next set of worksheets serves as tools for looking toward your financial future.

- We start with asking about when you would like to retire.
- Then we look at your risk profile as an investor.
- The next worksheet is for life insurance.
- Then we look at the resources you have for retirement including pension and social security.
- Next, we look at any special income you may expect such as inheritance income or divorce settlement income.
- We then look at any special expenses such as caring for a dependent parent or disabled relative as well as higher educational expenses for your children.

We then move on to information and input about your basic benefits package for your practice:

- Health insurance
- Disability insurance
- Saving for retirement in your qualified plan
- Long-term care insurance
- Life insurance.

We also provide you with tools to estimate your retirement savings needs and present funding levels.

CHAPTER 28

Financial Worksheets and Process Pages

Table 28.1 Personal Information Worksheet

Personal Information
Today's Date _____
Your Name _____
Your Age _____
Spouse's Name _____
Spouse's Age _____

© 2018, *Mastering the Financial Dimension of Your Psychotherapy Practice: The Definitive Resource for Private Practice*, Peter H. Cole and Daisy Reese, Routledge

Process Pages

An open space for journaling your feelings, thoughts, and emotional responses.

Object of Contemplation

Do you avoid dealing with financial issues?
If so, how does your avoidance work against you?

_____

_____

_____

_____

_____

_____

"We are here because there is, finally,
no refuge from ourselves."
—Scott Rutan

Table 28.2 Lifetime Financial Planning Objectives Worksheet

Your Objectives for Lifetime Financial Planning

In the space below, please check off and write down your objectives for lifetime financial planning.

- ☐ Maintain practice and other income at a level sufficient to maintain an agreeable lifestyle.
- ☐ Accumulate sufficient assets to maintain an agreeable lifestyle in the Elder Phase while working only as much as I desire.
- ☐ Accumulate sufficient assets to pay for the educational needs of my children.
- ☐ Reduce debt.
- ☐ Reduce tax burden.
- ☐ Ensure that the family will have sufficient income in case I become disabled.

For Disposition at Death

- ☐ Ensure that family has sufficient assets in case of my premature death or that of my spouse.
- ☐ Avoid unnecessary taxes at my death or that of my spouse.

Additional Lifetime Financial Objectives

_____
_____
_____
_____
_____
_____
_____
_____
_____
_____

© 2018, *Mastering the Financial Dimension of Your Psychotherapy Practice: The Definitive Resource for Private Practice*, Peter H. Cole and Daisy Reese, Routledge

Process Pages

An open space for journaling your feelings, thoughts, emotional responses.

Question

What feelings arise as you write down your financial goals?

_____

_____

_____

_____

_____

_____

_____

"Know your garden. It is time to speak your truth."
—*Hopi Elders*

© 2018, *Mastering the Financial Dimension of Your Psychotherapy Practice: The Definitive Resource for Private Practice*, Peter H. Cole and Daisy Reese, Routledge

The next worksheet is designed to be a snapshot of your practice. It asks that you think of your practice as a business in which one of the business expenses is your remuneration. The business of your practice must support not only your current lifestyle, but also the expenses of the business itself, along with funding your other life objectives.

Table 28.3 Private Practice Basic Worksheet

YOUR PSYCHOTHERAPY PRACTICE: BASIC WORKSHEET
Revenues
Psychotherapy: Individuals and Couples

Average Number of Client Hours Per Month	Average Fee per Session	Average Monthly Revenue From Individuals and Couples
A	B $	(A × B) $

Other Sources of Private Practice Revenue, (e.g., groups, consulting, teaching, interns)

Source of Revenue 1 Description	Source of Revenue 2 Description	Source of Revenue 3 Description	
Approximate Monthly Income $	Approximate Monthly Income $	Approximate Monthly Income $	Total Monthly Revenues From Other Sources $

Monthly Expenses

COMPENSATION	
Your Monthly Remuneration	$
BENEFITS	
Health Insurance	$
Disability Insurance	$
Retirement Investing	$
TAXES	
Federal Taxes	$
State Taxes	$
Local Taxes	$
GENERAL BUSINESS EXPENSES	
Liability Insurance	$
Rent	$
Furnishings	$
Business Equipment	$
Cont. Ed., Consultation	$

PROFIT or LOSS

Projected Revenues (monthly)	Projected Expenses (monthly)	Profit or Loss (monthly)
$	($)	=

© 2018, *Mastering the Financial Dimension of Your Psychotherapy Practice: The Definitive Resource for Private Practice*, Peter H. Cole and Daisy Reese, Routledge

Process Pages

An open space for journaling your feelings, thoughts, and emotional responses.

Creative Imagining

How can you manifest more fulfillment and prosperity with your psychotherapy practice?

_____
_____
_____
_____
_____
_____
_____
_____
_____
_____

"The million little things that drop into your hands. The small opportunities each day brings. . . ."
—*Helen Keller*

Now let's make an analysis of where you currently are in your financial life. The information we are gathering next encompasses your financial life in a broader spectrum beyond your practice. This includes the financial contributions of your spouse as well as other sources of revenue such as real estate, investments, trust income, and so on. In making use of this worksheet, let us suggest that you use it not only as a snapshot of where you are, but also as a tool for thinking creatively about increasing your income, reducing expenses, and adding to your net worth.

First, we will work with an income worksheet, which will detail all your sources of income as well as income tax deductions. Next, we will take an in-depth look at your assets and liabilities in order to determine your net worth. Next, we look in detail at your personal expenses including servicing any debt you may have. This is where we look at how you spend your money. After that, we will make an analysis of your cash flow.

INCOME WORKSHEET
(all values are annual)

Table 28.4 Income Worksheet

Earned Income	*Annual*
Your Private Practice Remuneration[1] (annual)	$
Salaried Income (e.g. work at a hospital, agency or clinic)	$
Spouse's Primary Earned Income	$
Spouse's Secondary Earned Income	$
Additional Income	
Bonus from your practice profit over and above your regular remuneration (annual)	$
Other non-salaried (income that will generate IRS form 1099) sources of income such as consulting, teaching.	$
Other Income from Spouse	$
Total Annual Earned Income	$
Interest, Dividends, Income from Investments, and Trust Income	**Annual Interest, Income, or Dividends**
CDs or Money Market Funds	$
Bonds or Bond Funds	$
Stocks or Stock Funds Dividends	$
Limited Partnerships	$
Investment Property Income	$
Total Annual Trust Income	$
Total Annual Income from Interest, Dividends, Income from Investments, and Trust Income	$
Deductions for Federal Tax Liability	
Charitable 50%	$
State Tax Paid	$
Property Taxes	$
Home Mortgage	$
Gross Deductions	$
Standard Deduction	$
Allowed Deductions	$
Personal Exemptions	$
Total Deductions for Federal Tax Liability	$

1 Please note that your private practice remuneration is not synonymous with your private practice revenue. Your remuneration is money specifically earmarked from your revenue for your salary.

© 2018, *Mastering the Financial Dimension of Your Psychotherapy Practice: The Definitive Resource for Private Practice*, Peter H. Cole and Daisy Reese, Routledge

Process Pages

An open space for journaling your feelings, thoughts, and emotional responses.

Top Dog and Underdog

Write from the voice of self-criticism about your financial situation.

_____
_____
_____
_____
_____

Now respond to the critical voice with self-compassion and self-acceptance.

_____
_____
_____
_____
_____

© 2018, *Mastering the Financial Dimension of Your Psychotherapy Practice: The Definitive Resource for Private Practice*, Peter H. Cole and Daisy Reese, Routledge

Table 28.5 Balance Sheet

	Balance Sheet		
	LIQUID ASSETS (do not include retirement plan assets)		
1	Cash in Bank Checking		
2	Cash in Bank Savings		
3	CDs		
4	Money Market		
5	Total Value of Stocks and Stock Mutual Funds (not in a retirement plan)		
6	Total Bonds and Bond Mutual Funds (not in a retirement plan) Description:		
7	Cash Value in Life Insurance		
	NON-LIQUID ASSETS		
8	Your Retirement Plan Assets		
9	Spouse's Retirement Plan Assets		
10	Your Automobile		
11	Spouse's Automobile		
12	Real Estate (home) Equity		
13	Real Estate (investments) Equity		
14	Furnishings—Home		
15	Furnishings—Office		
16	Other Hard Assets (e.g. jewelry, precious stones)		
17	Art		
18	(add lines 1 thru 14)	**Total Assets**	$
	LIABILITIES		
19	Mortgage on Home	Total Due	$
20	Mortgage on Investment Property	Total Due	$
21	Total Credit Card Debt (you and spouse combined)	Total Due	$

© 2018, *Mastering the Financial Dimension of Your Psychotherapy Practice: The Definitive Resource for Private Practice*, Peter H. Cole and Daisy Reese, Routledge

Balance Sheet cont.

22	Total Auto Loan Debt (you and spouse combined)	Total Due	$
23	Total Student Loan Debt (you and spouse combined)	Total Due	$
24	Other Misc. Loan 1 (you and spouse combined)	Total Due	$
25	Other Misc. Loan 2 (you and spouse combined) Description: Account #	Total Due Total Due	$ $
26	(add lines 19 thru 25)	**Total Liabilities**	**$**

YOUR ESTIMATED NET WORTH

27	(from line 18)	Total Assets	$
28	(from line 26)	Total Liabilities	$
	(line 27 minus line 28)	**Your Estimated Net Worth**	**$**

© 2018, *Mastering the Financial Dimension of Your Psychotherapy Practice: The Definitive Resource for Private Practice*, Peter H. Cole and Daisy Reese, Routledge

Process Pages

An open space for journaling your feelings, thoughts, and emotional responses.

Please journal about feelings that arise for you as you enter the information that constitutes your balance sheet.

Expenses

When dealing with your expenses, we want to separate the business expenses from the personal expenses in order to keep things organized. So, let us refer back to the basic worksheet for your practice to keep these expenses straight.

Expenses to Your Business
- Your monthly remuneration
- Health insurance
- Disability insurance
- Retirement investing
- Taxes on your practice income
- Liability insurance
- Office rent
- Business equipment
- Furnishings
- Continuing education
- Consultation
- Bonuses to you over and above your remuneration.

You can see from the list that your private practice has a lot to support—both your life and the private practice itself. Just as an aside, you might think about keeping this list in mind next time you are tempted to undercharge for your services. Remember, your time is a precious commodity; you cannot afford to give it away or undercharge for it!

Remember, it is OK to think like a businessperson *and* like a therapist. In fact, if you are in private practice, you have to. So, keep in mind that a basic rule of business is to reduce expenses while increasing revenue. Creative businesspeople are always asking themselves how they can reduce expenses. Look with fresh eyes at your business expenses, and see if there are ways that you can reduce them, even a little bit!

Personal Expenses

All of these expenses come out of your monthly practice remuneration or other sources of your or your spouse's take-home income.

We are listing personal expenses here. Nobody likes to look at their spending with a fine-toothed comb. It feels to most people about as pleasant as the sound of fingernails on a chalkboard. The fact is that looking at our spending is not unlike looking at our eating, or other activities that we sometimes do quite unconsciously. We are encouraged in modern society to spend unconsciously, without regard for consequences to our financial health, just as we are encouraged to eat junk food without regard for our physical health. The goal with looking at expenses is to find a balance between spontaneous support of what gives you pleasure, and on the other hand to pay attention to what is in the interest of your long- and short-term financial health. Staying conscious about how you spend may not be a lot of fun, but then again, neither is running up credit card debt.

Table 28.6 Personal Expenses Worksheet

PERSONAL EXPENSE WORKSHEET	
Rent	$
Groceries	$
Home Phone	$
Cell Phone	$
Car Maintenance	$
Mortgage or Rent	$
Clothes	$
Domestic Help	$
Restaurants	$
Movies	$
Other Entertainment	$
Vacations	$
Child Care	$
Alimony and Child Support	$
Furnishings for the Home	$
Gifts	$
Medical Expenses	$
Therapy	$
Health Club	$
Massage	$
Other (description)	$
Other (description)	$
Other (description)	$
Total Personal Expenses	$

© 2018, *Mastering the Financial Dimension of Your Psychotherapy Practice: The Definitive Resource for Private Practice*, Peter H. Cole and Daisy Reese, Routledge

Process Pages

An open space for journaling your feelings, thoughts, and emotional responses.

A space to journal as you work with your expenses.

"When all the doing is done,
I have to face myself in my naked reality."
—*Marion Woodman*

© 2018, *Mastering the Financial Dimension of Your Psychotherapy Practice: The Definitive Resource for Private Practice*, Peter H. Cole and Daisy Reese, Routledge

Table 28.7 Debt Maintenance Worksheet

DEBT MAINTANENCE WORKSHEET		
Mortgage Monthly Payment $ Years to Pay Interest Rate % ☐ Variable Rate ☐ Fixed Rate Total Due $ _____ Favorable Prepayment Terms?[1] ☐ yes ☐ no		
Credit Card 1 Monthly Payment $	Description: Total Due $	Account # Interest Rate %
Credit Card 2 Monthly Payment $	Description: Total Due $	Account # Interest Rate %
Credit Card 3 Monthly Payment $	Description: Total Due $	Account # Interest Rate %
Credit Card 4 Monthly Payment $	Description: Total Due $	Account # Interest Rate %
Auto Loan 2 Monthly Payment $	Description: Total Due $	Interest Rate %
Student Loan 1 Monthly Payment $	Description: Total Due $	Interest Rate %
Student Loan 2 Monthly Payment $	Description: Total Due $	Interest Rate %
OTHER Loans Monthly Payment $	Description: Total Due $	Interest Rate %
OTHER Loans Monthly Payment $	Description: Total Due $	Interest Rate %
Total Monthly Payment for Debt Maintenance $		

1   See our discussion on mortgage prepayment in Chapter 24.

© 2018, *Mastering the Financial Dimension of Your Psychotherapy Practice: The Definitive Resource for Private Practice*, Peter H. Cole and Daisy Reese, Routledge

Process Pages

An open space for journaling your feelings, thoughts, and emotional responses.

What comes up for as you detail your debts?

_____

_____

_____

_____

_____

_____

_____

_____

_____

"Remember the sky that you were born under. Know each of the stars' stories."
—*Joy Harho*

Now that we have established a worksheet for your expenses, we can plug in some important values. Let's look at your cash flow.

Table 28.8 Cash Flow Worksheet

CASH FLOW WORKSHEET (all values are annual and include both you and your spouse)	
1. Idle Cash on Hand	$
SOURCES OF CASH (inflow)	
2. Total Annual Earned Income (from personal income worksheet)	$
3. Total Annual Interest, Dividends, Income from Investments and Trust Income (from personal income worksheet)	$
4. **TOTAL CASH INFLOW (add lines 1 + 2)**	$
5. **TOTAL CASH AVAILABLE (add lines 1 + 2 + 3)**	$
USES OF CASH (outflow)	
6. Total Personal Expenses (from Personal Expenses Worksheet)	$
7. Total Debt Maintenance (from Debt Maintenance Worksheet)	$
8. Federal Taxes Paid	$
9. State Taxes Paid	$
10. Property Taxes Paid	$
11. Liability Insurance	$
12. Office Rent	$
13. Office Furnishings	$
14. Business Equipment	$
15. Cont. Ed., Consultation, Personal Therapy	$
16. Health Insurance	$
17. Disability Insurance	$
18. Retirement Investing	$
19. Other/Misc. Uses of Cash	$
20. **Total Cash Outflow**	$
21. **END OF YR Cash Balance** (line 5 + line 20)	$

© 2018, *Mastering the Financial Dimension of Your Psychotherapy Practice: The Definitive Resource for Private Practice*, Peter H. Cole and Daisy Reese, Routledge

Process Pages

An open space for journaling your feelings, thoughts, and emotional responses.

A space to journal as you work with your expenses.

© 2018, *Mastering the Financial Dimension of Your Psychotherapy Practice: The Definitive Resource for Private Practice*, Peter H. Cole and Daisy Reese, Routledge

At this point you should have a pretty good idea of where you currently stand. If the picture looks good, then you should be pleased—congratulations on doing things well! For those readers for whom the picture looks depressing, do not lose heart! Money is like any other issue in life; it can and will respond to your intention to work with it.

Your Financial Future

Now let's move on to looking forward into your financial future. First, take a moment to read through the overview on Social Security benefits and do some calculations about what you can expect when you reach retirement age.

Social Security and the Private Practitioner

The most common sources of income for retired therapists are Social Security, qualified retirement accounts, individual retirement accounts, annuities, and cash values in life insurance policies. Other sources of income might derive from other investments such as real estate or other businesses. It is not uncommon for therapists to continue to work past the traditional retirement age of 65. Many therapists love their work and do not want to give it up entirely in retirement. Other older therapists continue to work due to a continuing need for income. A combination of these two factors keep many therapists working well into their seventies. Please see a more detailed discussion of this in Chapter 6 on the Elder Phase.

Whatever your sources of income may be, it is important that you plan ahead so that you may prepare for a comfortable retirement income. A good place to begin your planning is with estimating your old age insurance with Social Security. You can go online and set up an online account with the Social Security Administration at www.ssa.gov. Online you get your Social Security statement, estimate future benefits, apply for benefits, and do just about everything you will need to do with the Social Security Administration.

When you go online and see your projected monthly social security benefits, you will see that Social Security is not designed to provide an adequate retirement income in and of itself. Instead, it is designed to provide a safety net that is supplemented with other retirement funds. You become eligible for social security payments through credit for qualifying quarters worked. Not all work is covered by Social Security, so you will need to clarify exactly what work you have done that qualifies. Your online account will detail the number of quarters you have worked that qualify.

How You Qualify for Social Security as a Solo Practitioner

If you are like most people in private practice, you probably run your practice as a sole proprietorship. The term "sole proprietorship" means that you are self-employed and not organized as a corporation or other entity such as a limited liability partnership—you are simply in business for yourself. As a sole proprietor, your business income is reported on IRS Schedule C. You pay self-employment (SE) tax based on your self-employed income. The self-employment tax is a Social Security and Medicare tax similar to the Social Security and Medicare taxes withheld from most wage earners. You figure your SE tax using Schedule SE (Form 1040). By the way, wage earners cannot deduct Social Security and Medicare taxes whereas sole proprietors may deduct half of SE tax in figuring their adjusted gross income.

In 2016 the SE tax rate is 15.3%. The rate consists of two parts: 12.4% for social security (old age, survivors and disability insurance) and 2.9% for Medicare (hospital insurance). Only the first $118,500 of your combined wages and net earnings in 2016 is subject to any combination of the Social Security part of the SE tax. All your combined wages, tips, and net earnings in 2016 are subject to the 2.9% Medicare part of SE tax. Again, you can deduct half of your SE tax in figuring your adjusted gross income. This deduction only affects your income tax. It does not affect either your net earnings from self-employment or your SE tax.

You must be insured under the Social Security system before you begin receiving Social Security benefits. Paying your self-employment tax enables you to be eligible for Social Security as a solo practitioner. You are insured if you have the required number of quarters of coverage. You can earn a maximum credit of four quarters per year. In the year 2016, you must earn $1,260 in covered earnings to get one Social Security or Medicare work credit and $5,040 to get the maximum four credits for the year.

With your Social Security benefit, between the ages of 62 and 70 you can decide when you want to begin taking the benefit. The Social Security Administration sets an age that it designates as your "full retirement age" based on the year you were born. In most cases, you will want to wait until your full retirement age to begin taking your Social Security benefit. The longer you wait, up to age 70, the higher your monthly benefit. Waiting beyond age 70 does not get you any additional benefit. I've been asked many times whether it is better to wait or take the benefit when you reach full retirement age. My answer is that if you think you are going to live to an old age, and can financially manage to wait, then by all means do! On the other hand, if you think for whatever reason that your time is limited, or you cannot manage financially to wait, then take the benefit when you reach your full retirement age.

Once you have opened your account with at www.ssa.gov you can estimate your benefits, so let's get started with the Social Security worksheet in the next table. Let's input your benefit if you take an early retirement at 62, your benefit at full retirement age, and your retirement if you wait until 70.

Table 28.9 Social Security Worksheet

	You	Your Spouse
Full Retirement Age Benefit	$_____	$_____
Age 70 Benefit	$_____	$_____

Table 28.10 Retirement Age Worksheet

Your Projected Retirement Age _____

Spouse's Projected Retirement Age _____

Table 28.11 Yearly Living Expenses Now and in Retirement Worksheet

Not including taxes. In today's dollars. For your household.

Now	$_____
Current Surviving Household	$_____
During Retirement	$_____
Single Retiree Survivor	$_____

Process Pages

An open space for journaling your feelings, thoughts, and emotional responses.

Feelings may arise as you think about the age at which you want to retire, and the money you will need to be comfortable.

_____

_____

_____

_____

_____

_____

_____

_____

"Now we are changed, making a noise greater than ourselves."
—*Kathleen Norris*

Table 28.12 Risk Profile Worksheet

☐ Conservative	
☐ Moderately Conservative	
☐ Moderate	
☐ Moderately Aggressive	
☐ Aggressive	

Table 28.13 Life Insurance Worksheet

	You	Your Spouse
Permanent life insurance	$_____	$_____
Term life insurance	$_____	$_____
Cash values (minus loans)	$_____	$_____

Table 28.14 Pension Worksheet

	You	Your Spouse
Defined Benefit Pension Plan	$_____	$_____
Anticipated Annual Amount	$_____	$_____
Starting Age	$_____	$_____
Increase Rate Before Retirement	$_____	$_____
Increase Rate After Retirement	$_____	$_____
Survivor Benefit	$_____	$_____

© 2018, *Mastering the Financial Dimension of Your Psychotherapy Practice: The Definitive Resource for Private Practice*, Peter H. Cole and Daisy Reese, Routledge

Process Pages

An open space for journaling your feelings, thoughts, and emotional responses.

Pension and Social Security

A place to journal your emotional response.

_____

_____

_____

_____

_____

_____

_____

_____

"Where does the lotus grow?
In the mud."
—*Marie Stuart*

© 2018, *Mastering the Financial Dimension of Your Psychotherapy Practice: The Definitive Resource for Private Practice*, Peter H. Cole and Daisy Reese, Routledge

Table 28.15 Special Income Worksheet

Special Income

Any sources of expected future income (e.g., inheritance or divorce settlement).

Description	Annual Amount	Annual Increase	Starting Year	Number of Years

© 2018, *Mastering the Financial Dimension of Your Psychotherapy Practice: The Definitive Resource for Private Practice*, Peter H. Cole and Daisy Reese, Routledge

Process Pages

An open space for journaling your feelings, thoughts, and emotional responses.

What comes up for you as you think about future income such as an inheritance? Feelings may arise in response to a lack of inheritance as well.

_____

_____

_____

_____

_____

_____

"We do not see things as they are; we see things as we are."
—*Talmud*

© 2018, *Mastering the Financial Dimension of Your Psychotherapy Practice: The Definitive Resource for Private Practice*, Peter H. Cole and Daisy Reese, Routledge

Table 28.16 Special Expenses Worksheet

Special Expenses
Any future expenses such as vacations, down payment on real estate, care for a dependent family member etc.
(*not including education expenses*)

Description	Annual Amount	Annual Increase	Starting Year	Number of Years

© 2018, *Mastering the Financial Dimension of Your Psychotherapy Practice: The Definitive Resource for Private Practice*, Peter H. Cole and Daisy Reese, Routledge

Process Pages

An open space for journaling your feelings, thoughts, and emotional responses.

Special expenses may be for things that you really value and want to make room for in your life.

_____

_____

_____

_____

_____

_____

_____

_____

"You must ask for what you really want,
Don't go back to sleep."
—*Rumi*

© 2018, *Mastering the Financial Dimension of Your Psychotherapy Practice: The Definitive Resource for Private Practice*, Peter H. Cole and Daisy Reese, Routledge

Table 28.17 Higher Education Expenses Worksheet

Higher Education Expenses for Dependents
In today's dollars

Name of Child	Years Until College	Cost per Year	Number of Years	Current College Fund Amount

© 2018, *Mastering the Financial Dimension of Your Psychotherapy Practice: The Definitive Resource for Private Practice*, Peter H. Cole and Daisy Reese, Routledge

Process Pages

An open space for journaling your feelings, thoughts, and emotional responses.

A financial gift such as paying educational expenses
can make a profound difference in the life of
a young person. Were you given this gift?
What feelings, memories, and associations
come up around this?

_____
_____
_____
_____
_____
_____
_____
_____

"We must be diligent today. To wait until tomorrow is too late."
—Buddha

© 2018, *Mastering the Financial Dimension of Your Psychotherapy Practice: The Definitive Resource for Private Practice*, Peter H. Cole and Daisy Reese, Routledge

If you have worked with the preceding worksheets, you now should have a sense of where you are financially, and some of the financial issues that you will need to prepare for. Let's move forward now, looking at a variety of issues that affect the financial life of your practice. In this next section we will discuss important business issues for your practice:

1) Federal tax deductibility issues for sole proprietors
2) Qualified plans of deferred compensation
3) Business overhead insurance
4) Medical and disability insurance
5) Personal liability insurance.

If You Are Structured as a Sole Proprietor, There Are Many Business Expenses That Are Deductible

Most therapists work under the structure that the IRS denotes as "sole proprietor." In today's environment, if you are working individually, setting your business up as a sole proprietor is both the most common business form and usually quite sensible. The main issue that I (Peter) have with the sole proprietor structure is that there is no separation between you as an individual and your business from the IRS's point of view. My thrust throughout this book is that your practice must be run like a business that will provide you, its owner, with a good living and benefits. In this sense you are both the employer and the employee. Therefore, in many cases of individual practice, it may be best for you to set up your practice as a sole proprietorship, but to think like a corporation in the sense that your practice should be conceptualized as a business that stands on its own, provides you with your remuneration, and also provides you with benefits including a retirement plan, health plan, and disability insurance.

Below is a list of practice expenses that are generally deductible to you if you are organized as a sole proprietorship.

- Employees' pay
- Reimbursement for employees' expenses
- Depreciation on business equipment

- Fire, theft, flood, or similar insurance
- Health insurance premiums
- Tax-qualified long-term care insurance
- Interest on debts related to your business
- Legal and professional fees
- Tax preparation fees
- Pension plans
- Rent expense
- Entertainment to a customer or client
- State income taxes directly attributable to your business
- Employment taxes
- State unemployment fund
- State disability fund
- Self-employment tax
- Personal property tax on property directly related to your business
- Travel, meals, and entertainment when traveling for business
- Business use of your home if you see patients in a home office
- Advertising
- Donations to business organizations
- Education expenses
- Licenses and regulatory fees
- Repairs to keep your office in normal operating condition
- Subscriptions to trade or professional publications
- Supplies and materials
- Utilities

The fact is that we solo practitioners have many financial difficulties and challenges, but we do have a wide array of deductions. Use them! These deductions are your right as a sole proprietor, and they are absolutely necessary in keeping your practice in good financial shape. Remember our social contract in the U.S. We have a limited amount of services provided by the government compared with the rest of the developed world. On the other hand, we have lower taxes. Nowhere is this clearer than in private practice. You have significant deductions as a sole proprietor—and you need them, because it is costly to buy your own social safety net

FINANCIAL WORKSHEETS AND PROCESS PAGES **255**

with private health insurance, long-term care insurance, disability insurance, retirement savings, and education savings.

Health Insurance

Health insurance is so political in America! Since writing the first edition of this book, the Affordable Care Act has made it much more possible for small businesspeople such as psychotherapists in private practice to find health insurance, especially those of us with preexisting conditions. However, we are writing this right at the time of the 2016 presidential election, and the Republican candidates are all promising to dismantle the Affordable Care Act, so where things will stand when this second edition goes to press is anybody's guess. We will go ahead and write about how things stand today with health coverage.

If you are self-employed and not covered by your spouse's insurance, then likely your best bet is to go through the Affordable Care Act exchange in your state. Depending on your adjusted gross income, you may or may not be eligible for a subsidy. Healthcare. gov is the federal website that famously was dysfunctional when it first came online in October 2013, but it has evolved into a very user-friendly site. If you follow the links to the section on Self-Employed (www.healthcare.gov/self-employed), you will find an excellent source of information about health insurance for the solo private practice psychotherapist.

Disability Coverage

The next vital issue is your disability coverage. As we discussed earlier in this book, earnings power is for most people their main source of income and livelihood, and likely their most valuable asset. Build disability coverage into your practice right from the start. As you move through the stages of your practice, with aging, the possibility of disability will likely feel more and more real. If you are faced with a health challenge that prevents you from working, it will be incredibly important that you are not also faced with financial failure. Here are some coverage guidelines:

If your state has short-term elective disability coverage, then you may want to look into purchasing the maximum coverage for the short term. Additionally, you may want to purchase business overhead coverage that will allow you to pay your office expenses in the event of illness and injury. By the way, if you are a sole proprietor, your business overhead coverage is deductible from your federal taxes. The third piece in the puzzle is to purchase disability insurance that will cover you for an extended period of time and will kick in after your short-term coverage has ended. Two leading providers of private disability coverage and business overhead coverage are Unum Insurance and Principal Insurance. You can find UnumProvident online at www.unum.com and Principal at www.principal.com. If you have a financial planner, he or she should be able to assist you in finding and designing appropriate coverage.

As we discussed earlier, make sure that your disability policy defines disability as an inability to return to your own profession, so that the insurer cannot force you to go into a new line of work or refuse to pay. I suggest also that you purchase coverage to the maximum allowable age and that you replace the maximum of your income allowable. One problem for therapists is that our expenses are very high and therefore our taxable income tends to be low. Because disability coverage is based on your taxable income, you will want to maximize the percentage of income being replaced. Although disability coverage is not generally a tax-deductible expense for a sole proprietor, the business overhead coverage is. In most cases benefits from your privately purchased disability coverage should be tax-free.

Saving for Retirement

Ok, now we have taken a look at your practice and its profitability, determined where you stand financially, your net worth, your income, expenses, and cash flow. We have discussed the vital importance of health and disability insurance to your financial well-being as a private practitioner. Now, we are going to make an analysis of how much you need in order to retire, and then how much you need to put away now in order to get there. These calculations are rather complex, and are usually done with computers. The program I use for my clients is called MoneyTree. You can find various calculators for retirement on a number of websites. To get a rough snapshot of your retirement savings needs, we have posted a financial calculator programmed for that purpose on our website (www.insightfinancialgroup.com). From our home page, go to the "Calculators" link, and choose the "Retirement Resources" calculator. Again, this calculator is not designed to give you the in-depth information you will get from a program like MoneyTree, but it should give you a ballpark idea of what you need to save now in order to reach your retirement savings goal.

Long-Term Care Insurance

If you are in your mid-fifties to mid-sixties, it is time to think about long-term care insurance. We discussed this coverage earlier in the book, and in this section we are going to get down to brass tacks and discuss how much coverage you need. Please review the section that covers whether long-term care is appropriate for you. If it is, then the first step is to call nursing homes in the area where you plan to retire. Find out how much a bed would cost in your geographical area on a daily basis. Next, you will want a policy that is designed to meet these needs. Make sure to purchase a policy with inflation protection and coverage for assisted living as well as home care. Finally, make sure that you have a tax-qualified policy so that you can deduct your premiums from your taxable income.

Just to give you a ballpark figure, I (Peter) ran a long-term care quote for a 55-year-old preferred risk in the state of Illinois with a major insurer for a 6-year policy with $150 per day, 100% home-care coverage, assisted living coverage, 5% compound inflation coverage and a 60-day waiting period. The premium came to $128 per month. The same policy for a 60-year-old came to $162 per month. For a 65-year-old, the premium is $212 per month. Obviously, your costs will vary, but I offer this to give you some kind of ballpark idea of the cost of long-term care insurance for you. As I mentioned in the earlier section on long-term care, I usually advise my clients to purchase long-term care insurance in their mid-fifties, but of course your individual circumstances determine what is most sensible for you.

Let's take an overall look now at the major items that you will need as a basic benefits package for yourself.

Table 28.18 Basic Benefits Package in the Life Cycle of Your Practice

	Launching Phase Ages 30–35	*Establishing Phase Ages 36–40*	*Prime Phase Ages 41–65*	*Elder Phase Age 66–?*
Health Insurance	Needed	Needed	Needed	Medicare Parts A + B will provide your basic coverage. Medicare supplemental insurance is often a good idea.
Retirement Savings	Fund according to estimates on calculator	Fund according to estimates on calculator	Fund according to estimates on calculator. Now is the time to make up for any shortfalls in earlier funding.	Hopefully you have put away enough at this point that no further funding is necessary.
Disability Insurance	Usually can wait until the Establishing Phase	Needed—usually replace 80% of net Schedule C income	Needed until about age 60, when resources can flow to long-term care insurance instead	Not applicable. Most disability policies only pay the benefit to age 65 or 67.
Long-Term Care	Usually not recommended until mid-fifties	Usually not recommended until mid-fifties	Recommended in mid-fifties	Usually recommended unless you have very few assets, have a very large estate, or do not care about leaving an estate to your heirs.
Life Insurance	Only needed if you have dependents. Getting an early start with permanent insurance may be a very smart move.	A must if you have a family that depends on your income. Permanent insurance will enhance your estate and provide a savings vehicle, while term insurance will provide basic coverage.	A must if you have a family that depends on your income. Evaluate your needs as they may change as you have more in retirement and your children are on their own financially.	If you have maintained a permanent policy, then you may want to let the cash value pay for the death benefit at this point so you do not have to keep paying a premium.

© 2018, *Mastering the Financial Dimension of Your Psychotherapy Practice: The Definitive Resource for Private Practice*, Peter H. Cole and Daisy Reese, Routledge

Process Pages

An open space for journaling your feelings, thoughts, and emotional responses.

Object of Contemplation:

If life were teaching you certain lessons by placing you in your current financial situation, what might those lessons be?

_____

_____

_____

_____

_____

_____

_____

"Of course there is no formula for success except perhaps an unconditional acceptance of life and what it brings."
—Arthur Rubinstein

© 2018, *Mastering the Financial Dimension of Your Psychotherapy Practice: The Definitive Resource for Private Practice*, Peter H. Cole and Daisy Reese, Routledge

CHAPTER 29

Looking Forward

WHERE TO GO FROM HERE

If you have worked your way through this book then you are now ready to move forward toward implementing your financial plan. You are armed with knowledge about your practice, investing, retirement planning, insurance planning, and estate planning. At this point, you can either implement your own plan based on the information you have gathered here, or you can consult with a professional financial planner. Our bias is that professional consultation can be a very worthwhile investment. Probably the strongest financial plans are developed when the client is deeply involved and informed about the issues, and seeks out professional consultation in the design and implementation of the financial plan. This is not unlike effective psychotherapy with an informed, interested patient who is willing to invest in treatment with a professional psychotherapist rather than going it alone.

A sound plan will address:

- Marketing and developing your practice
- Implementing a retirement plan
- Implementing appropriate investments within the plan
- Creating a thorough tax strategy to limit taxation
- Risk management with appropriate insurance coverage
- Estate planning issues
- Support for insight into the emotional material that colors your financial life.

261

SOME FINAL THOUGHTS

Really working with the material in this book is not easy, and we congratulate you on facing the issues that can be so challenging and yet are so critical to your financial well-being.

You can take charge of your practice and financial life at any stage of the game, but the truth is that the earlier in life you begin the process, the easier it is. If you are in the Launching Phase and reading this book, then you can put the time value of money to work for yourself, develop good financial habits, and start saving now for your future. You will thank yourself later in life if you do.

If you are in the Establishing Phase, then you still likely have plenty of time to put your financial plan in order. You may need to be a bit more aggressive if you haven't done any saving up to this point, but on the other hand, your income should be improving at this phase, hopefully giving you extra latitude in putting more away for retirement.

If you are in the Prime Phase, then hopefully you have been taking care of business in the earlier phases and just need to stay on track. If, however, you have not done a lot up to this point, then you may need to be aggressive in the funding of your retirement plan to make up for lost time. Again however, your earnings at this phase will hopefully give you the latitude to invest larger sums.

If you are in the Elder Phase, then you really have gotten to where you have been heading. If you took care of business, then you are likely in good shape and enjoying your life and practice as a labor of love. If you did not put enough away for whatever reason, there still probably are some good, creative options that you can explore, some of which we discussed in Chapter 6, "The Elder Phase."

Thinking holistically, that is, recognizing the connection between feeling, thinking, and behavior could be described as the essence of psychotherapy. We encourage you to use your understanding of your own emotional responses to enhance your financial self-care.

Throughout the worksheets, we have provided you with space to write down your thoughts, feelings, and associations to the material in the worksheets. We encourage you to look back on the process pages with a sense of creativity and openness.

If there are feelings that have come up for you around issues such as looking at the cash flow of your practice (fear, for example, or self-deprecating thoughts), then we encourage you to look at the connection between your process and your financial outcomes. The financial dimension is no different than any other aspect of your life in that your affective responses may have a profound influence on your effectiveness. If for example, you were working with the "Special Income" planner and had feelings come up about your family of origin with regard to your inheritance or lack thereof, these feelings are important and may be influential in how you deal with the nuts and bolts financial planning issues.

Psychotherapy is more than a profession, more than a behavioral science. It is a way of life that most of us find incredibly meaningful, heartfelt and rewarding. Those of us who love our profession feel that there is something deeply important to be gained when a person learns to be true to him or herself. The work we do with individuals ripples out into the larger world, helping to humanize an increasingly dehumanized world. Our mission in this book has been to help helpers take good care of themselves; we hope we have succeeded in being helpful to you.

A Buddhist approach to working with the financial issues in our lives and practices would embrace a feeling tone of compassion, self-acceptance, and self-exploration. If you can embrace such a feeling state, then the financial dimension of your practice can transform from a source of anxiety to a source of excitement, self-care, creativity, and self-development. Our hope is that you will find new energy for your practice and financial life as you work with the materials we are offering.

May your financial path be filled with learning and discovery.

ADDENDA

ADDENDUM I

Further Resources

LITERATURE FOR PSYCHOTHERAPY MARKETING AND PRACTICE DEVELOPMENT

Truffo, Casey. *Be a Wealthy Therapist: Finally, You Can Make a Living Making a Difference* (St. Peters, MO: MP Press, 2007). Tools to making a better living in private practice.

Barnes, Dorothy. *Independent Practice for the Mental Health Professional* (New York: Brunner-Routledge, 1999). Solid information about marketing, how to set up an office, and how to position yourself professionally.

Hartsell, Thomas and Barton Bernstein. *The Portable Lawyer for Mental Health Professionals: An A–Z Guide to Protecting Your Clients, Your Practice, and Yourself* (Hoboken, NJ: Wiley, 2013). Hartsell and Barton identify, explore, and present solutions to both the simple and complex legal questions that mental health practices must deal with daily.

Grodski, Lynne. *Building Your Ideal Private Practice: A Guide for Therapists and Other Healing Professionals* (New York: Norton, 2015). An inspirational and practical guide to marketing and building your private practice.

Kolt, Laurie. *How to Build a Thriving Fee-for Service Practice: Integrating the Healing Side With the Business Side of Therapy* (New York: Academic Press, 1997). How the field of therapy is changing, how to choose a specialty and market oneself, how to write a business plan and track one's business progress. The tone is practical and motivational.

Stout, Chris and Laurie Cope Grand. *Getting Started in Private Practice: The Complete Guide to Building Your Mental Health Practice* (Hoboken, NJ: Wiley, 2005). Contains all the tips and tools you need to build a successful mental health practice from the ground up.

LITERATURE ABOUT RETIREMENT

Dominguez, Joe and Vicki Robin. *Your Money or Your Life* (New York: Viking Penguin, 2008).

Mathews, Joseph. *Social Security, Medicare and Government Pensions: Get the Most Out of Your Medical Retirement and Medical Benefits* (Berkeley, CA: Nolo Press, 2016). Nolo Press is the venerable Berkeley-based publisher of self-help books. This is the 22nd edition of this book that has proven valuable to thousands of readers.

Haskins, Suzan and Dan Prescher. *The International Living Guide to Retiring Overseas on a Budget: How to Live Well on $25,000 a Year* (Hoboken, NJ: Wiley, 2014). A detailed guide to one of the least-known but most effective retirement strategies in today's chaotic economic environment: retiring abroad.

PUBLISHED BY PETER COLE AND DAISY REESE

Cole, Peter and Daisy Reese. *True Self, True Wealth: A Pathway to Prosperity* (New York: Simon and Schuster, 2008)

Cole, Peter. "Boundary Disturbances in Hospice Work." *Grounds for Gestalt II* (1996)

Cole, Peter. "Resistance to Awareness: A Gestalt Therapy Perspective." *Gestalt Journal* (1995)

Cole, Peter. "Affective Process in Psychotherapy." *Gestalt Journal* (Spring 1998)

Cole, Peter. "In the Shadow of the Leader." *Gestalt Review* (Fall 2013)

Cole, Peter and Daisy Reese. "Relational Development in Gestalt Group Therapy." *Journal of the Easter Group Psychotherapy Society* (Fall 2013)

INDEPENDENT FINANCIAL WEBSITES

Bloomberg Small Business (www.bloomberg.com/small-business)
MSN Personal Finance (www.msn.com/en-us/money/personalfinance)
CNN Money (www.money.cnn.com)
The Forum for Sustainable and Responsible Investment (www.ussif.org)

FINANCIAL WEBSITES FROM COMPANIES OFFERING FINANCIAL SERVICES

Insight Financial Group (www.insightfinancialgroup.com) This is the website of our company, Insight Financial Group. We have posted a series of articles written specifically for therapists on our website called "Clinicians Money Update." Also, we have links to most of the sites listed in this list, quotes, IRS publications, links to Social Security and Medicare, and a variety of calculators to help you make informed financial decisions.

Pacific Life (www.pacificlife.com) Pacific Life is a leading provider of life insurance and other investments. Go to their "educational information" link for lots of solid, user-friendly information on a variety of financial planning, insurance and estate planning issues.

Vanguard (www.vanguard.com) Vanguard is a leading provider of low-fee mutual funds and other investments.

WEBSITES ABOUT REAL ESTATE INVESTMENT TRUSTS

National Association of Real Estate Investment Trusts (www.reit.com) Information on real estate investment trusts from the National Association of Real Estate Investment Trusts.

WEBSITES FROM DISABILITY INSURANCE CARRIERS

Principal Financial Group (www.principal.com) Principal is a major provider of disability insurance.

Unum (www.unum.com) Unum Provident is another major provider of disability insurance.

GOVERNMENT WEBSITES

Medicare (www.medicare.gov)

Housing and Urban Development (http://portal.hud.gov) The official site of the U.S. Department of Housing and Urban Development (HUD). Search for "reverse mortgage" and follow the links for a thorough review of HUD's reverse mortgage program.

Social Security Administration (www.ssa.gov) The official site of the Social Security Administration. Chock full of useful information.

ONLINE BOOKKEEPING RESOURCES
QuickBooks® (www.quickbooks.com) The official site of QuickBooks, a leading accounting package used by many therapists.
Safeguard (www.gosafeguard.com) For therapists who do not want to use a computerized accounting program, Safeguard is the leading provider of non-computerized "one-write" accounting systems.

ONLINE RESOURCES FOR DEBT MANAGEMENT AND CREDIT
Credit Card Tune-Up (www.creditcardtuneup.com) A great site for comparing credit card rates and features.
U.S. Office of Federal Student Aid (www.studentloans.gov) Come to this site to get information on consolidating your student loans.
Bankrate.com (Bankrate.com) A great resource for comparing rates on any sort of consumer loan including credit cards, auto loans and mortgages.
Equifax (Equifax.com) Get your credit report here.
MyFICO.com (www.myfico.com) Find out your FICO score here. Your FICO score is a numerical assessment of your credit standing.

ONLINE CONSUMER INFO
Clark Howard (www.clarkhoward.com) Clark Howard is a wonderful consumer advocate on radio and the internet. Lots of good advice and resources here.
Consumer Reports (www.consumerreports.org) The venerable consumer magazine is now online.

ONLINE INSURANCE INFO
Insure.com (www.insure.com) Compare auto insurance quotes here.
Standard and Poor's (www.standardandpoors.com) The site for Standard and Poor's. Come to this site to get an independent rating of the financial solvency of insurance companies. A good place to visit before you commit to an insurance policy.

ADDENDUM I   **269**

ADDENDUM II

Using QuickBooks® for Your Bookkeeping

QuickBooks® by Intuit has become standard bookkeeping software for small businesses. It is quite adaptable and can readily be set up to help you with your private practice. There are of course excellent alternative to QuickBooks, and if you go to www.capterra.com and search accounting software, you will find lots of good alternatives.

In the first edition of this book, we recommended using QuickBooks for all facets of your practice. Now we suggest that you use a dedicated practice management program such as TherapyNotes, Valant, or SimplePractice for the day-to-day billing, scheduling, and operations of your practice. QuickBooks now has a broader role in your practice. It is not the program you will use to do the heavy lifting of billing, scheduling, or making credit card charges and keeping track of your client accounts. Your practice management program will do all of that. QuickBooks is where you will take the sum of all the checks, cash and credit cards you have taken in for the day, and enter them into your QuickBooks Revenue accounts.

The best version of QuickBooks will probably be QuickBooks Online for Self-Employed—currently priced at $10 per month. First, QuickBooks will ask you to set up your bank account, so that you can balance your bank account with QuickBooks. Next, you simply begin the process of tracking your income and expenses on QuickBooks. At the end of the day you will enter the total income you've taken in from checks, cash, and credit cards, and enter those amounts into QuickBooks as Business Income. And then you will detail all of your expenses so that you can be sure at tax time to get all of the deductions that you are due. A nice feature of QuickBooks is that you can run all kinds of reports and make an analysis of your income and your expenses. Additionally, Quick-Books integrates with TurboTax, which can help with keeping you organized at tax time.

ADDENDUM III

Glossary of Financial Terms

401(k)	A retirement plan that is funded by employee contributions and often with matching contributions from the employer. The contributions are taken pretax and grow tax-free until money is withdrawn. Please see individual 401(k).
403(b)	A retirement plan for public schools, colleges, and certain non-profits. These plans are self-directed. The employee makes a contribution that is sometimes matched by employer contribution. Tax-sheltered annuities are 403(b)s.
529 plan	State-sponsored college savings plans that provide tax-advantaged college investing. Each state has a 529 program set up—your state may also provide you with state income tax advantages if you use your own state's plan. You can use any state's plan for the federal income deferral.
amortization	The repayment of a loan (frequently used in reference to a mortgage) by the systematic repayment of interest and principal. In the early years of a mortgage, most of the payment goes to the payment of interest. An amortization schedule shows the pay-down of principal and the payment of interest with each mortgage payment over the life of the mortgage.
annual percentage rate (APR)	The Truth in Lending Act requires that lenders show the relationship of total finance charges associated with a loan. APR allows consumers to compare loans offered by competing lenders on equal terms, taking into account interest rates, points, and other finance charges as expressed in an annual percentage rate.
annuitant	When an annuity contract is set up to make a regular payment to the policyholder, the policyholder who receives the annuity payments is the annuitant.
annuity (fixed)	An annuity is a contract with an insurance company providing for tax-deferred growth on savings in the funding phase. When the annuitant is ready to retire, the contract is then "annuitized," meaning that regular payments are made to the annuitant. Fixed annuities earn interest that is tax-deferred until withdrawn.

annuity (variable)	Variable annuities provide for tax-deferred growth in separate accounts during the funding phase and payment on growth in the annuity when paid out. Variable annuities invest the policyholder's money in securities such as stocks and bonds that vary in value.[1]
appreciation	Appreciation refers to the increase in the value of an asset. For example, a stock that you bought at one price a year ago may have appreciated to a higher price today. Appreciation also commonly refers to real estate values.
asset	An asset is an item you own that has value, such as a stock, bond, real estate, or automobile.
asset allocation	A mixture of investments of various types that is designed to match the goals and preferences of the investor. Asset allocation models frequently vary from conservative, moderately conservative, moderate, moderately aggressive, and aggressive.
asset class	A category of investment type, for example stocks, bonds, real estate, or cash.
bear market	A period in which stock prices are declining. A bear market can last months or even years.
blue chip stocks	Equity issues of highly regarded companies that are well established. Many blue chip companies pay dividends in both bull markets and bear markets.
bonds	A formal certificate of debt issued by a government entity or corporation. Most bonds make a fixed payment at regular intervals, which is normally a fixed percentage of the face value of the bond. The face value is repaid when the bond matures.
bull market	A period in which stock prices are rising. A bull market can last months or even years.
cash	Cash is not just the money you have in your wallet or in the bank. As an asset class, cash refers to Treasury bills, short-term commercial paper, high-quality municipal debt, high-quality short term corporate debt, and other high-quality short term securities. Cash has the lowest volatility of all asset classes. See money market funds.
cash equivalents	Cash equivalents include money market funds, Treasury bills, and CDs.

---

1   Variable annuities are sold by prospectus only. Investors should read the prospectus carefully before investing. Annuities are long-term investments designed for retirement purposes. Withdrawals of taxable amounts are subject to income tax and, if taken prior to age 59½, a 10% federal tax penalty may apply. Early withdrawals may be subject to withdrawal charges. An investment in the securities underlying a variable annuity involves investment risk, including possible loss of principal. The contract, when redeemed, may be worth more or less than the original investment. The purchase of a variable annuity is not required for, and is not a term of, the provision of any banking service or activity. Guarantees are backed by the claims-paying ability of the issuer.

cash surrender value	The value of funds returnable at any given time to the insured upon the immediate surrender of a policy. Most life insurance and annuity contracts have significant deferred sales charges, making the cash surrender value less than the cash value. For this reason, such contracts only make sense if you are in them for the long haul.
cash value	The value of the savings element in permanent insurance.
certificate of deposit (CD)	CDs are low-risk investments offered by banks for varying durations of months or years. CDs are generally insured by the FDIC up to $100,000 per depositor and banking institution. Fees are usually assessed for early withdrawal.[2]
charitable remainder trust (CRT)	An irrevocable trust with one or more living income beneficiaries and one or more qualified exempt charitable organizations to receive the remainder of the trust upon expiration of the income interest. CRTs are often used with highly appreciated securities. A properly structured CRT permits the donor to receive income, estate, and/or gift tax advantages.
Chartered Financial Consultant (ChFC)	The ChFC designation has been conferred on more 40,000 financial professionals since its inception in 1982. ChFC designees have completed a comprehensive curriculum in financial planning and have met specific experience and ethical requirements.
common stock	A security that represents ownership in a corporation. Shares are bought by the stockholder who can, in turn, sell the share on a stock exchange.
compounding	A process whereby the value of an investment increases by using the principal plus the previously earned interest to calculate interest payments. Compound interest contrasts with simple interest that bases interest payments simply on the original principle, without including previously earned interest to calculate present interest payments.
conservator	A guardian and protector appointed by the court to protect and manage the financial affairs and/or the daily life of an individual who is not capable of managing his or her own affairs due to physical or mental limitations.
consumer debt	Debt that is incurred in the purchase of consumer goods, such as credit card debt, auto loans, and store-financed debt. Unlike most mortgage debt, most consumer debt is not deductible.
corporate bond	A formal debt security issued by a corporation. Most corporate bonds are offered with a $1,000 face value. Generally corporate bonds pay higher coupon rates than government bonds because of higher risk. Corporate bonds are rated for risk by independent rating agencies. As a general rule, the higher the risk, the higher the coupon rate of the bond.

2 CDs offer a fixed rate of return. They do not necessarily protect against a rising cost of living. The FDIC insurance on CDs applies in the case of bank insolvency, but does not protect market value. Other investments are not insured and their principal and yield may fluctuate with market conditions.

corporation	Legal structure for a business to act as an artificial person that can sue or be sued. A for-profit corporation may issue shares of stock to raise funds.
custodial care	A term used in long-term care and long-term care insurance. Refers to care that provides personal needs such as walking, bathing, dressing, eating, or taking medicine. Medicare does not pay for custodial care.
debt markets	The exchanges where debt securities such as U.S. government bonds, municipal bonds, and corporate bonds are bought and sold.
decedent	A legal term used in life insurance and estate planning term; a person who has died.
defined benefit pension plan	A pension plan in which the employer assumes investment risk and specifies the amount that will be paid to the employee in retirement. Such plans commonly provide a formula for the amount paid in retirement as calculated by the number of years served in relation to salary received. Such plans are expensive for employers and are becoming less common in the private sector than they were in years past, although such plans are still common in public employment.
defined contribution plan	In such plans, the employee assumes investment risk. The employer does not guarantee a given amount of income in retirement. Instead, contributions are made into the plan and benefits are received based on contributions made into the plan, performance of investments made by the plan, and vesting. These plans are considered less costly for employers than defined benefit plans.
depreciation	Depreciation is an accounting technique that represents the decline in value of an asset over time. For tax purposes a business owner writes off the cost of an asset over a period of time with charges made against earnings.
disability insurance	A policy designed to pay benefits based on a percentage of earned income if the insured becomes unable to work. Disability insurance is distinct from long-term care insurance and does not cover the same risks.
disposable income	Income that is available after taxes have been paid for spending or saving.
diversification	An investment strategy to spread risk among a variety of investments such as stock mutual funds, bonds, real estate, individual stocks of a variety of companies, and so on. The goal of diversification is to not put all your eggs in one basket, so that factors that may adversely affect one of your holdings will not have an adverse effect on all of your holdings. For example, concerns about terrorism and security may be bad for the airline industry, but lead to brisk business for companies that specialize in providing security.[3]

---

3 Although diversification doesn't guarantee a profit, it may be able to reduce the volatility of your portfolio.

dividends	A portion of a company's profit that is distributed to its shareholders. Dividend paying companies are frequently large and well established.
dollar cost averaging	A method of investing a fixed amount of money into an investment such as a mutual fund. Frequently, the money is transferred directly from a bank account into the investment on a monthly basis without regard to the price of the investment. The investor buys more shares when the price is low and fewer shares when the price is high. This may result in lowering the average cost per share.[4]
Dow Jones Industrial Average (DJIA)	A widely used indicator of the stock market, the DJIA has been computed since 1896. It is a price weighted average of 30 blue chip companies chosen by the Wall Street Journal. The DJIA currently includes GE, GM, HP, Coca-Cola, Microsoft, and ExxonMobil.
durable power of attorney for healthcare	A durable power of attorney for healthcare empowers the person you appoint to make healthcare decisions for you. You designate a person who makes medical decisions for you if you are unable to make them for yourself due to illness or incapacity. Most people choose to have a family member or close friend to act as the decision maker.
equity	In the context of stocks, equity refers to an ownership interest in a corporation in the form of common stock or preferred stock. In a real estate context, equity refers to the difference between the amount owed on the mortgage and the value of the property.
estate	All that a person owns. Upon death, "estate" refers to the total value of the decedent's assets. The value of the decedent's estate includes all funds, interest in businesses, real property, real estate, stocks, bonds, notes receivable, and any other asset the person may have possessed.
estate planning	The orderly and thoughtful preparation of a plan to administer and dispose of one's property so that after death, the people and/or institutions that the decedent favors will receive maximum benefit with minimum loss of assets to taxes.
estate tax	Tax levied on the transfer of property from the decedent to his or her beneficiaries and heirs. It is based on the amount in the decedent's estate and can include insurance proceeds.
executor	The person named in a will and appointed to carry out the desires of the decedent. Responsibilities include gathering up and protecting the assets in the estate, seeing to it that heirs and beneficiaries are treated according to the terms of the will, seeing to it that estate debts are paid, and managing the calculation and payment of estate taxes.

4 Dollar cost averaging neither guarantees a profit nor eliminates the risk of losses in declining markets and you should consider your ability to continue investing through periods of market volatility and/or low prices.

face amount	The amount to be paid upon death or maturity of a life insurance policy.
face value	In the context of a debt security, it is the amount paid to the bondholder when the bond matures.
fair market value	The amount that an asset would bring in the open market if put up for sale.
fiduciary	A party who occupies a position of trust such as a trustee, executor, or retirement plan administrator. Fiduciaries must follow the "prudent person rule," which states that those with responsibility to invest money for others should act with prudence, discretion, intelligence, and regard for the safety of capital as well as income.
financial planner	A professional who assists individuals, families, and organizations in reaching their financial goals.
fixed annuities	A contract between an annuity owner and an insurance company that can guarantee fixed payments over the life of the annuity. The annuitant can rely upon a fixed stream of income with the insurance company assuming the investment risk.
fixed investment	An investment such as a bond, CD, or note that pays a given rate of interest.
fixed rate mortgage	A loan on a property that is set and does not change over the life of the loan.
fluctuation	The variation in prices of stocks and other securities traded in secondary markets.
fund manager	A person (or team) who is responsible for making investment decisions related to a mutual fund or other formal portfolio such as a pension or insurance fund.
fundamental analysis	A method of stock valuation that studies the company's financial statements, operations, earnings, competition, and management strength. Fundamental analysis focuses on the company itself and is contrasted by technical analysis.
future value	Future value is a calculation relating to the time value of money. It calculates money's value in the future given the present value of the money, the number of years it will be held, the percentage rate at which it will grow, the number of times interest will be compounded per year, and the amount and number of payments that will be added over the years it is to be held. Inflation has the effect of reducing money's future value, while compounding of interest has the effect of increasing money's future value.
group insurance	Insurance issued to a group such as employees of a company or members of a credit union.
growth stock	A common stock whose price is considered likely to increase because the issuing company's business is poised for growth. Growth stocks generally do not pay dividends.

guardian	A term used in connection with wills and estate planning. A person named to care for another person, usually a minor.
healthcare advance directive	A document that expresses your general wishes about your medical treatment, in the event that in the future, you cannot speak for yourself. See durable power of attorney for healthcare.
home equity loan	A loan that is collateralized with the equity the borrower has in her home. The interest paid on home equity loans is sometimes deductible as mortgage interest.
illiquid	Assets that are not readily converted to cash such as real estate, collectibles, and limited partnerships.
illustration	An insurance term. A projection of how a specific permanent insurance policy or annuity is expected to perform over time, given certain inputs such as rate of return, premium payments, and length of time that premium payments are made.
income stock	A stock that historically has paid high dividends consistently.
individual 401(k)	New 401(k) plan established with the 2001 tax law. This plan allows individuals in solo practice and their spouses to establish a 401(k) with greatly reduced administrative requirements. See 401(k).
inflation	An economic term that describes a period in which there is an increase in the price of goods and services and that causes a decline in purchasing power.
in-force policy	An insurance policy that is sufficiently paid up as to be currently in effect and valid.
insurability	The degree to which an insurance company is willing and able to insure a particular person given his or her health status and other risk factors.
insured	A person upon whose death a life insurance policy pays.
interest rate risk	In a fixed investment, the risk that the interest being paid will be less than the going rate at a future date.
intestate	To die intestate is to die without a will. In such cases, state law determines the disposition of an estate.
investment portfolio	A mixture of securities and other assets that is designed to meet the needs of the investor. Refers to looking at the entire collection of holdings in their totality.
investment strategy	The approach an investor employs in making her investment decisions.
IRA	Individual retirement account. If one meets certain requirements set forth by the IRS, an individual may fund a Traditional IRA with pretax dollars that will grow tax-deferred and will be taxed when spent in retirement.

278 ADDENDUM III

IRA rollover	Certain retirement accounts may be "rolled over" into an individual retirement account held at a financial institution. For example, an individual who separates from service with a school district may be eligible to roll his 403(b) retirement account into a rollover IRA. The IRS has specified certain rules and penalties with regard to IRA rollovers, so be sure to consult with a financial professional before you roll over your retirement account.
junk bonds	Bonds issued by entities that receive a below investment grade rating from independent rating agencies such as Standard and Poor's. Junk bonds must pay higher coupon rates than investment grade bonds to attract investors.
Keogh	A tax-deferred retirement plan for self-employed individuals and the employees of sole proprietors. The Keogh is frequently used by sole proprietors for retirement saving.
leverage	Debt. A company that is highly leveraged is utilizing borrowed money. Similarly, an investor using leverage is utilizing borrowed money in his investing. The use of borrowed money in investing increases risk and may magnify gains and/or losses.
liability insurance	Insurance that covers the possibility of loss due to being held responsible for another's injury due to negligence or inappropriate action.
life expectancy	Based on actuarial tables, an insurance company's estimate of the insured's life span. Life expectancy is used in calculating life insurance premiums.
life insurance	Insurance that pays a specified amount on the death of the insured.
liquidity	The degree to which an investment is readily convertible to cash without penalty or loss.
living will	Document that specifies one's wishes with regard to medical treatment in the event the individual becomes incapable of making his or her own medical decisions. Commonly, living wills state that the individual does or does not want life support in the event that she can only be kept alive with the support of machines.
long-term care	Custodial, intermediate, or skilled nursing care provided to an individual who does not need acute care but cannot take care of his or her activities of daily living independently. Long-term care encompasses a broad range of help with daily activities that chronically disabled individuals need for a prolonged period of time.
long-term care insurance	A type of health insurance specifically designed to cover long-term care expenses. Some policies cover home health care and assisted living expenses. Benefits are triggered when the insured cannot independently take care of specified activities of daily living.
Medicaid (Medi-Cal in California)	Medical expense benefits for individuals and families deemed to be low-income and otherwise eligible by state and federal guidelines.

medical power of attorney	A document giving an individual (agent) the authority to make medical decisions on behalf the person assigning the power of attorney in the event that she becomes incapable of making her own medical decisions. The agent is usually a trusted friend or relative.
Medicare	Federal program that provides medical expense benefits for retired Americans. Medicare Part A provides coverage for in-hospital acute care. Part B provides outpatient coverage.
Medigap insurance	Insurance that covers some, but not all, areas of medical expense (gaps) uncovered by Medicare. Medigap insurance does not cover long-term care expenses. There are various levels of Medigap insurance that have been standardized by state insurance commissioners.
minimum distributions	In most tax-deferred retirement plans, there comes a point (age 70½ for most plans) when the retiree must begin to take money out of the plan and pay taxes on the portion that comes out. The minimum amount the retiree must take out is known as the minimum distribution.
money manager	Investment professional who buys and sells securities on behalf of his clients for a fee.
money market funds	Highly liquid and conservative funds that attempt to keep the value of one share to $1 with interest rates that vary. These funds invest in short-term debt obligations such as T-bills, commercial paper and certificates of deposit. Money market funds are neither insured nor guaranteed by the U.S. government.
mortality tables	Actuarial charts that insurance companies use to predict life expectancy of an applicant or insured individual.
mortgage backed securities	Securities that are backed by pooled mortgages. Government National Mortgage Association (Ginnie Mae), Federal National Mortgage Association (Fannie Mae), and Federal Home Loan Mortgage Corporation (Freddie Mac) are three entities that issue such securities.
municipal bonds	Debt securities issued by state, county, and local governmental entities including water districts and school districts. "Munis" are typically not subject to federal income tax and therefore offer lower coupon rates than taxable bonds. Their lower coupon rate typically makes munis inappropriate investments in tax-deferred accounts.
mutual fund	Open-end investment company that combines the investment dollars of many shareholders to manage a portfolio of securities— typically stocks and/or bonds. Mutual funds are used by small investors and large investors alike. They offer instant diversification, professional management, and the cost savings of sharing transaction fees among the shareholders. Mutual funds are sold by prospectus. The prospectus informs potential and current shareholders about the investment focus, fees, management, and performance of the mutual fund.

NASD	Established under federal law, the National Association of Securities Dealers is a private, not-for profit organization dedicated to bringing integrity to the markets and confidence to investors. Virtually every securities firm doing business in the U.S. is a member of the NASD. Among other responsibilities, the NASD acts as a provider of financial regulatory services to the U.S. securities industry.
net asset value (NAV)	Mutual funds hold many securities. At the end of each trading day, mutual fund companies must compute the value of a single mutual fund share. This computation involves adding up the total value of the underlying assets, subtracting the funds liabilities and then dividing by the number of shares outstanding.
net worth	An individual's total assets minus total liabilities equal his or her net worth.
pension plan	A qualified retirement plan. Defined benefit plans are more traditional pension plans that place the investment risk with the company, and pay a specific amount in retirement based on factors such as years of service, previous salary, and vesting. Defined contribution plans on the other hand place the investment risk with the employee, and benefits are based on accumulated account balances rather than a promise by the company to pay a specified amount. Popular defined contribution plans are 401(k)s and 403(b)s.
policy	An insurance contract between a policy owner and an insurance company that sets forth the terms and conditions of insurance.
policy loan	In permanent life insurance, loan to the policy owner by the insurance company that is secured by the cash value in the policy.
power of attorney	A document placing decision making power in the hands of a trusted person to act on behalf of the individual signing over this decision making power.
preferred stock	Dividend paying stock that is primarily held by corporations. Preferred stock takes precedence over common stock in the event of bankruptcy and liquidation. Dividends are paid to preferred stock before they are paid to common stock.
premium	Insurance term. The amount a policyholder pays the insurer to keep a life insurance policy in force.
principal	In a mortgage or other loan, the principal is the outstanding amount owed other than interest. When a payment is made, principal is the part of the outstanding balance that is thereby reduced. In an investment account, principal is the amount originally invested. When an investor says "I am not touching the principal," she is referring to leaving the original amount invested in the account, but leaving the option open of taking dividends or interest payments as income.
probate	Administration of the estate of a deceased person under the supervision of the court.

ADDENDUM III   **281**

profit sharing plan	A qualified retirement plan that allows individuals in private practice to put away a portion of their income on a pretax basis for retirement. The funds will grow tax-deferred, and will be taxed when distributed in retirement. If you have employees, you will have to contribute for them as well.
prospectus	In mutual fund and variable product separate account investing, a document, produced by an investment company that must meet the specific guidelines of the Securities Exchange Commission in describing in detail, the investment being offered. The prospectus provides terms, objectives, historical returns, costs, biographical information, and other information that is deemed useful in providing prospective investors with information helpful in making informed decisions.
qualified retirement plan	Qualified retirement plans are qualified by the IRS under section 401(a) to provide tax-advantaged retirement investing. Qualified plans are offered through one's employment. For sole proprietors in private practice, a qualified plan such as a 401(k) or Keogh can be established with the individual in solo practice acting both as employer and employee. Qualified plans require strict compliance with IRS rules, so it is advisable to seek professional advice in establishing and maintaining them.
refinance	In connection with a home or commercial mortgage, to take out a new loan on a property that replaces the old loan presumably with more favorable terms to the borrower.
registered representative	A person who has passed the appropriate NASD tests and is licensed in various states to sell securities as an agent through association with an NASD member broker/dealer.
rider	An optional feature on an insurance policy. The policyholder may choose a rider that she feels is in her interest in exchange for a higher premium. Example: On a permanent life insurance policy, an accelerated death benefit rider would allow for early partial payment of the death benefit to the insured during her lifetime if certain conditions are met.
Roth IRA	An individual retirement account that is funded with after-tax dollars. Money may be withdrawn tax-free in retirement. In contrast, the Traditional IRA is funded with pretax dollars and is then taxed when distributed in retirement.
rule of 72	A way to approximate when your money will double given a fixed annual compound interest rate. Divide 72 by the expected rate of return to approximate the number of years it will take to double your money. For example, if you are earning 5% compounded annually and you reinvest all of your interest, you will double your money in approximately 14.4 years.[5]

5 The rule of 72 does not guarantee investment results or function as a predictor of how your investment will perform. Returns will fluctuate and there is no guarantee that your investment will double in value.

282 ADDENDUM III

S&P 500 index	Standard & Poor's identifies 500 well-established American corporations for inclusion in this widely regarded measure of large-cap U.S. stock market performance. The S&P 500 attempts to include a representative sample of leading companies in leading industries.
safety of principal	An investment objective emphasizing that the original amount invested be as protected as is feasible given the risk characteristics of a given portfolio. The more aggressive the portfolio, the less emphasis there is on safety of principal. Conversely, the more conservative the portfolio, the more emphasis is placed on safety of principal. Safety of principal is assured up to the limits of FDIC protection with accounts in depository institutions that are covered by the FDIC.
second mortgage	A loan, collateralized by real estate, that is in addition to the primary mortgage. It carries rights that are junior to those of the primary mortgage.
Securities Exchange Commission (SEC)	The primary federal regulatory body for the securities industry. The SEC promotes full disclosure and is charged with preventing fraud and manipulative practices in the securities industry.
SEP IRA	A tax-advantaged retirement vehicle. The Simplified Employee Pension IRA is commonly used by therapists in private practice for tax-advantaged retirement investing.
skilled nursing care	In long-term care planning, skilled nursing care refers to a level of care needed by the patient that requires the supervision of a registered nurse 24 hours a day.
skilled nursing facility (SNF)	A SNF is primarily engaged in providing skilled nursing care to its residents.
small cap	Small capitalization stocks are those of smaller, publicly traded companies. This asset category is generally more aggressive and growth oriented than the stocks of more established companies with larger capitalization.
stock dividend	The common stocks of certain companies regularly pay shareholders a portion of income earned called dividends. Although some common stocks customarily and regularly pay dividends, corporations are not legally obligated to pay dividends on common stock.
stocks	A stock certificate signifies an ownership position or equity in a corporation. The amount of ownership the stockholder has in the corporation is proportional to the percentage of the stock he owns relative to total stock outstanding.
stock exchange	A market where stocks, bonds, and other equities are bought and sold. Major American stock exchanges include the New York Stock Exchange, the American Exchange, and NASDAQ.

suitability	The suitability of an investment refers to its appropriateness for a particular investor given her risk tolerance, financial circumstances, and life circumstances. Registered representatives are required by the NASD and other self-regulatory agencies to only sell investments that are suitable for their client.
surrender value	In variable life insurance or variable annuities, the surrender value is cash value of the policy minus any deferred sales and surrender charges. Most variable life insurance and variable annuities have substantial surrender charges and are therefore only suitable for people who intend to hold the policy over the long term.
tax credit	A dollar-for-dollar, direct reduction that offsets other income tax liabilities. Certain investments offer tax credits as their primary selling point.
tax deduction	A reduction in total income relative to the individual's tax bracket. A tax deduction is subtracted from adjusted gross income in determining taxable income. Contributions to qualified plans, state and local taxes, and charitable gifts are commonly used tax deductions.
tax-deferred	In tax-deferred accounts such as qualified plans, the contributions to the accounts go in on a pretax basis, and the taxation on the money is deferred until it is withdrawn in retirement.
tax-sheltered annuity (TSA)	Tax-sheltered annuities are offered by certain non-profit organizations, school districts, and hospitals as tax-deferred retirement plans.
tenants in common	The holding of property by two or more people, usually a couple, each of whom has an undivided interest in their portion of the property. One person may sell her share or leave it in a will without the consent of the other owner or owners. If a person dies without a will, his share goes to his heirs, not to the other owners.
term life insurance	Life insurance that has no cash value and is time limited. Term life insurance is contrasted with permanent life insurance, which is priced to last until the insured's death at which time it will pay a death benefit and which carries a cash value. Term insurance is significantly less expensive than permanent insurance.
testamentary trust	A trust created under the provisions of a will. A testamentary trust takes effect upon the death of the grantor.
ticker symbol	A combination of letters that is shorthand for a security. Some famous ticker symbols include MSFT (Microsoft), GM (General Motors Corp.), JNJ (Johnson & Johnson), and GE (General Electric).

time value of money	A calculation of compound interest over a given number of years with a given interest rate and given contributions. Time value of money refers to the concept that a given amount of money will be worth more in the future than it is now because of money's capacity to garner interest.
total disability	In disability insurance, some policies define total disability as the inability of the insured to perform any work for which he or she is qualified. Other policies define total disability as the inability of the insured to perform the duties of his or her own occupation. Some policies may change occupation definitions after a specified period of disability. In choosing a disability policy it is important to understand how your insurer defines total disability.
Treasury bill	A debt security offered by the U.S. Department of Treasury that has a duration of less than 1 year. Treasury bills are guaranteed by the government for repayment of principal and interest if held to maturity.
Treasury bond	A debt security offered by the U.S. Department of the Treasury that has a duration of more than 10 years. Treasury bonds are guaranteed by the government for repayment of principal and interest if held to maturity.
Treasury note	A debt security offered by the U.S. Department of the Treasury that has a duration of between 1 and 10 years. Treasury notes are guaranteed by the government for repayment of principal and interest if held to maturity.
universal life insurance	A kind of permanent life insurance that offers flexibility of premium payments. Universal life offers a death benefit along with a tax-advantaged savings component. The policyholder may borrow against the cash value in the policy without paying taxes on the borrowed sum. As long as the policy stays in force, the loan may not need to be paid back. At the time of death, if a loan is outstanding, the death benefit will be reduced by the amount of the outstanding loan.
unlimited marital deduction	In estate planning, the unlimited marital deduction refers to the fact that married people can leave unlimited assets to their spouses without incurring estate taxes. The estate taxes are eventually collected when the spouse dies. A common mistake is encountered when the deceased leaves everything to his spouse (employing the unlimited marital deductions) and eventually, estate taxes are levied upon the death of the spouse who now has all the assets in her name alone. Estate planners employ a variety of strategies to avoid this mistake.
value stocks	Stocks that are thought to be a good buy primarily because the price of the stock is considered to be underpriced when subjected to fundamental analysis of the earnings and overall health of the issuing corporation.

variable investment	An investment in a security that can gain or lose in value. Stocks and bonds are variable investments in that their value can and does vary when sold in the secondary stock and bond markets.
variable rate mortgage (VRM)	A mortgage whose rate changes with interest rates. Generally, variable rate mortgages are available at lower initial rates, because the borrower is assuming the risk that rates will rise. In contrast, fixed rate mortgages are generally more expensive because the lender is assuming the risk that rates will rise.
variable universal life insurance	Life insurance that combines a death benefit with a tax-advantaged investment component. The insured self directs the investment among the separate accounts that are offered within the policy. The separate accounts are typically managed by the same money management firms that manage large mutual funds and pensions. The policyholder may borrow against the cash value in the policy without paying taxes on the amount borrowed. The amount borrowed may not need to be repaid as long as the policy remains in force. If the insured dies with the policy in force and with borrowed funds outstanding, the death benefit is reduced by the outstanding loan amount. Variable universal life policies typically have steep deferred sales charges that decline and disappear over time. These polices are only appropriate for long-term investors.
vesting	Retirement accounts frequently include both employee contributions and employer contributions. Vesting refers to the schedule set out in the retirement plan by which the employee acquires ownership in the retirement funds contributed by the employer. Employee contributed funds are always fully vested.
viatical settlement	If a person with a terminal illness such as cancer or AIDS owns a life insurance policy, that policy may be sold in a viatical settlement that gives the insured less than the death benefit for use while still living. The purchaser of the policy pays the premium and receives the death benefit on the death of the insured now. At the height of the U.S. AIDS epidemic in the 1980s, viatical settlements were commonly used by AIDS sufferers to meet their financial obligations.
whole life insurance	Permanent insurance that has both a death benefit and a cash value that accrues over time.
zero coupon bonds	Bonds that do not make regular coupon payments, but instead are sold at a discount and pay face value at maturity.

INDEX

Page numbers in italics indicate figures and tables.

401(k) 26, 134, 146, 147, 148, 154, 157, 161
403(b) 60, 61, 194
529 plan 146, 151, 152

ACA *see* Affordable Care Act
Addiction Equity Act 108
advanced medical directives 12, 46, 203, 210–11, 214
Affordable Care Act (ACA) 2, 16, 108–10, 112, 256
age and wisdom 48–9
ambiguity and incompletion 50
amortization 182, 183, 184
annual percentage rate *see* APR
annuitant 151
annuities 57, 60–1, 134, 150n2, 194; variable 150n3, 150–1, 162
appreciation of property 207
APR (annual percentage rate) 179
asset allocation 3, 4, 10, 11, 12, 26, 36, 36n2, 130, 138, 153, 156–8, 159, 163, 166, 167, 172; with 40% in bonds and cash *44*; with 50% in bonds and cash *45*; with 60% in bonds and cash *46*; conservative *59*; Elder Phase *59*; growth *36*; inappropriate 136–7; maximum growth *15*; Prime Phase 43–5
asset classes 97, 155, *156*, 159, 166, *167–8*

assets 61, 64, 97, 139, 155, 182, 192, 196–7, 214, 218, 222, 227, 256; estate planning 46, 203, 204; living trusts 205; pour-over will 206; retirement 126
autos and auto loans 189–91; expenses 189

balance sheet *290–1*
bank CDs *see* certificate of deposit
bear market 154, *155*
benefits package *259*; *see also* disability insurance and business overhead insurance; health insurance; life insurance; long-term care insurance; retirement savings
Bly, Robert 106
bonds 26, 36, 43, 45, 59, 95, 149, 157, 163–5, 185, 195; asset allocation with 40% in bonds and cash *44*; asset allocation with 50% in bonds and cash 44, *45*; asset allocation with 60% in bonds and cash *46*; corporation *156*, 163, 164; junk *156*, 164; municipal *156*; treasury 165
bookkeeping 4, 10, 26, 127–8, 169; QuickBooks 4, 26, 119, 120, 122, 128; resources 128; Safeguard 128
Buddhism 20, 263

bull market 154, 155
business expenses 141, 182, 224, 225, 233, 254–7
business overhead insurance 201

Capterra.com 119
cash 56, 74, 89, 90, 91, 92, 166, 169, 172, 173, 180, 189; and bonds 43–5; *see also* surrender for cash
cash equivalents 157
cash flow 128, 169, 227, 257, 263; worksheet 218, *239*
cash instruments 165–8; *see also* certificates of deposit; money market funds; mutual funds; real estate
cash surrender value 56, 57
cash values 55, 56, 141, 149, 193, 194–5, 241
CD *see* certificate of deposit
Centers for Disease Control and Prevention 108
certificate of deposits (CD) 165, 166, 166n1
certified financial planner (CFP) 96–7
CFP see certified financial planner
characterological defenses around money wounds 76–82; malignant narcissistic defense 77–8; masochistic defense 79–80; narcissistic defense 76–7; oral defense 78; repetition or healing 81–2; schizoid defense 80–1; symbiotic defense 79
chartered financial consultant (ChFC) 96, 97
ChFC *see* chartered financial consultant
Child Protective Services 14
Co-dependent 70, 71
Cole, Peter H.: *True Self, True Wealth* 70
common stock 162, 163
community property 209, *210*
compounding 160, 161
conservator *208, 209*

corporate bond *156*, 163, 164
corporation 98, 151, 162, *167*, 175, 242, 254; bonds 163, 164
couple's money 87–93, 207, 208, 210; communication 86, 88–93; concrete communication 91; difficulties in the relationship 90; emotionally informed 91–2; flexible and effective 92–3; gifts 62; interpersonal issue 87–8; rigid communication 88, 90–1
CPAs (certified public accountants) 26, 97, 147
credit and debt issues *see* debt and credit issues
credit cards and debt reduction 78, 177, 178–81

debt and credit issues 176–91; autos and auto loans 189–91; credit cards and debt reduction 78, 177, 178–81; getting help for debt and credit problems 177–8; home mortgage 181–5; keeping on top of your credit 177–81; student loans 185–9
debt maintenance worksheet *237*
decedent *210*
defined benefit plan 61
depreciation 254
dialectical behavioral therapy 106
Direct Consolidation Loan program 185
disability insurance and business overhead insurance 42, 198–201, 256–7; business overhead insurance 201; cost-of-living adjustments 200–1; definition of disability 199; duration of disability 200; elimination period 200; guaranteed renewability 200; partial disability benefits 199–200
disposable income 169
diversification 158–9, 166, 172
dividends 35n1, 160, 162, 163, *167*, 172, 194, 228, *239*
divorce 136, 218

dollar cost averaging 154n1, 154–6;
   combining with asset allocation
   157n4, 157–8
durable power of attorney 204,
   211–12, *212*

economic times, sustaining your
   prosperous practice through
   changing 103–7; be confident
   104; be flexible 104–5; don't
   be too proud 105–6; focus
   on ground game 106; try new
   things 106
education expenses 95, 131, 151,
   152, 218, 252
Elder Phase 36, 48–64, 262; age
   and wisdom 48–9; ambiguity
   and incompletion 50; asset
   allocation 59; financial planning
   51–9 (*see also* financial planning
   in Elder Phase); health insurance
   62–4; higher net worth therapists
   estate planning issues 61–2;
   mortality issues 51; required
   distributions 60–2; rewards for
   work well done 11–12; slowing
   down but not stopping 49–50
EMDR *see* eye movement
   desensitization and reprocessing
Emling, Shelly: *Your Guide to
   Retiring to Mexico, Costa Rica
   and Beyond* 58
equity 162; car 190; home 56, 177,
   181, 182, 183 (*see also* Home
   Equity Conversion Mortgage;
   real estate investment trust)
Establishing Phase 28–36, 262;
   beginning to build 10–11;
   importance of self as instrument
   28–31; importance of self as
   instrument: emotional 30–1;
   importance of self as instrument:
   intellectual 29–30; importance
   of self as instrument: physical
   29; importance of self as
   instrument: spiritual 31;
   investment considerations 33–4;
   professional confidence 31–2;

real estate 33–4; savings 34–6;
   setting fees 31–2; weaving the
   whole cloth 32–3
estate 42, 149–50; expenses 62;
   preservation 43; taxes 60, 62,
   152n4, 194, 210, 212, 213, 214
estate planning 4, 12, 46, 195,
   202–14, 261; advanced medical
   directives 12, 46, 203, 210–11,
   214; choosing best method of
   ownership 206–10; common
   techniques 204; common tools
   203; community property 209,
   210; durable power of attorney
   for healthcare 211–12, *212*; fee
   simple estate 207, *207*; higher
   net worth therapists issues
   61–2; joint tenancy with right
   of survivorship (JTWRS) 207–8,
   208, 209; life insurance 212–14;
   living trusts 204–5; living will
   204, 211–12, *212*; planning for
   your practice 214; portability
   210; pour-over will 204, 206;
   revocable living trust 206;
   tenancy in common 208–9, *209*
Equifax.com 177
executor 206
expenses 26, 35n1, 120, 122, 128,
   132, 136, 142, *143*, *144*, 149,
   176, 177, 227, 233–4, 239, 257,
   270, 271; auto 189; business
   141, 182, 224, *225*, 233, 254–7;
   education 95, 131, 151, 152,
   218, 252; estate 62; family 95;
   living 56, 60; major 80; medical
   139; office 257; overhead 1,
   131, 201; personal 233–4, *235*;
   retirement 135; special 218, *250*;
   unexpected 169; worksheet 218;
   yearly living *244*
eye movement desensitization and
   reprocessing (EMDR) 106

Facebook 113, 116, 117
face value 163, 164–5
family expenses 95
fee setting 31–2

INDEX **289**

fee simple estate 207, *207*
FICO score 177; Equifax.com 177; MyFICO.com 177
financial future 218, 241–3
financial planner 1, 4, 26, 42, 55, 64, 94–8, 134, 137–8, 140, 141, 178, 192–3, 199, 200, 201, 203, 218, 257, 261; certified financial planner (CFP) 96–7; chartered financial consultant (ChFC) 96, 97; how to choose a highly qualified 96–7; how to pay 97–8
financial planning in Elder Phase 51–9; estimating retirement resources needed 54–5; foreign retirement 58–9; life expectancy 54; life insurance policy annuity contract 57; life insurance policy living benefits 56; life insurance policy loans 56–7; life insurance policy surrender for cash 56; living simply 57–8; retirement age 51–4; retirement funds shortfall 55–9; reverse mortgages 56
financial mistakes 130–45; excessive tax liability 141–5; failing to obtain adequate insurance 139–41; inappropriately allocating assets in retirement plan 136–8; take care of future self 134; treating all income as money to be spent 131–3; underfund retirement plan 133–6
financial well-being 43, 46, 64, 81, 83–6, 98, 133, 176, 198, 257, 262; family rules around money 86; introduction to lifetime plan 217–19; money in the family system 84–5
fixed rate mortgage 138, 182, 185
fixed rate of interest 164
fixed rate of return 194, 195
foreign retirement 58–9
Freud, Sigmund 50, 88
Friedlander, Rachel 125, 126
future value 55n2, 163

gender impact on retirement plan 135–6
Gestalt therapy 20, 24, 82
Goldstein, Margaret J.: *The World's Top Retirement Havens* 58
Google 114, 118
Great Depression 81, 103
Great Recession 137, 138, 181
growth stock 162
guardianship of minor children 203, 206

health insurance 16, 36, 43, 108, 131, 139, 140, 256, 259; Elder Phase 62–4; *see also* Affordable Care Act
higher education expenses 152, 192, 218; worksheet *252*
higher net worth therapists estate planning issues 61–2
Hillman, James 106
Home Affordable Refinance Program (HARP) 138
home equity home 56, 177, 181, 182, 183
Home Equity Conversion Mortgage (HECM) 56
home mortgage 181–5; amortization 182, *183*, 184; not all mortgage payments are created equal 182–3; prepayment of principal 184–5; *see also* Home Equity Conversion Mortgage; reverse mortgage

illiquid 169, 172
income worksheet *228*
individuation: "pseudo" financial 84–5; psychological intertwined with financial 84
inflation 54–5, 59, 134, 159, 163, 165, 167, 197, 258
insured 57, 64, 108, 149n1, 165, 166n1, 193, 195n1, 199, 213, 242; FDIC 165; uninsured 108
internet 25, 113, 114, 190

Internship Phase 13–16; financial dimension 15–16; maximum growth asset allocation *15*

Intuit: QuickBooks 4, 26, 119, 120, 122, 128

investment portfolio 138, 157, *163*, 175

investment strategy 3, *95*, 138, 158

IRAs (individual retirement accounts), catch-up contributions 148; education 151–2; Roth 60, 61, 146, 147–8, 184, 185; SEP 126, 134, 146, 147, 148, 150; Traditional 147–8

IRS 60; estimated taxes 141; funding limits and income restrictions 148; Schedule C 242; securities losses 138; sole proprietor 254; tax advantaged plan 148; variable universal life insurance 150; website 146

Jackson, Phil 134

joint tenancy with right of survivorship (JTWRS) 207–8, *208*, 209

journaling process pages 221, 223, 226, 229, 232, 236, 238, 240, 245, 247, 249, 251, 253, 260

JTWRS *see* joint tenancy with right of survivorship

Jung, Carl 37, 38, 85

junk bond *156*, 164

Keogh Profit Sharing Plan 134

Knorr, Rosanne: *The Grown Up's Guide to Retiring Abroad 58*

knowledge gap 125–9; bookkeeping resources 128; putting your financial house in order 127–8; responsibility to yourself 129; "seat of the pants approach" approach 126, 127; treating your practice as a business 128, 129, 131, 224; underdeveloped financial skills 3, 125–6

knowing yourself 22–3

Launching Phase 17–27, 262; beyond consulting room 24–5; combining passion with non-attachment 19–22; financial dimension 26; knowing yourself 22–3; laying a foundation 10; managed care 18–19; marketization 23–4; non-attachment 19–22; office—to share or not 17–18; practice management software and bookkeeping 26; retirement plan 26

leverage 175, 189

liability insurance 131, 140, 233, *254*

life expectancy 54, 55, 61

life insurance 140–1, 153, 192–6, 206, 213, 241, *259*; annuity 57; cash values *55*, 56, 241; death benefit 62, 149, 150, 213; estate planning 212–14; evaluate 35; how much to get 192–3; irrevocable trust 213–14; living benefits 56; loans 56–7; permanent 56, 57, 141, 194; premium 62, 149; purchase 11; temporary 193; trust 62; types 193–6; variable universal 148–50, 149n1, 162, 193, 194–5, 195n1; what kind to get 193–6; whole 149, 194; who needs it 192; worksheet *246*

lifetime financial planning objectives worksheet *222*

LinkedIn 113, 116, 117

liquidity 166, 173

living expenses 56, 60

living trusts 204–5

living will 204, 211–12, *212*

long-term care insurance 11, 42–3, 64, 196–8, 199, 219, 255, 258

major expenses 80

malignant narcissistic defense 77–8

managed care 18–19, 40, 105, 106, 120–1, 122; empowerment

INDEX **291**

model 110–12; making it work for you 108–12

Markowitz, Harry 158–9

masochistic defense 79–80, 99

Medicaid 64, 109, 111, 112, 196, 196

Medi-Cal 196–7

medical expenses 139

Medicare 62–3, *63*, 109, 111, 112, 196, 242; Part A 62, 63, *63*; Part B 62, 63; Part C 63; Part D 63

Medigap 63

Mental Health Association 22

Mental Health Parity 108

mentoring 10, 11, 13, 20, 22, 30, 41–2, 82

mid-life 41, 48, 78, 85; career change 17; crisis 37

minimum distributions 61, 62

Modern Portfolio Theory 158–9

money: consciousness 67–71; definition 73; manager 97, 165

money as a transference object in therapy 99–100

money in the family system 84–5; family rules around money 86; pseudo financial individuation 84–5; psychological indivuation intertwined with financial indivuation 84

money market fund 157, 166, *168*

MoneyTree 257–8

money wounds, characterological defenses around 76–82; malignant narcissistic defense 77–8; masochistic defense 79–80; narcissistic defense 76–7; oral defense 78; repetition or healing 81–2; schizoid defense 80–1; symbiotic defense 79

mortality issues 46, 51, 202

municipal bond *156*

mutual funds 97, 162, 165–7, 166n2, 174; REIT 173

MyFICO.com 177

narcissistic defense 76–7, 78

Nelson, Willie 37

net asset value 173

net worth 61–2, 64, 72, 197, 202, 218, 227, *257*

non-attachment 19–22, 24

office 10, 11, 34, 131, 136, *255*; buying the building you practice in 170–1; expenses 182, 257; to share or not 17–18

online presence 113–18; social media presence 116–18; various pages of a therapist website 115–16; your website 113–15

oral defense 78

overhead expenses 1, 131, 201

ownership: car 189, 190; choosing best method 204, 206–10; community property 209; cross-213; fee simple 207, *207*; joint tenancy with right of survivorship 207–8, *208*; mutual funds 166; proportional 166; real estate 172; stocks 162–3, 166; tenancy in common 208–9, *209*

payment for therapy 99–100

pensions 126, 135, 193, 218, *247*, 255; worksheet *246; see also* Simplified Employee Pension; Social Security

permanent life insurance 141, 194; loans 56–7; trading permanent for annuity 57

personal expenses 233–4; worksheet *235*

personal information worksheet *220*

policy loans 56, 57

pour-over will 204, 206

power of attorney, durable 204, 211–12, *212*

practice as a business 128, 129, 131, 224

practice management software 26, 119–22, 128

premium 62, 63, 139–40, 149, 190–1, 194, 197, 198, 200–1, 214, 258

Prime Phase 36, 37–47, 262; asset allocation 43–5; characterological patterns 46–7; crossroads 37–8; estate planning 46; financial planning 42–3; generativity 41–2; integrating theory and authenticity 38–9; mentoring 41–2; reaping rewards 11; shaping your practice 39–40

principal 149n1, 150nn2–3, 152n4, 166, 166nn1–2, 173, 181, 182, 183, 186, 195n1, 214; fixed- 165; prepayment 184–5; value 195n1

Principal Insurance 257

private practice basic worksheet 225

probate 149, 203, 204–5

procrastination 70, 128, 140

profitability tracking 120, 142–5, 143–4

prospectus 149n1, 150n3, 166n2, 195n1, 273n1

psychological dimensions 24, 72–5; definition of money 73; object relations perspective 73–5

psychological individuation intertwined with financial indivuation 84

Psychology Today 113, 117–18

putting your financial house in order 127–8

qualified retirement plan 150n2, 160, 161, 182, 241

RAND Corporation 108

real estate 11, 33–4, 137, 168–73, 192, 194, 227, 241; buying the building you practice in 170–1; investment trusts 15, 36, 43, 44, 44, 45, 45, 46, 59, 168; limited partnerships 173; mutual funds that hold REITs 173; securities 171–3; stocks 172; *see also* real estate investment trust

real estate investment trust (REIT) 43, 44, 45, 168, 172; mutual funds 173

Reese, Daisy: *True Self, True Wealth* 70

refinance 182, 183, 184

REIT *see* real estate investment trust

responsibility to yourself 129

retirement: expenses 135; gender impact 135–6; *see also* annuities; financial planning in Elder Phase: estimating retirement resources needed; financial planning in Elder Phase: retirement age; financial planning in Elder Phase: retirement funds shortfall qualified retirement plan; financial mistakes: inappropriately allocating assets in retirement plan; financial mistakes: underfund retirement plan; foreign retirement; gender impact on retirement plan; IRAs; Launching Phase: retirement plan; qualified retirement plan; savings: retirement; Social Security

retirement age 51–4

revenues 34, 120–1, 122, 130, 131–3, 132, 133, 135, 140, 142, 198, 227, 233; worksheet 143, 144, 225,

reverse mortgage 55, 56

revocable living trust 206

rider 197

risk profile worksheet 246

Roth IRA 60, 61, 146, 147–8, 184, 185

S&P 500 155, 156, 156n2, 163

salary 130, 131; deferrals for 401(k) 147

savings 182, 200; accounts 165; college 151, 152; education 146; incentive match plan for employees (SIMPLE IRA) 147; monthly needed to reach retirement goal of $1 million 34–6, 36; retirement 42, 54–5, 126, 147, 219, 257, 258, 259; tax 141; tax-advantaged 161;

tax-deferred versus taxable 159; whole life insurance 194
schizoid defense 80–1
seasons of the therapist 9–12; Elder Phase—rewards for work well done 11–12; Establishing Phase—beginning to build 10–11; Launching Phase—laying a foundation 10; Prime Phase—reaping rewards 11
"seat of the pants approach" approach 126, 127
securities: losses 138; real estate 171–3; *see also* bonds; stocks
self-employment (SE) tax 62, 242
self-exploration 37, 48, 263
SEP *see* Simplified Employee Pension
Simplified Employee Pension (SEP) 60, 147, 160; IRA 126, 134, 146, 147, 148, 150
skilled nursing facility 197
Skype 25
small cap funds *167*
socially responsible investing 109, 174–5, 195
Social Security 54, 55, 58, 63, 127, 135, 199, 218, 241–3; Administration 54, 241, 243; chart of retirement ages with reductions for early retirement 52–3; and private practitioner 241–2; worksheet *244*
sole proprietorship 3, 26, 146, 205, 242, 257; deductible business expenses 254–6
special expenses worksheet *250*
special income 218; worksheet *248*
stockbrokers 97, 137
stock exchange 172
stock market 137, 154, 155, 156n2, 158, 162
stocks 26, 36, 43, 44, 45, 59, 165, 166, 167; common stock 162–3; growth stock 162; real estate 172; tips 97–8; value 163; *see also* asset classes; securities
stock value 163

student loans 185–9; Direct Consolidation Loan program 185; repayment plans *186–8*
surrender for cash 56
sustaining your prosperous practice through changing economic times 103–7; be confident 104; be flexible 104–5; don't be too proud 105–6; focus on ground game 106; try new things 106
symbiotic defense 79

taxable vs. tax-deferred on $7,500 in income *161*
tax-advantaged investing 134, 141
tax-advantaged investing for self-employed psychotherapists 146–53; 401(k) for individuals 147; 529 plans 152; catch-up contributions to IRAs 148; education IRAs 151–2; employment-based vehicles 146–8; insurance-based vehicles 148–51; IRS funding limits and income restrictions 148; savings incentive match plan for employees (SIMPLE IRA plan) 147; tax-advantaged education saving plans 151–2; Traditional and Roth IRA 147–8; variable annuities 150–1; variable universal life insurance 148–50
tax deduction 227
tax deferred 34, 35, 60, 61, 141, 150, 150n2, 152, 159–61, *161*, 164
tax liability 131, 141, 171
tenancy in common 208–9, *209*
time value of money 26, 34, 159–61, 262
total disability 199
treasury bill 164, 166
treasury bond 165
treasury note 164–5

underdeveloped financial skills 3, 125–6
unexpected expenses 169
Uniform Gift to Minors 62

Uniform Transfer to Minors 62
universal life insurance 146, 194, 195; variable 148–50, 162, 174, 193, 195
U.S. Census 108
U.S. Department of Education 185–6, 189
USSIF 174

value stock 163
variable annuities 150n3, 150–1, 162
variable universal life insurance 148–50, 162, 174, 193, 195

website: About 115–16, 117; Book an Appointment 116; Contact 116; Fees and Insurance 116; Forms 116; Home Page 115; Services 115; Useful Links 116; various pages of a therapist website 115–16; your website 113–15
Whitaker, Carl 30, 49
whole life insurance 148, 193, 194
why a financial planning book for therapists 1–5
WordPress 114

Helping you to choose the right eBooks for your Library

Add Routledge titles to your library's digital collection today. Taylor and Francis ebooks contains over 50,000 titles in the Humanities, Social Sciences, Behavioural Sciences, Built Environment and Law.

Choose from a range of subject packages or create your own!

Benefits for you
- » Free MARC records
- » COUNTER-compliant usage statistics
- » Flexible purchase and pricing options
- » All titles DRM-free.

REQUEST YOUR FREE INSTITUTIONAL TRIAL TODAY
Free Trials Available
We offer free trials to qualifying academic, corporate and government customers.

Benefits for your user
- » Off-site, anytime access via Athens or referring URL
- » Print or copy pages or chapters
- » Full content search
- » Bookmark, highlight and annotate text
- » Access to thousands of pages of quality research at the click of a button.

eCollections – Choose from over 30 subject eCollections, including:

Archaeology	Language Learning
Architecture	Law
Asian Studies	Literature
Business & Management	Media & Communication
Classical Studies	Middle East Studies
Construction	Music
Creative & Media Arts	Philosophy
Criminology & Criminal Justice	Planning
Economics	Politics
Education	Psychology & Mental Health
Energy	Religion
Engineering	Security
English Language & Linguistics	Social Work
Environment & Sustainability	Sociology
Geography	Sport
Health Studies	Theatre & Performance
History	Tourism, Hospitality & Events

For more information, pricing enquiries or to order a free trial, please contact your local sales team: **www.tandfebooks.com/page/sales**

 Routledge
Taylor & Francis Group

The home of Routledge books

www.tandfebooks.com